Contemporary Psychoanalysis and Eastern Thought

SUNY Series, Alternatives in Psychology

Michael A. Wallach, Editor

Contemporary Psychoanalysis and Eastern Thought

John R. Suler

State University of New York Press

Published by
State University of New York Press, Albany

For information, address State University of New York Press,
State University Plaza, Albany, N.Y. 12246

Production by M. R. Mulholland
Marketing by Bernadette LaManna

Library of Congress Cataloging-in-Publication Data

Suler, John R., 1955–
    Contemporary psychoanalysis and Eastern thought / John R. Suler.
        p.   cm.—(SUNY series, alternatives in psychology)
    Includes bibliographical references and index.
    ISBN 0-7914-1577-5 (hard : alk. paper).—ISBN 0-7914-1578-3
(pbk. : alk. paper)
    1. Psychoanalysis and religion.   2. Zen Buddhism—Psychology.
3. Taoism—Psychology.   4. Psychotherapy.   I. Title.   II. Series.
BF175.5.R44S85   1993
150.19′5—dc20   92-30817
                                                                        CIP

10 9 8 7 6 5 4 3 2 1

For Debra

Contents

Preface

I intended this book as a kind of collage. It collects a variety of ideas from psychoanalytic and Eastern disciplines. It gathers together my own experiences as a researcher, clinician, martial arts player, and student of Eastern philosophy. Because knowledge comes in all shapes and sizes, the text places side by side theoretical analyses, case studies, empirical data, literary references, anecdotes, and story-telling. I hope that, like a good collage, each of the pieces has its own individual tale to tell that embellishes those of the other pieces, even as the whole assemblage points to insights that are greater than the sum of the parts.

Many motifs resurface throughout the course of the book. To do justice to the abundant meanings of certain themes, I attempted to approach them from several different perspectives. At the same time, there is a clear progression from beginning to end. The first two chapters provide the backdrop for this East/West study, followed by three chapters that delve into essential theoretical issues—especially the paradox of the self/no-self polarity. From that point on, the discussion moves toward more pragmatic topics: meditation, the personality dynamics of Eastern students and teachers, and frameworks for understanding psychotherapeutic technique and process. Finally, the last chapter describes the vision quest, a practice that allows any individual, without formal psychotherapy or spiritual training, to tap a transformative realm of human experience. This practice is not Buddhism, Taoism, or psychoanalysis, nor is it specifically Eastern or Western. For that reason it may seem out of place in this book. But it points to universal processes that underlie all forms of transformation—including, and perhaps especially, the transformations in everyday life. This chapter was my way of ending the book on the note that "Zen is one's everyday mind."

Earlier versions of some chapters or material from some chapters have appeared in journal articles. Paradox in psychological transformations: The Zen koan and psychotherapy appeared in *Psychologia: An International Journal of Psychology in the Orient*, 1989, *4*, 221–229; Psychodynamics of the vision quest in *Voices: The Art and Science of Psychotherapy*, 1988, *24*, 83–90; Wandering in search of the self: A contemporary version of the vision quest in *Journal of Humanistic Psychology*, 1990, *30*, 73–88; Images of the self in Zen meditation in *Journal of Mental Imagery*, 1990, *14*, 197–204; finally, Zen Buddhism and psychoanalysis, *Psychoanalytic Review*, is in press.

My thanks to George Atwood, Mark Finn, Edward Katkin, Jeffrey Kauffman, Murray Levine, Richard Noll, Alan Roland, Jeffrey Rubin, Jeffrey Rutstein, and Lloyd Silverman for their advice and encouragement; to Arlene Burrows, Nancy McWilliams, Karel Rubenstein, and Howard Tennen, who taught me psychoanalytic psychotherapy; to Susanna and Guy DeRosa who taught me Tai Chi Chuan; to Joseph Masling, who never much liked Eastern philosophy but always supported me; to William Cates and Thomas Altizer, who strongly influenced me early in my academic life; to John and Doris Suler; and especially to Debra Finnegan-Suler.

1

Chasing Two Rabbits?

Comparing the Disciplines

A martial arts student once said to his teacher, "In addition to studying your system, I'd like to improve my skills by learning another style." The teacher's reply was matter-of-fact. "The hunter who chases two rabbits," he stated, "catches neither one."

By comparing and attempting to integrate psychoanalysis and Eastern practices such as Zen, are we indeed chasing two rabbits? Surely, a first glance at these two disciplines reveals many disparities. Zen is a spiritual system for attaining enlightenment; psychoanalysis is a psychotherapeutic method for curing mental illness. To reach enlightenment, Zen advocates the dissolution and transcendence of the self; to cure psychopathology, psychoanalysis—especially object relations theory and self psychology—upholds the need to fortify the cohesion and continuity of the self. Whereas Zen speaks of the need to negate all desires and forms of self-centeredness, psychoanalytic approaches such as self psychology maintain that ambitions, ideals, and the grandiose/exhibitionistic components of the self play a crucial role in the development of psychological well-being. Patients talk about their childhood, about their fears and hopes, whereas Zen students meditate their way toward an empty mind.

The very effort to compare and integrate Eastern and Western ideas will alienate some people. Some psychoanalysts will claim that a reexamination of their theory in the light of Eastern thought will result in our completely missing the boat as to what constitutes the essence of psychoanalysis. They may claim that we have stretched the theory out of shape, ignored its key elements, or watered it down with unnecessary notions from a foreign, incompatible world. Some Zen devotees will raise similar objections: Our efforts are a misunderstanding and even a bastardizing of their discipline, too.

But are we really chasing two rabbits? One of the single most

important insights of psychoanalysis is the realization of the unconscious. Exactly what constitutes this thing called the unconscious has
been the subject of many debates. By the broadest and most comprehensive definition, it indeed is a thing, or an It ("das Es," as Freud
suggested)—a collection of processes, properties, experiences, or
meanings—that defies appellation. Mysterious, hidden, this It nevertheless is part of us—the most important part, looming larger than
our experience of I-ness, that in fact shapes the thoughts, feelings,
and actions of the "I" without the "I" even knowing it. Along with
Copernicus's revelation that we are not the center of the universe and
Darwin's discovery that we are but a part of a larger organismic flow,
the psychoanalytic exploration of the It exposes the corresponding intrapsychic insight that the mind as usually experienced is superseded
by a deeper, more expansive Mind.

Is this insight much different from the Eastern vision of the It—
whether we call it the Void, No-Mind, or Tao—that lies hidden beneath us, yet permeates all that we see and do, a force greater than
the I to which the I ultimately must yield? Without doubt, there are
specific psychoanalytic conceptualizations of the unconscious (e.g.,
repressed affects) that differ substantially from the Eastern view of
the unconscious. But perhaps the fullest, most far-reaching vision in
psychoanalysis parallels that in Eastern spirituality. Perhaps there is
only one rabbit to chase.

If psychoanalysis and Zen overlap in this vision of the unseen
realm that underlies identity, then they are similar, too, in their aim
toward this realm. Fromm (1959; Fromm, Suzuki, & DeMartino, 1960)
noted that they share the premise that knowledge—knowledge of the
self—leads to transformation. The psychoanalytic goal of exploring
the unconscious, of letting ego be where id was, may correspond to
the Zen intention of "awakening" within the unconscious (Suzuki,
1949). The unconscious that is realized in these two disciplines may
differ in content, but the underlying process of awakening is similar:
To get in touch with the unconscious is to get in touch with reality,
with the truth. It is to wake up. One contacts and gains knowledge of
a wider, deeper reality—a knowledge, Fromm stated, that is more
than intellectual or even affective. It is an experiential knowledge.
When pursued to its fullest conclusion, this knowing blossoms into
an awareness that expands beyond previously known boundaries:

> If one pursues the aim of the full recovery of the unconscious—
> then this task is not restricted to the instincts, nor to other lim-
> ited sectors of experience, but to the total experience of the total

man; then the aim becomes that of overcoming alienation, and
of the subject-object split in perceiving the world; then the uncovering of the unconscious means the overcoming of affective
contamination and cerebration; it means the disappearance of
the state of repressedness, the abolition of the split within myself between the universal man and the social man; it means
the disappearance of the polarity of conscious vs. unconscious; it
means arriving at the state of the immediate grasp of reality,
without distortion and without interference by intellectual reflection; it means the overcoming of the craving to hold onto the
ego, to worship it; it means to give up the illusion of an inde-
structible, separate ego . . . (1959, pp. 95–96)

The very heart of psychoanalysis lies close to that of Eastern
thought. Yet contemporary psychoanalytic approaches, especially object relations theory, self psychology, intersubjectivity theory, and
psychoanalytic phenomenology, draw the evolution of the psychoanalytic movement even closer to the ancient oriental practices than was
possible within the context of traditional drive theory. When Kohut
(1977) made his controversial progression from self psychology in its
"narrow" sense to its "broader" sense, he no longer conceptualized
the self as simply a content of the mental apparatus or the product of
drive cathexes, but as the center of the psychological universe, the
very cornerstone and overarching organizing principle of personality
dynamics. The ideas of earlier theorists such as Erik Erikson, George
Klein, Karen Horney, and Erich Fromm, as well as object relations
theory, set in motion this shift to the self as a central psychoanalytic
concern. Rather than being preoccupied with unlocking and redirecting instinctual drives—a theoretical fixation that prevented an empathic understanding of the religious experience—psychoanalysis
devoted itself to investigating and developing the self. This theoretical shift opened a new, more compatible path to Eastern traditions,
which, for several thousand years, have also focused on the exploration and realization of that something called the "self." Buddha himself lost interest in the religious metapsychological explanations and
ascetic practices that dominated his time. He wanted to know how
the mind works here and now. He wanted to understand the most
basic, essential experience of the self.

As compared to traditional psychoanalysis, the epistemology
of contemporary psychoanalytic systems more closely echoes that of
Zen. Although there are many intricacies in the relationship of theory
to clinical observations and some doubts about whether pure, theory-

free observations are possible, self psychology and intersubjectivity approaches do emphasize an "experience-near" understanding of the patient that sets aside conceptualizations which create distance between the patient's and therapist's experience. Classical theory viewed the clinician as a detached, objective observer of the patient, which Freud symbolized in his image of the analyst as a surgeon performing an operation, and "Aaron Green" (Malcolm, 1980) captured in his analogy of the analyst as a car mechanic. Instead, the contemporary approaches advocate an empathic-introspective immersion into the patient's subjective world in which the observer participates in the observed. Only within this "intersubjective field" (Stolorow, Brandchaft, & Atwood, 1987) can the self be explored. These theories highlight an idea that skilled clinicians (both psychoanalytic and humanistic) have known all along: that we understand and transform people most effectively when we experience life in their shoes.

Zen similarly calls for an abrogation of all theories and abstractions, claiming that self-realization is only possible through what is intuitive, immediate, subjective. In contrasting the objective and subjective epistemologies, Suzuki (1960) recited Tennyson:

> Flower in the crannied wall,
> I pluck you out of the crannies;
> Hold you here, root and all, in my hand,
> Little flower—but if I could understand
> What you are, root and all, and all in all,
> I should know what God and man is.

and contrasted this poem with Bashō's (1644–1694) haiku:

> When I look carefully
> I see the nazuna blooming
> By the hedge!

Both Tennyson and Bashō sense the same mystery in the flower, experience the same awe for the Being it expresses. But they approach the secret very differently. The Western, objective strategy with which we are so familiar (but which we rarely recognize as a strategy) tears an experience from its ground and holds it at arm's length to understand it—a method that inadvertently causes the thing observed to wither and die within our grasp. It is no longer what it was before we intervened. On the other hand, Zen, like the contemporary psychoanalytic methods that emphasize empathic introspection, attempts to enter right into it, to see it, as it were, from the inside, thereby closing the gap between the knower and the known. "The basic goal of Zen is to come in touch with the inner workings of one's being, and to do this in the most direct way possible, without resorting to anything external or superadded." This quote, from Suzuki (1949, p. 43), could easily have been the words of Kohut, Winnicott, or Bion.

The Starting Points

To find a convergence of psychoanalysis and Eastern philosophy, we must define the respective points of departure. The problem with any definition is that it begins by offering us clarity and precision, and ultimately ends by enslaving us to its boundaries. From the West, our starting point is psychoanalysis, and surely many definitions of this discipline are available. Rather than confining us to any one of them, I attempt to draw on a wide range of psychoanalytic approaches. However, like anyone else, I have my biases. As evident in the discussion so far, I often accentuate ideas from those schools that emphasize the *self* (rather than drives) as the phenomenon of central importance in the intrapsychic world. It is a self that possesses intrinsic intentionality, always being shaped by its relationship to the object (other), and one that invariably strives to actualize its own internal design. As such, object relations theory, self psychology, intersubjectivity theory, and psychoanalytic phenomenology often serve as the home base from which we push toward the East. The advantage of these approaches lies first of all in the fact that the concept of the self is an important link between West and East, and second, that this concept, unlike many others, is sufficiently powerful and versatile to serve as such a link. At the same time, I do not completely abandon classical theory. It holds many valuable concepts for an East/West study, and is the developmental origin of contemporary theory. One must not discard the baby with the bathwater or ignore one's roots.

Rather than defining psychoanalysis as the study of a particular type of intrapsychic dynamic (e.g., structural, oedipal, economic, etc.), I emphasize its unique epistemological characteristics as a vehicle for studying intrapsychic events. In the tradition of psychoanalytic phenomenology (Atwood & Stolorow, 1984; Stolorow, Brandchaft, & Atwood, 1987) and psychological hermeneutics (Messer, Sass, & Woolfolk, 1988), I consider it a disciplined subjectivity rather than a natural science. Its method is founded on the premise that the knowing subject is enmeshed with the object of observation, that clinical investigators necessarily must draw on their own experiences and self-knowledge to guide their understanding of the lives they study. More than being simply a collection of techniques, the psychoanalytic approach, via empathy and introspection, creates an intersubjective field where the worlds of the observer and the observed interweave, where the observer becomes the observed. Understanding one's sub-jectivity—one's own psychological dynamics, values, preferences, even historical context—is part and parcel of understanding the frame of reference that dictates the how, when, and why an observation occurs.

To facilitate the convergence of East and West, other key fea-tures of psychoanalysis need to be highlighted, features that readily translate into Eastern styles of thinking. Three of its essential char-acteristics are its emphasis on psychic determinism, unconscious mental functioning, and primary process (Pine, 1988). Ultimately, it is mind—an unknown and in some respects unknowable realm of mind—that determines all that we see and do, that accounts, per-haps, for reality itself. The path to this unconscious psychic realm follows not reason and rationality, but the primary process functions of symbol, metaphor, and illogical connections among ideas that defy conventional truths. Loewald's (1976) definition of primary process, as distinguished from secondary process, reveals how closely the psychoanalytic vision of how the mind works, at its deepest level, can parallel the oriental view:

> Mental and memorial processes are primary if and insofar as they are unitary, single-minded, as it were undifferentiated and non-differentiating, unhampered, as Freud has described it, by laws of contradiction, causality, and by the differentiation of past, present, and future and of subject and object, i.e., by the differentiation of temporal and spatial relations. Mental pro-cesses are primary to the extent to which they are non-splitting, to the extent to which they do not manifest or establish dual-ity or multiplicity, no this and/or that, no before and after, no ac-tion as distinguished from its agent or its goal or its object. The secondary process is secondary insofar as in it duality becomes established, insofar as it differentiates; among these differentia-tions is the distinction between the perceiver and the perceived. (p. 319)

Other characteristics of psychoanalysis also resonate with the East. Similar to oriental philosophy that warns us of our tendency to take illusion for reality, psychoanalysis points to transference, or, more generally, to the illusions and self-deceptions that distort our view of the world and ourselves. Heeding the Eastern vision of the *yang* and *yin*, it points to resistance—the stubborn intrapsychic blockades against any change—as well as to the internal nuclear program that awaits the opportunity for actualized development, despite the odds. Finally, psychoanalysis speaks about the alleviation of suffering through self-knowledge, a principle that unites it with many spiritual and philosophical disciplines that grapple with the travails of being human.

Some people will not be satisfied with the definition of psychoanalysis that I here offer as our starting point from the West. Is it too broad, too vague? Does it miss the indisputably essential qualities of the theory? As Goldberg (1986) stated, perhaps there are a few fortunate people who truly know what psychoanalysis is and is not. For the rest of us, it remains an open-ended discipline, free from orthodoxy, that allows for, even encourages, creative flexibility.

As difficult as it may be to define psychoanalysis, it is no more difficult than defining what we mean by "Eastern discipline." Eastern philosophies may resemble each other as closely as, say, psychoanalysis resembles behaviorism. Some scholars even abhor the very term *Eastern philosophy*, for they claim that no such animal exists—in effect, that I am chasing dozens of rabbits. But it would be hard to deny that there are similar themes that weave throughout the Eastern philosophies, or that there is a common denominator among those in the West. Freud and Skinner both adopted the scientific attitude of logical positivism, and both their theories were decidedly deterministic. Many, if not all, Eastern philosophies speak of the importance of selflessness or egolessness—a theme that is central to this book.

While trying to define a starting point in the East, I found selecting a title for this text to be one of the more difficult tasks. The term *Eastern philosophy* seemed inappropriate because it tends to underplay the psychological insights offered by the Orient, yet the term *Eastern psychology* grated on both my aesthetic and scientific nerves. The term *Eastern religions* also seemed inadequate because the range of this book covers issues outside those involving spirituality, God, and transcendental existences. Even *Eastern thought* is deficient in its connotation of reason, logic, and rationality—activities that Eastern practices want to downplay, even nullify. Throwing up my hands in defeat and leaving that portion of the title completely blank might have been an easy solution—and essentially correct in its depiction of the core Eastern vision. Nevertheless, practicality dictated that words of some kind be etched in. The term *Eastern disciplines* seemed most appropriate. Like psychoanalysis, the oriental schools—particularly Zen—are not just philosophies. They are rigorous systems with specific training methods for producing a transformation in consciousness.

I focus mostly on two Eastern disciplines: Zen and Taoism. One reason is primarily pragmatic: This is what I know best. But there is also a more academic rationale. For good reasons, scholars often have chosen to compare Western psychological theories with Zen. Of all religions, East or West, Zen in its purest form is perhaps the least "religious." It barely resembles institutionalized religions as we know them in the West. There is no ideology, no dogma or preachings. There are no rituals or bibles. There is no God to believe in or afterlife to attain. Even words, which supposedly cannot capture the essence of Zen, are avoided. As Herrigel (1960) noted, it is a *method*, a process of altering consciousness to create "enlightenment." Zen is not concerned with metaphysics and spiritual doctrine, but with the very mechanisms by which consciousness becomes transformed. It aims to disclose the underbelly of how we experience ourselves in our immediate world. It points to the mind in its purest form. To facilitate this process, it employs a variety of specific strategies: meditation, koan study, the unique relationship between master and student. All these characteristics—the shunning of metaphysical speculation, the emphasis on experiential process, the application of specific transformational techniques, and especially a distinctive interaction between master and student (not unlike that between clinician and patient)—make Zen ripe for a comparison with contemporary psychoanalysis, especially those theories that stress experience-near understanding.

In many of its most basic premises, Taoism resembles Zen. Historically, the two are intertwined: Indian Buddhism processed through Chinese Taoism became Japanese Zen (Smith, 1965). However, there are some striking differences between the literature on these two philosophies. The writings on Taoism contain few references to specific schools or training methods. Other than the descriptions of expressing Taoist principles through painting, poetry, dietary cuisine, or the martial-arts style Tai Chi Chuan, there are few accounts of how, exactly, people learn Taoism. The teacher/student relationship is underplayed, as compared to the numerous stories about disciples' encounters with Zen masters; and although Taoist meditation techniques do exist, most books rarely mention them. Of course, the paucity of information on specific training methods and teacher/student interactions may not reflect Taoism itself, but instead may be one of the damaging outcomes of the Chinese Cultural Revolution—or it simply may reflect the dearth of Western translations of Taoist texts.

If such features indeed are underplayed in Taoism, it may mark Taoism's strength, as well as its weakness. One pure, undistracted Taoist goal is the study of change and transition as manifested in nature—in the movement of water, the activity of fire, the dynamics of earth and sky. These processes of change reflect the more universal patterns of transformation and serve as models for understanding all types of changes—environmental, social, psychological, transcendental. If Taoism is anything, it is the revealing of how things evolve, shift, and transmute into other things. Tao *is* the archetype of all processes of change. For this reason Taoism can serve as fertile ground for the cross-fertilization of Eastern ideas with psychoanalysis, which epitomizes the Western "science" of intrapsychic changes. In fact, the most basic of the Taoist principles parallel those in psychoanalysis. Taoism's emphasis on images as powerful, multifaceted expressions of hidden truths overlaps with the psychoanalytic emphasis on the imagistic quality of unconscious processes, as in dreams. Its inquiries into the vibrant polarity of *yin* and *yang* that underlies all processes of change reflects the psychoanalytic exploration of the dynamic polarities in personality. The doctrine of *wu wei*—employing creative nonaction to allow an unfolding of things according to their own design—resembles some of the fundamental principles of psychoanalytic technique. And *Te*—the virtue of harmony, naturalness, and spontaneity, of things being the way they were meant to be, the everyday manifestation of Tao—may very well be the ultimate goal of any form of psychotherapy.

Although this book aims to compare and integrate psychoanalysis with Zen and Taoism, other theories and philosophies should not be ignored in any East/West study. No one discipline owns the market on the exploration of the self. Humanistic psychology, existentialism, phenomenology, deconstructionism, Indian and Tibetan Buddhism, Sufism, Christian and Judaic mysticism, Yoga, analytic psychology, Hinduism—all of these (just to name a few), as expressed in art and literature, as well as formal academic treatises, can fortify our efforts. At various points I draw on ideas from such disciplines. I also hope the text will trigger further associations in the reader that enhance his or her understanding at those points where the text may be lacking. Consider psychoanalysis, Zen, and Taoism to be the nucleus, the center focus, of this East/West study. Also important, if not more important, is the surrounding field of ideas and insights that provide the complex backdrop to this focus—a backdrop that sustains and enriches the nucleus. Keeping in mind this inter-weaving dynamic between a figure and its multifaceted ground makes good sense while undertaking an exploration of any kind. It also lies at the center of the marriage between Eastern and Western thought. One rabbit IS many rabbits.

Some Obstacles

Striving for an integration of psychoanalysis and Eastern philosophy one runs headfirst into some rather stubborn deterrents. The history of this endeavor is riddled with misunderstandings, prejudice, mud-slinging, and even a primitive form of territoriality. Early psychoana-lytic theorists passed off Zen and mystical practices in general as pathological regressions to a condition of merger with the mother. Psychoanalysts are not alone, because the prejudice against Eastern practices runs rampant in Western culture as a whole. This became very clear to me during an undergraduate lecture on Zen when the class of suburban, middle-class students, downright outraged, unani-mously proclaimed that Zen must be "brainwashing."

The airs of misinformed prejudice and superiority blow from the East as well. One Zen student (see Matthiessen, 1987, p. 160), who suggested to a master that Zen and psychotherapy had similar effects in overcoming suffering, met with a sharp reply. The master insisted that the psychotherapist is just another patient. "Can he cure this bowl? This table? Zen can do! Can psychotherapy cure birds? Or only, perhaps" (anticipating, as Matthiessen suggested, a familiar Japanese joke) "some kind of monkey?" Apparently, his evaluation is shared by other masters as well. Matthiessen mentions a Zen teacher who claimed that psychotherapy deals with "twigs," whereas Zen aims "straight into the root."

Obviously, many psychotherapists, even those inclined toward the East, will not take kindly to such remarks. Psychoanalysts, es-pecially, who spend their professional lives delving into the uncon-scious, will not appreciate the estimation of their work as mere tinkering with twigs. Such comments reveal the naiveté of those who have not experienced the unlocking of the unconscious during in-depth intrapsychic exploration. Although there may be a dimension of truth to what these Zen masters have to say—a truth that can clar-ify and enrich the psychoanalytic purpose—it is the attitude by which it is conveyed, and the underlying close-mindedness, that is destruc-tive to all concerned, including the masters.

Fortunately, many Zen teachers do recognize this problem.

They warn their students against falling into the "stink of Zen." Usually this expression refers to the self-conscious, self-indulgent, self-aggrandizing forms of spiritual pursuit—a preoccupation that reflects the exact attitude of self-importance (narcissism, in psychoanalytic terms) that Zen aims to negate. In a more general sense, the stink is the overall tendency to take oneself, and Zen, too seriously. Some astute teachers are quick to counteract this problem. For example, students have come to bow before the master, only to find a large pumpkin sitting on his cushion. Masters have been known to hang their underwear out in the garden in order to shock the students into thinking that someone had dared to defile the sanctity of their monastery.

So, too, the true believers in psychoanalysis may distort their faith into an all-consuming preoccupation that foils the scope and clarity of their vision. I am reminded of the eminent psychoanalyst who congratulated one of his students on her recent engagement. Admitting that she was happy, the student nevertheless expressed worry about the fact that her fiance had never been analyzed. "Analyzed—smanalyzed!" he retorted. "He's a great guy, marry him!" The necessity of not taking one's devotion to an ideology too far was expressed by Freud himself in his now-famous remark: Sometimes a cigar is just a cigar.

Zen and psychoanalysis are both pathways that lead somewhere. The destination is what is important. Zen compares itself to a raft that carries you across a river. Once you're there, you can leave the raft behind. Otherwise, you cling to something that is of no use to you—and you get nowhere. Being willing and able to abandon the raft is the type of attitude that will make an integration of East and West possible. It is this kind of outlook that will overcome what Rubin (1992a) describes as "Eurocentrism" and "Orientocentrism"—the pervasive tendency to view the world through blinders while clinging rigidly to one of the two hemispheric viewpoints; to distort the views of the other camp according to your own preconceptions; or simply to devalue the other side without a second thought. The knee-jerk tendency to reject the unfamiliar must yield to the realization that what appears as heresy may be enlightenment in disguise.

One issue that affects integrating East and West makes some psychoanalytic clinicians especially edgy. They are not comfortable with discussions about "transcendental" or "transpersonal" realms. Some people roll their eyes at the mere mention of religion and spirituality. Perhaps this discomfort is simply the result of conflicting paradigms. Transpersonal concepts run against the grain of a theory that historically has focused almost exclusively on intrapsychic events and their social ramifications. Perhaps the discomfort reflects a more personal, narcissistic injury inflicted by the possibility that there is something beyond psychological dynamics as we traditionally conceptualize them, work with them every day in our practice, and believe them to exist in ourselves. And then, of course, perhaps the eye-rollers are correct: Ideas about transcendental existences may be pure poppycock.

To the contrary, several notable theorists (e.g., McDargh, 1983; Meissner, 1984; Rizzuto, 1979) have shown that psychoanalysts need not feel uneasy with issues about God, faith, and religious experiences. At the very least, these theorists demonstrated how we can study the psychological manifestations and consequences of the belief in spiritual realms, as well as the experience of spiritual realms. Implicitly, they also reveal that the transcendental world is not as otherworldly as it may seem. Psychological theory does have access to it.

Zen would add that everyday people also have access to such realms. If there is any one message that is clear in Zen, it is that enlightenment is near at hand, that it is one's "everyday mind." As Matthiessen (1987) noted, the "mystical" only seems mystical if we assume reality is limited to what can be measured by the intellect and senses. Knowing does take other important forms—as in that thing called *intuition* that is the staple of every clinician's professional diet.

It also is important to emphasize that the East has many ideas to offer other than those concerning transcendental spheres of existence. The beauty of oriental thought is its ability to translate spiritual issues into practical, down-to-earth concerns. Buddhism contains a rich analysis of emotional and mental phenomena. Zen illuminates the perceptions, attitudes, and actions of day-to-day living. Taoism, as evident in the classic *I Ching*, comprehensively investigates the benefits and hazards revolving around a wide variety of social and psychological situations, and it offers strategies for contending with those situations. Although we may spend some time with our head in the clouds pondering the metapsychological and transcendental implications of spirituality, we must not overlook the vital, pragmatic connections between Asian knowledge and the insights of psychoanalysis.

We also must not forget that any theory or discipline is rooted in the social/historical context in which it developed. We cannot escape how our civilization influences our ideas, personality, and spirituality any more than we can escape the air we breath. The features of psychoanalysis, Zen, and Taoism reflect the cultural backgrounds that nourished them. Even the basic definitions and personal experience of the self is culture-bound in the East and West (see Roland, 1988). Perhaps theories can never fully transcend their social/historical context, even cross-cultural theories. Lifting oneself up out of one's own boots may be impossible. But any attempt to integrate Eastern and Western ideas without taking heed of this dilemma undoubtedly will run into misleading or faulty conclusions.

Integrating and Pointing

There are several pathways to follow while attempting an integration of Eastern and Western ideas. Eastern ideas can be assimilated into a Western framework by interpreting them through the lens of our psychological theories—a strategy often employed in psychoanalytic studies, particularly in efforts to explain transpersonal experiences. Often, we deal with novel and seemingly strange concepts by trying to comprehend them in terms of our own familiar concepts. This is a viable integrative method, and one that I employ in this book. But there are drawbacks. Simply translating an Eastern concept into its Western equivalent sometimes can sink into a stale form of algebra in which words are substituted for other words. Searching for Eastern ideas that are comparable to Western ones—that is, the ideas that are most readily integrated—also may lead us to ignore the disparities between East and West. More insidiously, this approach can degenerate into a form of Eurocentrism in which we explicitly force round pegs into square holes and implicitly proclaim, by assuming our Western concepts can cover all bases, that our ideology possesses more explanatory power than theirs.

Starting from the other hemisphere, we may also cast Western concepts into an Eastern framework—a scheme less common in psychoanalytic work than it is in humanistic and transpersonal psychology. The chapter on Taoist imagery in this book attempts such an integration for psychoanalysis. Of course, coming from the East, we run into the same pitfall as we did from the West. Orientocentrism—overvaluing and idealizing Eastern ideas—can become just another set of blinders that leads us to ignore or distort what could be a clear, fresh view of Western theory.

The most ideal form of integration encompasses a drawing together from both sides simultaneously. It involves a fluid shifting back and forth between interpretations from the East and interpretations from the West. We must look for the areas of overlap where the two camps seem to be revealing the same sorts of insights, a mirroring of ideas that offers consensual validation. To accomplish this, we may need to accentuate the similarities while, for the moment, minimizing the differences: To translate one system into a foreign system first requires a zooming in on even the smallest areas of similarity. What may begin as a simple comparison or translation may develop into a subtle blending of the shades of meaning from both systems.

We must also clarify, rather than ignore, the areas of disparity. These regions of contrast may be the fertile ground that expands and enriches each side via the exploration of thesis, antithesis, and synthesis. Only by understanding the differences as well as the similarities between oriental and psychoanalytic approaches can we establish a truly synergistic, complementary integration in which the two not only support and validate each other, but also balance and embellish each other by filling in their respective deficiencies.

One reviewer of this book commented that it was an attempt to compare apples and oranges. This is both true and necessary. For without comparing apples and oranges, without exploring their complementarity, how would we ever arrive at the concept of 'fruit?' Exploring the ways in which two things are both the same and different is the only means by which we arrive at a higher-order concept that integrates the two. It is the method of triangulation by which we use two known points to determine the position of an as-yet undetermined third point.

Reaching for this integration of East and West will guide us into unfamiliar territory that presents some potentially anxiety-provoking challenges. We must risk a modification of traditional theories without falling into the trap of stretching them into farfetched shapes that lose their strength. We must walk a delicate balance, applying Eastern and Western ideas without clinging to either side. If we are successful, we move into a peripheral zone that is not conventional psychology nor traditional Eastern practice. It is a neither-here-nor-there territory that has the disadvantage of placing us into a marginal status. Hybrids are not easily accepted by either side. But it is a zone that also offers a transitional space for creative ventures and the establishment of a new, revitalized identity. Maintaining this identity requires that we not succumb to a narcissistic investment in one system, assuming that the other system must somehow yield to it. It demands the self-confidence that allows us to acknowledge the limitations of our old world view and the acceptance of new ideas that lie outside it. It compels us constantly to question our basic assumptions and cherished ideals.

Bodhidharma, one of the patriarchs of Buddhism, crossed the Himalayas to China—not an easy feat for an old man (it is also the subject of a Zen koan: Why did he do it?). Years later, the emperor, who had taken a keen interest in Buddhism, invited Bodhidharma to the palace. Over a cup of tea the emperor encouraged this great religious man to discuss his insights. "What is the essence of the holy teachings?" he inquired insistently. "No holiness, only nothing," Bodhidharma replied. Skeptical and frustrated, the emperor pressed on, "Who stands before me?" The old master's reply was simple and straightforward: "I know not."

Surely Bodhidharma was no dolt. His reply indeed communicated the core of his teachings, a message we need to hear in our attempts to integrate East and West. "No" can be the only reply when we ask if we have touched the essence of any profound teaching. Not-knowing must take precedence over knowing. To not-know points us in the direction of the thing to be discovered. It is to acknowledge the essence of the unknown that continually slips away from us as we continually pursue it. Not-knowing constitutes the basic attitude of the "beginner's mind" described by Suzuki (1970): the mind that is open, limitless, ready for new prospects. For the beginner's mind there are many possibilities, whereas for the expert's mind there are few. When we start from a position of not-knowing, we experience wonder and awe rather than the stale taste of the familiar. To see new vistas we must learn to undo and transcend our old concepts in what becomes an "art of unknowing" (Kurtz, 1989). This strategy always will leave a realm of obscurity and uncertainty at the center of our study—intentionally so. As Bruner (1959) suggested, there also is an "art of ambiguity" that enriches rather than detracts from any discipline. Allowing ambiguity at exactly the crucial spot points us in the right direction, fuels the creative imagination, offers a hint of what lies beyond our understanding without forcing a prejudiced grasp of what is not yet graspable.

The ancient masters compared Zen to a finger that points to the moon. We also may think of psychoanalysis and the Eastern disciplines in general as pointing fingers. We can analyze their details, compare and contrast them, look for similarities and differences, but we should not focus on the fingers to the exclusion of where they are pointing. We should not mistake the fingers for the moon. I once had a dog, Duncan, who loved to bark (in a befriending way) at cats outside our front door. When I saw one, I would energetically motion to the door with my finger, hoping to direct his attention to the cat. Invariably, he would sense the excitement in my voice and stare at my finger. There is a bit of Duncan in all of us. Despite the efforts of psychoanalysis and Eastern disciplines, we sometimes concentrate on the concreteness of the pointer, rather than see the more elusive thing to which it points.

Finally, before progressing into an academic study of Eastern thought, we must consider how to handle the ancient masters' warning that the intellect will always fail to grasp the essence of Zen and Taoism. Some masters even have relegated scholarly and literary people to the lowest rung among Zen students. If this is true, is an academic attempt to integrate Eastern and Western ideas at all viable? Should all books—including this one—be taken only as idle ruminations that lack true insight? Perhaps. Yet perhaps intellect, an undeniably integral human attribute, also is an expression of the Tao that must be recognized for what it is—simply intellect, with all its strengths and weaknesses.

2

East Meets West

The History of East Meeting West

Around 600 B.C. the son of an Indian king became disillusioned with the luxuries of his upbringing. Deeply troubled by the suffering of everyday life that he saw outside the palace walls, he decided to abandon his inheritance and wander the countryside in search of an explanation. For many years, under the tutelage of spiritual masters, he ardently practiced meditation and asceticism, and he studied the traditional philosophical and religious systems. But he was not satisfied. His training, no matter how thorough or intense it seemed, did not reveal to him a solution for human suffering. One day, in desperate determination, he sat under a tree to immerse himself in meditation, vowing never to get up unless he absolutely understood the dynamics of the mind that created suffering. He sat there for several days.

Finally, a profound realization befell him. It transformed him. He now was the "enlightened one" whose life mission was to pass on what he had learned, and, most important, to directly stimulate in others (and thereby transmit) the psychic transformation he had experienced under that tree. His teachings spread throughout India. He passed down his insights through his lineage of disciples, who then carried them to China, Southeast Asia, and across the waters to Japan. Eventually, the momentum broke through the hemispheric barrier to Europe and the Americas. With each move, from country to country, culture to culture, the teachings blended with new ideas, divided into different schools, and evolved according to the needs of the society.

But the basic ingredients of the original teachings, which were both robust and versatile, remained the same. His system was psychological rather than metaphysical, because it directly addressed human nature and human problems; it was therapeutic in its design to end pain and suffering; it was pragmatic in its attention to practical predicaments that required solutions; it was both "empirical" in its emphasis on direct, personal experience as the final test for truth and "scientific" in using such experience to uncover the cause-and-effect relationships that order existence; it was directed to the individual because it made an appeal to each person to find his or her own way (Smith, 1965). It emerged as one of the most influential philosophical and religious systems in history.

Some 2500 years later, just before the turn of the twentieth century, a German physician turned his attention away from the conventions of his training in neurology and toward the problem of mental suffering. He grew dissatisfied with the popular psychiatric explanations of psychological illness and ventured into new scientific territory. Through the analysis of his patients' psyches—and, more astoundingly, through the prolonged, systematic probing of the depths of his own mind—he beheld intellectual and personal revelations that launched his new vision of human nature. At first his insights were rejected by the scientific community; but the luminance of his ideas inevitably attracted disciples. His mission was to pass on to his followers not only his conceptual knowledge, but also to give them the direct, personal experience of a rigorous exploration and transformation of their own psyches. He and his followers transported the heritage to England, throughout Europe, and into the Americas. The teaching blended with other philosophies, separated into different schools, and progressed in its subtlety and complexity.

In contrast to the somatogenic emphasis of traditional psychiatry, the new approach was distinctly psychological. It had a powerful theoretical structure, but was also distinctly therapeutic and pragmatic. Its hypotheses were tested empirically, through the personal experiences of the case study method. The results led to scientific conclusions about the cause-and-effect relationships that regulate the psychological world. It was always directed to the individual, because it assumed that each person must use the method to find his or her own way. It became one of the most influential intellectual and therapeutic systems in history.

In the telling of legends, as in these two, archetypal themes are deliberately highlighted. Buddha and Freud were both charismatic leaders who spoke to the underlying needs of their times that cried out for attention. Each in his own way addressed the issue of suffering. The similarities between the histories of the traditions they founded, and the sheer momentum of ideas that they set in motion, made it inevitable that their disciplines would someday converge.

What is so surprising is not that Buddha and Freud eventually shook hands, but that it didn't occur until some 100 years after the birth of psychoanalysis. Before that time, psychoanalysis showed either indifference or a mildly devaluing attitude toward Eastern religions. This less-than-enthusiastic greeting originated partly from Freud's reductionistic criticisms of religion in general. In such works as *The Future of an Illusion* (1927) and *Civilization and Its Discontents* (1930), he viewed religion as a cosmology whose explanations of the world eased infantile feelings of helplessness, as a system of rewards and punishments that attempted to substitute for adaptive superego functions, and as an unhealthy recapitulation of parent/child relationships, especially the oedipal drama. He labeled religion as a neurotic, often obsessional acting out of unconscious conflicts. He claimed it had evolved into a wish-fulfilling illusion that undermined rationality and deceptively channeled sexual and aggressive drives.

Freud sketched this view of religion based mostly on his study of Christianity and Judaism. He knew very little about the East. His brief intellectual excursion into this area was stimulated by his correspondence with the French poet and author Romain Rolland, a student of Hinduism, who encouraged Freud to examine meditation from a psychoanalytic viewpoint. Unfortunately, Freud's (1930) conclusion echoed his general tendency to reduce religion to pathology. He explained the meditative experience of "oneness with the universe" as a regression to the preverbal, symbiotic union with the mother and the revival of unbounded narcissism. This concept of the "oceanic feeling" remained uncontested for many years. A variety of theoretical and historical analyses (e.g., Horton, 1974; Kovel, 1990; Shafi, 1973) identified it as a lightning-rod theme in the psychoanalytic position on contemplative states of consciousness, a position that placed psychoanalysis at odds with Eastern traditions.

On the wider theoretical landscape, in the first half of the twentieth century psychoanalysis moved in a direction that was generally incompatible with Eastern styles of thinking. Freud's abandonment of hypnotic technique in favor of free association set in motion an important historical transition (Kris, 1950). The psychoanalytic emphasis shifted from altered states of consciousness to waking consciousness, from primary process to secondary process, from images to words. The analysis of transference became the primary therapeutic objective. To achieve this goal, the analyst was advised to rely solely on the ego functions of reason and rationality. Pursuing hypnotic and meditative reveries was considered a distraction from the verbal, rational exploration of the patient's transference reactions to the analyst. Even dream interpretations focused mostly on verbal as-sociations. Words and language, which appeared more amenable to objective, scientific investigations, became the primary tools of the ego in its psychotherapeutic quest to master the unconscious. But psychoanalysis was not alone in this transition. During the early 1900s, academic psychology as a whole was shifting its emphasis to the mechanisms of language, logic, and reason, rather than the seem-ingly quixotic realm of mental images and introspective daydream-ing, the topics that were its heritage (Holt, 1964).

Beginning in the 1940s and reaching a peak in the 1950s, the tide began to turn, and a wave of appreciation for Eastern philosophy surfaced among psychoanalysts. Many of them were drawn to Zen. The essays of D. T. Suzuki, a renowned Zen scholar from Kyoto, were translated into English and European languages. His ideas became a beacon for many Western thinkers. Akihisa Kondo, a Japa-nese psychiatrist who trained in the United States, introduced a num-ber of psychoanalysts to Suzuki—most notably Karen Horney and her colleagues, as well as Erich Fromm. Fromm, in turn, influenced a number of members of the William Alanson White Institute in New York City, and invited Suzuki to speak in New Mexico in 1957. Hor-ney's group, which included Harold Kelman, David Shainberg, and Antonio Wenkert, were previously inclined toward Eastern philoso-phy because of their interest in Hasidic Judaism and the existential philosophy of Martin Buber (Roland, 1988). Horney first applied ideas from Zen in her book *Our Inner Conflicts* (1945). In 1952, shortly before her death, she traveled to Japan with Suzuki to observe first-hand the life at a Zen monastery and to lecture at Jikeikai Medical School in Tokyo, where she compared psychoanalysis to Morita ther-apy, a treatment designed by Shomo Morita, who worked at Jikeikai and was heavily influence by Zen. In her posthumously published *Final Lectures* (1987), she called on psychoanalysts to learn from the ideas and traditions of Buddhism.

During the late 1950s and early 1960s, a surge of articles ap-peared (see Haimes, 1972). In 1959 Fromm published his ideas on Zen and psychoanalysis in *Psychologia,* an international psychology jour-nal originating from Kyoto University that became a showcase for English-language articles on Zen, psychoanalysis, and East/West studies in general. In 1960 Fromm revised his paper and published it with those of Suzuki and Richard DeMartino, a professor of religion, in the now-classic book *Zen Buddhism and Psychoanalysis.* Harold Kel-man, who became president of the American Institute for Psycho-analysis and editor of the *American Journal of Psychoanalysis,* published a string of articles (1958, 1959a, 1959b) that clearly revealed the strong influence of Eastern thought on his view of psychoanalysis, particularly on his ideas concerning the experience of communing and relating to others. Other psychoanalytic works, which, unfortunately, have not received as much recognition in historical analyses, appeared by Westerners such as Maupin (1962), Fingarette (1958), Van Dusen (1957, 1958), and Weis (1960), and by Easterners such as Doi (1962), Kondo (1952) and Sato (1957). Koji Sato founded the journal *Psychologia*, met with Fromm and Horney, and wrote prolifically on Zen and psychology, including a comprehensive review paper in 1968 that contained many references on psychoanalysis.

Of course, a review of how East met West would not be complete without mention of Carl Jung, who took a keen interest in Eastern philosophy. In 1958 he met with Shinichi Hisamatsu, a Japanese psychiatrist and Zen philosopher. A short dialogue between Jung and Hisamatsu was published in 1969 in *Psychologia*. Unfortunately, as Haimes (1972) suggested, the two doctors appear to have had difficulty communicating with each other, which, in addition to a strange translation, made the dialogue sound "Alice in Wonderland-ish." Jung was also drawn to Chinese Taoism. He was intrigued by the *yin/yang* philosophy, the *I Ching* (for which he wrote the foreword in the standard Wilhelm/Baynes translation), and the phenomenon that he called "synchronicity" (Jung, 1951/1971). Jung's attraction to Eastern philosophy reflected his overall fascination with mysticism and the occult—a preoccupation that contributed to his clash with Freud and his exit from the inner psychoanalytic circle in 1927.

During the 1950s, an important theoretical shift within psychoanalysis made it a more fertile ground for Zen influences to take root. The unconscious was no longer viewed simply as a reservoir of repressed memories, fantasies, and affects that had to be mastered by the powers of the ego's rationality. As in the Zen viewpoint, the unconscious was recognized for its power to offer new ways of perceiving and knowing. It was a potential source of intuition and creativity, even of wisdom, that could expand and enrich the conscious mind. This was the major thesis of Fromm's (1959) paper on Zen and psychoanalysis and an idea that Jung had long endorsed. Although still dwelling on the notion of regression, Kris (1950) and later Schafer (1958) proposed that a "regression in service of the ego" enabled one to tap the unconscious as a fountain of artistic inspiration. The illogical, nonrational modes of unconscious thinking could be a gold mine, rather than a devious pest that needed to be subjugated to reality's demands. As evident in the works of Lewin (1950) and Ehrenzweig

(1971), "oneness" experiences—the result of an immersion into un-conscious modes of perception and affect—were no longer pegged as strictly pathological, but as a potential catalyst for health and creativ-ity. In the early 1960s, Bion would emerge as the great psychoanalytic mystic who idealized the transformative powers of the unconscious. In her work as an artist, Milner (1957) similarly charted the uncon-scious as a realm of mystical creativity and revelation. These ideas, later blending with the emphasis on subjectivity and the "self" in ob-ject relations theory and self psychology, and with the growing recog-nition of the potentially salutary effects of religious and mysti-cal experiences (Jones, 1991; Finn & Gartner, 1992; Lovinger, 1984; Meissner, 1984; Rizzuto, 1979; Rubin & Suler, 1992), further ripened psychoanalysis for its dialogue with the East.

The theoretical changes within psychoanalysis during the mid-1900s and its growing interest in the East reflected an even wider cul-tural transition that affected all of Western philosophy, literature, and science. In the 1950s and 1960s the writings of Alan Watts, Aldous Huxley, R. H. Blyth, Christian Humphreys, Thomas Merton, and Eu-gen Herrigel roused the Occident's curiosity about religious experi-ences, mysticism, and Zen. The existential philosophies of Nietzsche, Kierkegaard, Tillich, Buber, and Heidegger, as well as the literary works of Herman Hesse, D. H. Lawrence, and James Joyce, were gaining popularity. Their ideas attacked rationalism, emphasized subjectivity and phenomenology, and probed the perplexing balance and inseparability of opposites. William James's turn-of-the-century classic, *Varieties of Religious Experience,* was rediscovered. Bergson pro-posed a philosophy of radical intuitionism. Gödel in mathematics and Heisenberg in physics pointed out the limits of reason and objectiv-ity. The beat generation waved Zen as its banner, paving the way for the 1960s, when mysticism, altered states of consciousness, and ex-cursions into the psyche became a fashionable way of life.

The burgeoning investment in Zen was not just faddish, nor simply speculative and intellectual. The Japanese Zen masters Nyo-gen Senzaki, Nakagawa Soen, Hakuun Yasutani, and Shunryu Su-zuki came to the United States to develop Zen training centers. A few devoted Westerners who began their training then, such as Rob-ert Aitken, Richard Baker, Bernard Glassman, Philip Kapleau, and Maurine Stuart, were later ordained as full-fledged teachers. Many Americans, including psychotherapists of various backgrounds, were drawn to the opportunity for a firsthand, serious study of Zen. Some were fascinated by meditation. Others found their way to Zen through the martial arts, which were rapidly gaining popularity.

It would be a mistake to conclude that Zen was the only path by which psychoanalysis encountered the East. Given the amenability of Zen philosophy and practice to the psychoanalytic method, it was perhaps an easier path to follow than others. But Taoism, Hinduism, Indian Buddhism, and Tibetan Buddhism, among other disciplines, all have influenced Westerners. Zen and psychoanalysis were two points of contact within a more expansive rendezvous between East and West. They also were not monolithic entities that simply met head-on. Each drew upon and evolved out of a variety of other disciplines. Zen was born in China from the wedding of Indian Buddhism and Chinese Taoism. Many psychoanalysts who originally reached out for Zen were heavily influenced by existentialism or humanistic psychology. Zen and psychoanalysis converged as two rivers fed by other tributaries and by the watershed of entire regions.

A Progression of Selfobject Relationships

Randall (1984) once described the various selfobject relationships— mirroring, alter ego, and idealizing—that exist between religion and psychology. Just as narcissistic dimensions of relatedness abide within the individual self, so, too, they operate within the structure of group-selves such as religion and psychology. With all the beliefs, practices, and activities that comprise its complex organization, the group-self is driven by the basic narcissistic need to survive as a unique entity. It uses the existence of other group-selves to define itself, activate itself, and bolster its own cohesion.

Randall's analysis applies to psychoanalysis and Eastern thought as well. The history of their encounter roughly corresponds to the progression from archaic to mature forms of selfobject relationships.

Both psychoanalysis and Zen have brandished their own versions of infantile grandiosity. At the most primitive developmental level, each has been guilty of making grandiose, monistic claims about solely owning the inside story on the "truth" of how the mind works and the essence of human suffering. For psychoanalysis, everything can be explained according to the principles of the unconscious; for Zen, the mystical experience of "no-mind" determines all. Both have believed that only those who participate in their faith truly see the light. They tolerated only those other disciplines that deferentially mirrored and supported their viewpoint. At this level of development, any competing system of thought is completely ignored because it introduces new questions and uncertainties that threaten the stability of the self. If the alien system does present challenges that cannot be avoided, the reaction is a counterattack of criticism and devaluation driven by narcissistic anger: The group-self wants to do away with its perceived menace.

In a less archaic form of the grandiose self, psychoanalysis and Zen believe that the other is of value, and does have a separate existence, although the other's view is limited in scope. The Zen experience is valuable, but it does not take into account the individual's overall psychological and social development, as does psychoanalysis. Psychoanalysis does much to reveal the unconscious functions of the individual self, but it falls short of the larger Zen vision that transcends the individual self. Each discipline believes that the other should respect and mirror its fuller knowledge. Each may defend against this underlying grandiosity by presenting what appears to be an alter-ego attitude toward the other. Zen is actually a psychological system, like psychoanalysis, that can be explained by and reduced to psychoanalytic concepts. Psychoanalysis, in the long run, strives toward a religious and spiritual understanding of people, something Zen has been doing for a long time. Although a grandiose attitude underlies such statements, these alter-ego positions do reveal some form of connectedness with the other through assumed similarities to the narcissistic self.

Psychoanalytic thinkers have at times idealized Eastern thought by what Randall (1984) called a "borrowing" form of idealization. By merging with the acclaimed Eastern discipline, participating in its unique insights, and adopting those ideas, they sought to secure and expand the psychoanalytic self structure. At times bowing to the East's grandiosity, some clinicians and theorists have accepted the idea that the East's vision surpasses that of the West, that psychoanalysis should be remolded in the shape of Eastern philosophy. The reverse idealization of psychoanalysis by Eastern thinkers has not been as frequent or as strong. At a well-known institute for East/West studies, a respected American Zen master once conducted a workshop entitled "Zen Is Not Psychotherapy."

Randall's (1984) call for healthy selfobject relations between religion and psychology applies also to psychoanalysis and Eastern thought. Psychologically healthy individuals and group-selves thrive within a matrix of supporting selfobjects. In recent years this goal seems to be within reach. There was evidence of it, for instance, in the 1984 Inner Science Conference held at Amherst College, at which the Dalai Lama and Western scientists exchanged ideas. The healthy mirroring between Eastern and Western thinkers provides a sense of motivation to carry out one's ambitions; increased self-esteem follows the applause of one's achievements. Healthy alter-ego responses create continuity between selves and between group-selves, thereby encouraging camaraderie and open dialogue. Healthy idealizations provide guidelines for directing the creative tensions that arise from the need to actualize nuclear ambitions and ideals. Such enriching dynamics between East and West are still in the nascent stage.

Historical Themes

Examining how psychoanalysis and Zen progressed toward their inevitable encounter with each other uncovers several important historical themes. These themes pertain to the parallel aspects of their development as separate disciplines that addressed similar issues concerning human nature and human suffering. They reveal the developmental facets of Zen and psychoanalysis as "selves" that strive for inner cohesion, stability, and continuity over time.

Routinization

The sociologist Max Weber (1947) described how religious and social movements begin with a charismatic leader who speaks directly to the underlying needs and emotions of the times. The leader is set apart from ordinary people and treated as being endowed with exceptional powers of intellect and insight. The charismatic experience is spontaneous, inspirational, mesmerizing—but unstable. After the leader dies, the descendants scurry to preserve the teachings by incorporating them into the rituals and routines of an institutional structure. Those descendants who attain legitimacy and power derive their status from being linked to the original charismatic experience that is encoded into and perpetuated through the social structures. The teachings survive, but often at the cost of the founder's original experiential insight becoming diluted and routinized within the bureaucracy. Over time, the discipline may stagnate; the group-self loses its vitality, stiffens, and cracks.

Both Zen and psychoanalysis had their origins in charismatic phenomena. Both, at times, have faced the threat of the original inspirational insights becoming stagnant through excessive routinization and bureaucratization. Matthiessen (1987) described how many masters in Japan feared that Zen practice had become overly institutionalized, rote, and stale. Shortly before her death, in her presidential address to the Psychoanalytic Division of the American Psychological Association, Helen Block Lewis lamented that candidates at psychoanalytic institutes were far more creative in their thinking before they began their training than when they finished. Zen and psychoanalysis, both rooted in an initial passion for exploring and transforming the psyche, at times have sunk into passionlessness.

Zen and psychoanalysis also share the emphasis on lineage as an idealized feature of their institutional structure. One's legitimacy and authority are determined to a large extent by belonging to a recognized school and by tracing one's connection to a recognized figure. Z was analyzed by Y, who was analyzed by X; C received dharma transmission from B, who received it from A. Ideally, one's ancestral line extends back to one of the truly great teachers, or to the original charismatic figure himself, Freud or Buddha. This emphasis on lineage is a double-edged sword. On the one hand, it maximizes continuity in transmitting the elusive experiential component of the teachings. On the other hand, it cements credibility and authority almost exclusively within the institutional structure. Some critics have devalued Alan Watts's and D. T. Suzuki's contributions in bringing Zen to the West because, not having received dharma transmission from a recognized master, they did not qualify as true lineage holders.

Transplantation

One way Zen and psychoanalysis have avoided excessive routinization is by moving to a new culture. Bodhidharma, one of the patriarchs of Buddhism, must have understood this when he carried the teachings from India over the Himalayas to China. While taking root in foreign soil, a discipline absorbs new ideas. It must adapt in order to survive the challenge of an alien climate. It discovers which of its characteristics have enough vitality to handle the new environment, which ones are flexible enough to evolve, which ones must be discarded as no longer useful. During the transplantings of psychoanalysis, England gave birth to object relations theory and the United States to self psychology. The Chinese and Japanese boiled down the complex rituals and spiritual speculations of Buddhism into the simplicity of Zen. When Japanese Zen eventually showed signs of becoming excessively routinized, some masters believed that it could be revived by moving it to the United States. There, among other benefits, the American emphasis on individuality could help counteract the authoritarian and militaristic qualities of Japanese Zen that had threatened its vitality. Like a swimming shark, a discipline must keep moving to stay alive.

Schisms and Debating the Essence

"Religions are always splitting," Smith (1965, p. 132) stated in his classic text, *The Religions of Man*. This holds true for many social, philosophical, and intellectual systems as well. The group-self may fracture in reaction to the extreme routinization of its practices and belief system. What turns rigid often cracks and fragments. Schisms arise from ideological conflicts and differences of opinion about new avenues of development. Even what were previously considered the most elemental principles may be challenged and discarded by revisionist schools. Psychoanalysts debate whether the drives or the self is the essence of personality dynamics, whether psychological problems are primarily the result of repressed conflicts or intrapsychic deficits, whether the pathogenic kernels are trauma or unconscious fantasy, whether interpretation or empathy is the most curative vehicle. Zen masters disagree over whether enlightenment is attained suddenly or gradually, and whether koan study is necessary to intensify training (Rinzai school) or "just sitting" in meditation (Soto school) is enough. A few masters have even questioned the necessity of meditation, which traditionally has been considered the *sine qua non* of Zen. Instead, they suggest that a person can be led to enlightenment by "direct pointing" during question and answer exchanges with the master (Watts, 1975b). Some masters underplay the importance of enlightenment itself: Suzuki (1970) does not even mention it in his well-known book, *Zen Mind, Beginners Mind*.

Wars among the schools are ubiquitous. For psychoanalysts, they have led to intellectual attacks, personal attacks disguised as intellectual attacks, and overt personal attacks. In feudal Japan, competing Zen teachers sometimes killed their rivals.

Paradoxically, a search for the essence of the discipline, for its purest expression, and for its most unitary foundation is what drives the development of schisms. The debates address theoretical principles and abstract ideals. For psychoanalysis and Zen, which are both therapeutic systems, the debates also focus on what is the most powerful technique for inducing intrapsychic transformation. Each school tends to view the others as relatively ineffectual. Curiously, though, an extended analysis of the differences between the schools often reveals that they are all correct and not as different as they seem. The selfhood of the discipline advances and learns to balance itself when it tolerates fragmentations, digests trial and error, and accepts the ambiguity of opening up unfamiliar territory.

Rebels, Heretics, Outcasts

Healthy disciplines successfully balance orthodox conservatism and progressive liberalism. Heretics and rebels often fuel the latter. Weber's (1947) theory proposed that charismatic leaders with revolutionary insights often arise from outside the existing institutional structure. If they appear from within the bureaucracy, they may be shunned as outcasts, who are then forced to cultivate their own following. The rebelling camp may be reabsorbed into the tradition, thereby modifying it; it may eventually itself become routinized; if it lacks vitality or proves to be a vagary, it will die. Both Zen and psychoanalysis—which themselves started off as renegades—have had their share of dissenters, mavericks, and iconoclasts within and outside the discipline. By proclaiming a new theory to supersede the traditional drive/conflict model, Heinz Kohut, previously a highly respected psychoanalyst, was labeled a pariah and given little support from the establishment. Nevertheless, he eventually developed a following that grew in strength, and finally reentered the mainstream as an influential force.

Approaching his death, Hung-jen, a sixth century Zen master, wanted to pass down his robe and bowl to a successor. He suggested that all candidates for the position should demonstrate the quality of their Zen insight by writing a poem. The most learned and recognized disciple submitted a worthy piece. However, a verse written anonymously onto the monastery wall revealed a far superior mind. Determined to find out who the author was, Hung-jen finally discovered it was written by Hui-neng, a lowly kitchen worker who pounded rice for the meals. In secret, the master passed down his robe and bowl to Hui-neng, who fled the monastery when the rival and his cohorts threatened to kill him. Hui-neng survived the ordeal and later became a renowned master.

Esoteric or Exoteric Direction

In the evolution of the discipline, as its doctrines and practices become more complex, more abstruse, there is a tendency toward esoteric withdrawal. At the most extreme pole, the teachings become private, secretive, the rights of only a privileged few; it is assumed that outsiders will not understand, or that the knowledge is too powerful for laymen to handle. Although the majority of members within the discipline may not resort to such self-preoccupied isolation, smaller subgroupings within it may do so with fanatical fervor. At a less extreme level, the esoteric movement creates experts who are unable to converse with outsiders, or inner factions with specialized interests that have difficulty communicating with other factions.

Being intrapsychically directed as well as scholarly, psychoanalysis and Eastern disciplines both are especially susceptible to esoteric drift. Psychoanalytic extremists may narcissistically withdraw into their intellectual pursuits and a self-preoccupied obsession with the workings of their own minds. The history of Zen and Taoism is filled with stories of hermits meditating in the forest.

But being also systems designed to alleviate suffering, sectors of psychoanalysis, Zen, and Taoism remain rooted to exoteric, altruistic strivings. As theoretically intricate as psychoanalysis may get, it originated as and will continue to be a method whereby one person attempts to therapeutically treat another. Zen, which attempted to shed the theological complexities of Buddhism, insists that it is designed to help ordinary people actualize their "everyday mind."

In their legends and philosophies, the Eastern disciplines have specifically addressed the esoteric/exoteric dilemma. According to myth, Lao Tsu, a wise sage who lived around 500 B.C., fled the mishaps of civilization to retreat into the mountains. Before disappearing forever into the wilderness, he was persuaded by the frontier warden to write down his ideas for posterity. The result was the *Tao Te Ching*, one of the pillars of Taoism. In Buddhism, the two major schools, Theravada and Mahayana (of which Zen is a sect), divided on the issue of esoteric or exoteric emphasis. The Theravada philosophy values the *Arhat*, the highly trained monk who renounces the world and immerses himself totally in inner exploration and the pursuit of perfected enlightenment. The Mahayana doctrine values the *Bodhisattva*, the searcher who brings himself to the brink of complete enlightenment and nirvana, but renounces the prize so that he may return to the world to show others the way (Smith, 1965). Whereas the Theravadan "Little Raft" is meant for a privileged few, the Mahayanan "Big Raft" is intended for the masses. Perhaps a glimmer of this distinction is evident in the psychoanalytic debates about whether "true" psychoanalysis is only for candidates in training and the fortunate patients who are "YAVIS" (young, attractive, verbal, intelligent, successful) or whether it can benefit everyone.

Extinction and Revival

Old ideas die, only to be reborn. The histories of Zen and psychoanalysis are marked by great teachers who are forgotten, then rediscovered and reassimilated decades or centuries later. Matthiessen
(1987) described how the reputation of Dogen, a thirteenth century
Zen master, had completely vanished until Tetsuro Watsuji, an eminent twentieth century Japanese philosopher, happened upon his
writings. According to Matthiessen, contemporary scholars have attempted comparisons of Dogen to Heidegger and Whitehead, believing him to be one of the greatest minds in human history. In the
world of psychoanalysis, Arthur Deikman, who pioneered the empirical study of meditation, is barely mentioned in contemporary, high-
profile studies. The existential psychoanalytic theories of the early
1900s, which are often ignored today, may someday prove to be valuable to current phenomenological and intersubjective approaches in
psychoanalysis.

The extinction and revival of old ideas often is driven by the dynamic polarity of *yin* and *yang*. According to Taoist philosophy, opposites blend into and counterbalance each other; they give rise to each
other and are inseparable. An idea is challenged by an opposing idea,
which gradually gains strength, replaces the old idea, and then is itself challenged by a revival of the old idea (which is now "new"). The
cycling of opposites, Watts (1975b) pointed out, would become repeti-
tious and boring if not for the fact that remembering also cycles with
forgetting. Psychoanalysis, for example, sways with the perennial
movements of the nature/nurture, somatogenic/psychogenic philosophies. Psychiatry, the father of psychoanalysis, is distinctly biological
in emphasis. Freud (1895) himself began his work with a neurological
theory of the mind. But psychoanalysis eventually evolved into the
premier psychological model of human nature. Currently, theories
about the biological foundations of temperament, object-relatedness,
and predispositions to mental illness are regaining their foothold.

A mixture of devaluing and selective perception may prolong
the defunct status of past approaches. We may focus on the faults of
our predecessors and globally devalue them as a way to bolster our
own sense of self as "modern" thinkers. It may be a type of oedipal
rivalry in which we strive to surpass our forebears. There is a tendency among some contemporaries to devalue or ignore predecessors
simply because they are predecessors. The belief that all things de-

velop over time leads to the self-deluding idea that the people of the past are somehow inferior to the people of the present.

A paper frequently cited in the psychoanalytic literature on Eastern thought is Alexander's (1931) "Buddhist training as an artificial catatonia." Concentrating on the title of his paper and rarely discussing its contents, writers have conjured him up as evidence of the early psychoanalytic tendency to misunderstand and pathologize meditation and the "oneness" experience. His analysis at times does smack of biased, Eurocentric tendencies. He labels *nirvana* as an intensely regressive experience in which the world is denied, making Buddhism, unlike psychoanalysis, an asocial practice that does not seek adjustment to the world. He claims that psychoanalysis is superior to Buddhist meditation because it supplements subjective knowledge with objective knowledge. He states that the central core of Buddhism "can be understood in its deepest meaning only in the light of psychoanalytical interpretation" (p. 138).

Selectively focusing on such comments, we could easily conclude that Alexander is guilty of pathologizing Buddhism and idealizing psychoanalysis. However, he also proposes ideas that not only parallel contemporary views, but in some respects surpass them as more liberal and bold. He suggests that Buddhist meditation corresponds to the chronological path of a well-conducted analysis, but goes further: It leads to a recollective knowing of the unconscious that is unlimited by time and space. This knowing is "endopsychic" (p. 143); it entails a recollective awareness of one's embryonic development, when ego and id were identical, when mind and body first evolved. This knowing moves even deeper to retrace the phylogenic events of primordial times that are encoded in embryonic development. Alexander hints that one directly experiences the interchanges between psyche, biology, and matter. It is a realization that transcends the mind/body/matter distinctions and leads to a direct knowing of the world and how one is mirrored in it.

The seed of new ideas lies in the past. According to the Taoist philosophy of *yin* and *yang*, it is even possible that the kernel of a new theory is embedded in an old theory which appears to be its opposite. Contemporary thinkers look back to discover the origins and reflections of their notions in the work of their predecessors, including those who held opposing viewpoints. Psychoanalytic revisionists can find support for their hypotheses somewhere in what Freud said long ago. Zen locates the germ of its philosophy in the incident when

Buddha, rather than speaking about his insights to a gathering of followers, simply raised a flower in the air.

Historical Themes of the Individual Self

Both the psychoanalytic and Eastern disciplines strive for the transformation of the individual self. To better understand this transformative process, the two disciplines can reflect on their own histories as group-selves. The themes that emerge in an historical analysis of how the Eastern and Western disciplines developed, and how they met, apply also to the dynamics of the individual self as it develops and encounters other selves. If, as Buddhist philosophies suggest, the self mirrors the world and the world mirrors the self, then phylogenic and ontogenic development will parallel each other. To focus on only historical or individual development is to overlook the Buddhist vision of the identity of the universal and the particular.

Like the group-selves of the psychoanalytic and Eastern disciplines, the individual self may succumb to a routinization of its structures. Over time, intrapsychic patterns that dictate thought, feeling, and behavior become ritualized, stale, rigid. Although those structures initially evolved to encode a vitally important experience, the essential meaning of the original experience may fade from consciousness with the process of routinization. Pathological symptoms are extreme examples of psychological structures that have solidified into unyielding, life-draining parasites that constrain intrapsychic development. Everyday life routines and habits also may be the product of a routinization process that has carried consciousness far from the inspirational experience which originally touched off underlying thoughts and feelings, and stimulated a potential change in the intrapsychic system. Like the charismatic phenomenon, such inspirational experiences tend to be spontaneous, unstable, short-lived. The attempt to capture and preserve the experience by encoding it into psychological and behavioral habits eventually dwindles in effectiveness.

Transplantation of the self may overcome the effects of excessive routinization. The transplantation may involve the pursuit of a new body of knowledge, a new life activity, or living in another culture. In each case, the self confronts new ideas that challenge the old ones. Some ideas may resonate with and affirm previously unconscious dimensions of the self. In the process of acclimation, the person assimilates novel viewpoints, develops new self structures, tests the flexibility of old ones, and discards self-concepts that are unadaptive.

The search for one's identity becomes intense when immersed into foreign territory. In his psychoanalytic investigation of the Westernizing of Indians and Japanese, Roland (1988) described this process as the "expanding self," which incorporates new organizational structures and paradigms from another civilization or from profound changes within its own culture. Mountain (1983) suggested that Zen itself is an experience of being homeless, of always detaching from the routine patterns of where one lives, both physically and psychologically, in order to reveal new directions for the self.

The expanding self leads to the realization of distinct sectors, schisms, and potentials within self structure. The schisms may be previously repressed or dissociated components of the self, or they may arise from the development of new structures that conflict with the old. Rebels, heretics, and outcasts within self structure are as vital to the overall evolution of the self as are the more conventional, stable self-representations. The goal is not necessarily to abolish or merge the competing concepts, but to harmonize them as interlocking images that will balance the self's long-term development.

This development will entail a variety of historical processes: the cycling between the extinction and revival of self-representations; the realization of how the seeds of newly evolving self structures were present in earlier versions of self structure; the self-affirming or self-transformative encounter with opposing viewpoints; the appearance of "fads" in self-concepts which, lacking a connection to deeper structures, die out; the attachment to a lineage of family or mentors as selfobjects that stabilize the continuity of the self; the devaluing and idealizing of predecessors as a means to define self-identity; the oscillation between esoteric withdrawal—when one becomes self-preoccupied and either unwilling or unsure about being revealed to others—and exoteric engagement, when one pursues a communicative, perhaps altruistic, connection to others.

The self's historical process is a search for its essence. Reenacting the legend of a Freud or Buddha, one becomes a pioneer of self-examination, looking for an answer to questions about one's identity and the meaning of one's suffering. The journey is a widening of the self beyond what it previously knew, a questioning of everything one previously assumed or cherished. The process leads to higher levels of organization. Similar to the group-selves that are Zen and psychoanalysis, the unfolding of the individual self follows a basic Buddhist principle: there is no abiding self. The self is continually changing. The only self is the self that is becoming.

3

Self and No-Self

The Self/No-Self Controversy

Across the entire spectrum of contemporary psychoanalytic theorizing—including self psychology (Kohut, 1977, 1984), object relations theory (Greenberg & Mitchell, 1983), psychoanalytic phenomenology (Atwood & Stolorow, 1984; Stolorow, Brandchaft, & Atwood, 1987), and developmental approaches (Mahler, Pine, & Bergman, 1975; Stern, 1985)—one consistent theme stands out, despite the internal complexities within the theories and the territorial battles between them. The goal of development, as well as the psychotherapeutic attempt to correct thwarted development, is the striving for an integration or enhancement of the self. There are a variety of ways to describe what this process involves: It is a unifying of conscious and unconscious, a harmonizing of self and object representations, an integration of cognitive-affective schemata, of introjections and internalizations, or of id, ego, and superego structures. Regardless of what terms are used, all theories emphasize the need for unity, cohesion, or concordance among the constituents of the self. For Kohut, the survival and development of the self and its nuclear program was the most basic motivating force in personality dynamics.

Invariably, clinicians find themselves, at a very deep level, face to face with this fundamental force in their patients—a face-to-face encounter similar to that of the Zen master and student. Atwood and Stolorow (1984) described this elemental need to maintain the organization of experience in terms of the patient's attempts to affirm, encapsulate, and "concretize" experience in the form of dreams, symbolic objects, symptoms, and behavioral enactments. Especially when a precarious self structure teeters on the edge of disintegration, the person may cling to these concretizations of experience, and to defensive and compensatory structures, or even fragments of the self, to maintain some measure of self-cohesion, even though fragile and/

or maladaptive. At all costs, throughout psychotic, borderline, neurotic, and "normal" conditions, people strive to preserve some, if only marginal, feelings of self-integration and cohesion. It reflects a need for identity, predictability, and continuity across time, a need to attach meaning to one's experiences and to organize those meanings into an overall sense of self that embodies purpose and direction.

Of course, this psychoanalytic emphasis on an integrated self imbued with meaning and purpose does not strike an entirely new chord in the history of psychology. Humanistic theories have long spoken of the basic human need to achieve a harmonious, unified self. This concept is the foundation of self-actualization theories (Maslow, 1971; Rogers, 1963). But even predating psychology, this theme weaves throughout the history of Western philosophy. It is one of the earliest, most fundamental of philosophical ideas. In the *Symposium*, for example, Plato's description of ascending the ladder of knowledge toward higher and higher organizations of truth stood as a metaphor for the increasingly integrated conditions of selfhood.

If we shift now to the East, a very different picture emerges. Across the entire spectrum of Eastern philosophies and religions including Indian, Chinese, and Japanese traditions, one important theme stands out, despite the complexities within these traditions and the ideological conflicts between them: The self is an illusion. To rid ourselves of this illusion, we must be rid of the self. The first three Buddhist Noble Truths are that life is filled with suffering, that this suffering is caused by self-centeredness, and that the only remedy for suffering is to be free of the self. Rather than heralding the need to strive for an enhancement or integration of the self, the Eastern traditions emphatically call for its abrogation. It is not an easy task to accomplish; the Eastern masters recognized, as did Western psychologists, the basic human fear of the loss of one's identity and the pressing motivation to maintain organization and coherency in self-experience. The attempt to anchor a threatened self can reach desperate proportions, as in the middle stages of prolonged meditation, when one experiences extremely vivid memories, intense physical sensations, hallucinatory images, or feelings of omnipotence and omniscience that are elements of the archaic grandiose-exhibitionistic self. Driven by the basic need to avoid disintegration anxiety and stabilize self structure, the meditator feels tempted to hold on to these concretizations of self-experience, as pathological as they may sometimes be. But the Zen master's response is clear: Do not cling. Do not cling to the self or any of its fragments. "Clinging," a Zen word that overlaps with the concept of "concretizing," is a seeking of permanence—and permanence of the self is an illusion.

Here lies the most basic dilemma in the East/West literature. The fact that psychoanalysis advocates the affirmation of self, whereas Zen calls for its negation, stands as a formidable stumbling block in the attempts to marry Western psychology and Eastern philosophy. For some researchers this ideological contrast served as an intriguing springboard for exploring why the East and West differ and how this difference can be transcended. For others, it served as the mud for slinging criticisms at the seemingly misguided ideas of the other camp.

If we are looking for quick answers, one relatively easy solution is at hand. When Zen speaks of self-negation, it may be referring to the need to abolish what psychoanalytic theorists have called the "false self"—the outer, superficial layers of personality formation that are constructed as a defense against inner experience and unconscious conflicts, or as a compensatory structure to offset internal fragility, depletion, and hollowness in the experience of self. For the neurotic or normal person, self-negation means dropping the facade we carry throughout the day—the self as a commodity that we use to persuade, impress, and barter with others. Instead, in the words of the human potential movement, we should "be real." In self psychology, the self to be negated may be the narcissistically pathological, grandiose self, the self that is wrapped in unrealistic, unmodulated feelings of omnipotence and invulnerability, that clings to its false perceptions of having attained perfection in and by itself, without needing assistance from the outside, that glorifies its own sense of agency. This false self, a protective device, ultimately must yield to allow the surfacing and eventual reparation of the inner self, which is fragile, depleted, precariously dependent on its selfobjects.

Self psychology's concept of the grandiose self and its pathological dynamics do indeed epitomize Zen's warnings against the dangers of the egotism of the self. However, Zen's suggestion that the self must be negated goes beyond the need to overcome blatant narcissistic disturbance, just as it goes beyond the need to "be real" by abolishing the false, neurotic self. Self psychologists recognize that the grandiose-exhibitionistic self is an important feature of all, including normal, developmental paths. Narcissistic dynamics are universal. In fact, narcissism—the structuralization of the self—is the primary feature of development. By contrast, Zen takes a radical position. Even healthy narcissism that is tempered and fruitfully integrated into the developing self must be negated. When Zen advocates the abolishing of self, it advocates the reversal of the most basic and supposedly "healthy" narcissistic striving for the unification of self.

Consider the following story from Janwillem van de Wetering's

A Glimpse of Nothingness (1978), in which he describes his experiences in a Japanese Zen monastery:

> In an unreal green forest you are walking next to the old master. You reach a brook. The master touches your shoulder and you know he wants you to sit down. He points at a piece of cork floating past; it has been in a fire and half of it is black. "That piece of cork is your personality," the master says. "At every turn, at every change of circumstances, at every conflict, defeat or victory, a piece of it crumbles off." You look at the piece of cork. Pieces of it detach themselves and disappear. "It's getting smaller," you say, nervously. "Getting smaller all the time," the master answers, "until nothing is left of it." He looks quiet and pleasant. He appears only as a little man who wants to point something out to you. You will lose your name, your body, and your character. Your fear diminishes. If it has to happen it will happen. Nothing will remain. And nothing you will be. (p. 35)

If this story accurately reflects Zen's philosophy, then Zen speaks of a complete, thorough abolishing of the self—a radical notion that slaps the face of psychoanalysis. For psychoanalysis the true self is the whole self. For Zen the true self is no self at all. In this chapter we explore how this apparent contradiction may be resolved. But as we engage this discussion, we should keep in mind the traditional Zen warning. Ultimately, the discussion may point to insights that can be felt intuitively, but may not be fully graspable by words and concepts. Perhaps this intuitive realization is what Zen—and psychoanalysis—is all about.

Facets of Selfhood

Before beginning a discussion of how the self/no-self dilemma might be resolved, we must clarify what we mean by this thing we call the 'self.' The task is easy to propose, but not so easy to accomplish. Nor is it by any means new. Trying to define the self *is* the history of philosophy and psychology, and if this history has revealed anything, it is the fact that attempting to conceptualize the self turns into a complex, slippery juggling act. Within psychoanalysis alone, there have been many prominent theorists who have tackled this task (e.g., Atwood & Stolorow, 1984; Erikson, 1963; Gedo & Goldberg, 1973; Hartmann, 1939a; Jacobson, 1964; Kahn, 1974; Kernberg, 1975; Klein, 1976; Kohut, 1977; Lichtenstein, 1977; Loewald, 1960; Menaker, 1982;

Winnicott, 1974), to name only some. The fact that so much effort has been devoted to understanding the self is itself revealing. Either the great minds in history are chasing rainbows, or they (and perhaps all of us) intuitively sense that there is something important here to pursue, regardless of how elusive and mysterious this thing called the 'self' seems.

Rather than attempt the encyclopedic mission of reviewing all the philosophical and psychological theories, I would like to tease out just a few definitions that will be helpful to us throughout this book. By no means are these definitions mutually exclusive, for they do, indeed, overlap. They may be considered different perspectives or facets of selfhood, which intertwine with each other. And by no means are they exhaustive. As stated in Taoism, once we take that first step in dividing the one into two, invariably, further discriminations follow until the two become ten thousand things. In the world of intellectualizations, there are categories within categories within categories, distinctions heaped upon distinctions—but ultimately they are all aspects of the same thing, whatever it is.

The five facets of selfhood I discuss are: the observing self, the experiencing self, the willing self, the self-as-structure, and the superordinate self.

1. The Observing Self

Starting with Freud, at various points in the history of psychoanalysis, theorists have commented on the ego's curious ability to observe not only phenomena outside its psychic sphere (events in the external environment), but also intrapsychic events within its own realm (e.g., Greenson, 1967; Miller, Isaacs, & Haggard, 1965; Sterba, 1934). The most basic analytic technique—free association—relies on this ability of the ego to observe its own processes, as vividly portrayed in Freud's analogy of undertaking self-observation as if one were sitting on a train, watching and describing the views outside the window as they pass by. The ego can "split" or "dissociate" itself into a part that observes and a part that is observed, and then rejoin itself. By allying themselves with the observing egos in their patients, therapists establish the essential working alliance that makes interpretations and insight possible.

But we do not have to tie ourselves to the framework of traditional psychoanalytic theory and conceptualize this observing process strictly as an ego function. As more recent theorists (e.g., Atwood & Stolorow, 1984; Bach, 1984; Deikman, 1982) have pointed out, it is the *self* that has the curious ability to observe itself. We are not simply playing with words here by substituting "self" for "ego." By saying that the self can observe itself, we place the observing self at a much more influential position. It *is* selfhood, not simply an ego function within the structures of the self. Again, the concept is not new, for psychology and philosophy have long heralded humankind's unique talents for self-reflection. As we will see later, the special qualities of this observing self make it a powerful concept for tackling the self/no-self dilemma.

2. The Experiencing Self

The splitting of the ego results in the observing ego and the experience that is observed. The origin of this experience is the "experiencing ego" (Greenson, 1967). For example, a patient feels angry and shouts at his therapist. At that moment there is no thinking about, observing, or analyzing of the anger and the shouting. It is simply experienced. Afterwards, with the help of the therapist, the patient splits off into the observing self that enables the patient to gain distance from and discuss the experience. Oscillating between the experiencing and observing egos—between experiencing something and then understanding it—constitutes the course of psychotherapy. Traditional psychoanalytic theory (e.g., Sterba, 1934) described the experiencing ego as cathected with instinctual or defensive energy. As before, we do not need to limit ourselves to drive theory or the conceptual framework of ego functions. Selfhood itself embodies the facets of experiencing and observing. The experiencing self is the stage on which all experiences take form—including behaviors, perceptions, sensations, feelings, and the variety of felt psychophysiological concomitants of these phenomena. The experiencing self is the *living within* these experiences. Afterwards, we may (or may not) observe or reflect on them. When a spoon falls from the table, we see it and catch it. There is no detached observing of the event at the moment—there is only the experiencing of it.

3. The Willing Self

At some vital level the self is an agent, a doer, an initiator of action. Although psychotherapy strives for insight, a modulation of instinctual impulses, alterations in self and object representations—whatever terms are used—the ultimate goal is to get the patient to do something differently, to change. Psychotherapy aims to activate the willing self, as Freud (1923) suggested by claiming that the therapist's basic task is to free the patient's ego to choose one way or another.

The notion of will and a self-as-doer has its roots deep in philoso-phy—for example, Aristotle, Kant, Nietzsche, Schopenhauer—but psychoanalytic thinkers (e.g., Horney, 1950; Menaker, 1982; Rank, 1945; Stern, 1985; Wheelis, 1956) and a variety of other psychological theorists (Farber, 1966; May, 1969; White, 1959; Yalom, 1980) have also explored the vicissitudes of will and agency. To will change, one must weigh alternatives, be aware of the wishes, wants, and feelings that underlie the alternatives, decide, choose, and ultimately take re-sponsibility for the outcome. Willing encompasses the desire to mas-ter and change oneself, as well as one's environment. It involves freedom.

But, as Zen would ask, who is it that acts, does, and wills things? Exactly where this homunculus lives within the intrapsychic world has always troubled philosophers and psychologists alike. The very idea flies in the face of deterministic personality theories, includ-ing psychoanalysis. For the rationalist philosophers such as Spinoza and Hobbes, the willing self is an illusionary, subjective state. For psychoanalytic theorists such as Atwood & Stolorow (1984), only the experience of agency is analyzable, whereas the ontology of agency lies beyond the scope of analytic inquiry.

Despite the philosophical conundrums, we have a hard time shaking the intuitive sense that a willing self exists, and the concept of a willing self invariably creeps into even deterministic theories. As Kohut (1977) suggested, the self appears as a fundamental motivator, organizer, and center of initiative that is more than simply a content, structure, or experience within the mental apparatus.

4. The Self-as-Structure

An important theme in object relations theory and self psychology is that the self is a structure consisting of self and object representa-tions, and the more basic cognitive-affective schemata that comprise these representations (Atwood & Stolorow, 1984; Blanck & Blanck, 1974; Horner, 1979; Kernberg, 1975; Kohut, 1971, 1977; Mahler, Pine, & Bergman, 1975; Winnicott, 1974). These self and object representa-tions, which encapsulate affect, meaning, and purpose, and often are coded as "good" or "bad," arise from the internalization of in-teractions with significant others. Patterns of representations are con-solidated into larger systems that constitute the larger intrapsychic structures which are experienced, consciously or unconsciously, as the self. These structures endure through time, providing a sense of continuity to the self. The degree of cohesion, harmony, and flexibility of self-experience coded within these structures marks the level of psychological health. Essentially, the notion of the self-as-structure is the "nuts-and-bolts" perspective on selfhood.

Although the metapsychology of defining such things as "structure" and "representations" runs the theorist into troublesome tautologies, the concepts nevertheless make intuitive sense and are clinically useful (Schafer, 1968). Psychoanalytic phenomenologists (Atwood & Stolorow, 1984; Stolorow, Brandchaft, & Atwood, 1987), in fact, prefer the concept of structure and distinguish it sharply from the idea of the self as an experiencing subject and agent who initiates action—an ontology of self that they believe lies beyond the scope of psychoanalytic inquiry. One reason they make this distinction is to avoid the paradoxical, theoretically troublesome statements that sometimes creep into self psychology, such as, "The fragmented self strives to restore its cohesion." Can the pieces of a self strive toward self-restoration? They state that patients, viewed objectively by the therapist, always seem to be acting and doing. What is relevant from the empathic-introspective vantage point is whether patients have the *experience* of personal agency, which is a basic component of structural self-organization, and therefore open to psychoanalytic inquiry.

5. The Superordinate Self

If the self as presented in the previous definitions seems intangible, mysterious, or metapsychologically impenetrable, then this last concept surely will raise the skeptic's eyebrows. Here we envision the self as a superordinate organizing principle of the psyche that embodies and unifies all the facets of selfhood. Several psychoanalytic theorists have spoken of a superordinate principle (e.g., Erikson, 1963; Hartmann, 1939a; Lichtenstein, 1977). Kohut (1977, 1984) is one of the most controversial figures who proclaimed that the self is the primary organizing feature of personality. When he made his theoretical progression from self psychology in its "narrow" sense to its "broader" sense, he no longer conceptualized the self as simply the product of drive cathexes or a content of the mental apparatus (the self-concept within self structure), but as the center of the psychological universe, the cornerstone and overarching organizing principle of personality dynamics. On the broadest scale, we may think of this superordinate self as the glue or container that unites the willing, observing, experiencing, and structural facets of self.

Exactly what this overarching self is or where it comes from is indeed mysterious. If gestalt psychology is correct in its assumption that the whole is greater than the sum of its parts, then the superordinate self transcends the components and processes of the intrapsychic world—a mystical idea that feels comfortable to transpersonal and humanistic theorists, but not to many psychoanalytic thinkers.

Now that we have outlined these five facets of selfhood, let us briefly consider some of the problematic questions introduced by these definitions. Whenever we create alternative conceptual categories, we beg the question, "Which is most important?" Can there be several core aspects of selfhood, or is one of these more fundamental than the others? Do the distinctions really hold, or are the various facets perhaps reducible to one "true" self? For example, if we conceptualize "structures" as configurations at a slow rate of change, as did Rapaport and Gill (1959), then the self-as-structure may actually be a process or action with its origin in the willing self. Can there even be a "structure" of experience without an experiencing self somehow embedded in that structure to make it an experience? Isn't the observing carried out by the observing self actually another type of experience embodied by the experiencing self? Can there be any observing or experiencing without the motivating force of a willing self to drive that process?

All these problems stem from an epistemological dilemma. According to Zen, attempting to think, analyze, or conceptualize the self, as required by theory development, inevitably misses the mark and results in the fragmenting of the self—which is why Zen shuns all abstractions, and self psychology optimistically strives for a theory-free, "experience-near" understanding of the patient's inner world. Attempting to conceptualize the self within the context of subjectivity as required by Zen and self psychology alike inevitably opens up an epistemological can of worms. Conceptualizing requires a splitting between a distant, objective thinker and the object of the thought, a duality that is incompatible with the subjectivity of the empathic-introspective immersion into self-experience. Western languages themselves consist of a splitting of subject, predicate, and object that biases our attempts to realize the self's core. Because language is tightly woven into the cognitive-affective schemata of self structure, it shapes, perhaps inaccurately, our experience of the self. In its search for the core of personality, contemporary psychoanalysis often explores the self's earliest origins at the preverbal level—a core self that, as Zen agrees, is not accurately described with words.

What would be a Zen master's reply to the debates about the self as being either a willing, observing, experiencing, structured, or superordinate thing? Most likely the kind of mystical, paradoxical statement that does not fit neatly into the cognitive-affective schemata of

Western, including psychoanalytic, theorizing. Perhaps something like, "The true self is all and none of these things" or, in an even more mystical fashion, "The self neither is nor isn't any of these." Zen's reply might also be a deceptively simple question. As described by Kapleau (1980a), Zen students are often asked, "Who is it that has this thought, feeling, or attribute?" Concerning the five facets of selfhood, we similarly might ask, "who is it that observes, experiences, wills, or has these structures and superordinate things?" When we turn around to find this "who," it slips away: where there is a self there is nothing, no self there.

All these replies indeed seem inaccessible to psychoanalytic thought—which is perhaps why Atwood and Stolorow (1984) section off certain ontologies of self as beyond the scope of psychoanalytic inquiry, and why Heinz Kohut considered the self, at its deepest level, the final bedrock through which psychoanalysis could not pass. In his epilogue to *The Restoration of the Self* (1977), Kohut refused to assign a firm meaning to the term *self* or to define its essence. He stated that its essence, like that of reality, is unknowable. "We cannot, by introspection and empathy, penetrate to the self *per se;* only its introspectively or empathically perceived psychological manifestations are open to us" (1977, pp. 310–311).

Kohut's comments echo Watts's (1975b) description of the Tao. Like electricity or "energy," it cannot be neatly pinned down by conceptual explanations. None is adequate. It is an ultimate, to be taken as a fundamental thing. All other things can be explained from it, but not *it* itself. As Lao Tzu states at the outset of the *Tao Te Ching*, the Tao that can be named is not the eternal Tao.

Despite these conceptual puzzles and unknowable dimensions of selfhood, the basic dilemma in the attempts to unite East and West still stands before us: How can the Western emphasis on the self be reconciled with the Eastern focus on no-self? Without a solidly convincing, unanimously acceptable definition of the self, we are off to a precarious start. Nevertheless, with the five definitions in hand we can approach several possible, though ultimately tentative solutions to the problem. As with our five definitions, by no means should these solutions be considered the only possible ones—and by no means are they totally independent of each other. If, indeed, there is a core, "true" self that somehow intrinsically is related to no-self, then these solutions can only be overlapping perspectives on that one vision.

In the sections that follow, the first two perspectives involve attempts to conceptualize the no-self as the observing self, and as the self rooted in spontaneity and unity. The third is a developmental model that postulates the cohesive self-as-structure as a prerequisite for reaching the condition of no-self. The last sections describe possible mechanisms of how self and no-self interact. We may postulate the existence of intrapsychic balances and "oscillations" between the two. Or, following Kohut's lead, we can explore how the subjective epistemology of Zen and psychoanalysis overlap at a deeper, more paradoxical level of the core self, at the point where its first manifestations surface from the ontologically unknowable bedrock. As indicated by the hypothetical Zen master's replies to the analytic debates about selfhood, it is a level where the self's primary manifestations assume the form of dualities—apparently contradictory dualities of is and isn't. In the last two sections I discuss the "interpenetration" of self and no-self, self and object.

The No-Self as Observing Self

The most convincing argument for identifying the no-self as the observing self was presented by Deikman (1982), who also pioneered the experimental research on meditation (Deikman, 1963, 1966a). He began by pointing out the misconception among psychological theorists, as well as among laypeople, that the true self is an object, a thing, of sorts. Early in life children come to believe that their body, with all its sensations and feelings, is a self-contained object that constitutes the self. An equation forms: Body = Self. Later in development, thinking and reasoning join the bandwagon concerning this self-contained thing, so that the equation becomes more sophisticated: Body and Mind = Self. This "object self" is experienced as finite, distinct from other entities, localized somewhere in psychic space, continuous over the temporal dimension of past, present, and future. It is experienced as an object, like automobiles and trees. Even when the sense of "I" emerges in development—when the child becomes aware of the willing self—this "I" also comes to be treated as an object, a distinct doer-of-things separate from other doers. Essentially, this object self is the self-as-structure, with all its complex constellations of self and object representations, including the representations of the self as an experiencing, willing thing. The object self is functional, even necessary for survival, because it serves the need to present oneself to and act within the external environment—but once created, this object self does not give up control easily, and ultimately dominates consciousness.

Psychological theorists and people in general tend to overlook the subjective awareness of the observing self that makes the experience of the object self possible. Whenever there is a feeling, an action, a thought, or a sensation, there is always the ability to be aware of that phenomenon as an aspect of the object self. But whatever we notice or conceptualize is the object of awareness, not awareness itself, which always seems to jump back a step when we experience the object. We can even become aware of the fact that we are aware of something—and once this happens, the secondary awareness itself becomes an object of experience. But we cannot be aware of the source of awareness during the act of being aware. We cannot directly observe the observing self. It is the transparent center of subjectivity that is incapable of being objectified. It leaps away in an infinite regression of awarenesses each time we turn to observe it. We cannot detach ourselves from awareness in order to observe it because we *are* that awareness. It is the core experience of selfhood.

Deikman (1982) believed the word *transcendent* must be used to describe this mysterious, observing self, because it forever remains apart from the contents of consciousness. It is of a fundamentally different nature—featureless, limitless, without boundaries, not affected by the world any more than a mirror is affected by the images it reflects. It is not an objectifiable self-as-thing, as we typically think of the self. It is no-self.

Deikman described how the Yogic discipline of Ramana Maharsi prescribed the exercise of "Who am I?" to demonstrate that the observing self is not an object that belongs to the realm of thinking, feeling, or acting. If I lost my arm, I would still exist; therefore, I am not my arm. If I lost my vision, my hearing, even forgot my name, I would still exist; therefore, I am not any of those things. Ultimately, I am not any object thing that can be named or thought, not even this very thought itself at this very moment. The essential me is the act of being aware, the observing self. Descartes' "I think, therefore I am" must yield to the more essential statement that "I am aware, therefore I am." A contemporary version of this Yogic exercise was described by Yalom (1980) as the "dis-identification" exercise, in which one draws up a list of all the things one believes oneself to be in response to the question "Who am I?" Then, one by one, the items are crossed off and one tries to imagine who one is without being those identities. When the last item is crossed off, who is left? Zen masters similarly demand that students show them the "who" who feels, thinks, or acts. Where and what is this who? We sense that there must be a self there, but it is the no-self that cannot be grasped.

Undoubtedly, there is a mystical quality to this observing no-self that does not sit well with Western psychology, including many psychoanalysts. Deikman claimed that Western science mostly has ignored this transcendent no-self, assuming that the observer and the observed are phenomena of the same order. He cites the story from the Vedantic literature about a group of peasants who ford a river. Afterwards, concerned that someone might be lost, the leader counted the group, but inadvertently omitted himself from the count. He came up one short. Each member of the party also counted in a similar fashion, and all came up short. Now worried, they searched up and down the river looking for the lost person. Finally, a passerby helped solve the problem by suggesting that the leader count himself. Relieved that no one was missing, they proceeded on their way.

We always miss the obvious. The observing self is forever present, but easily overlooked, simply because it lives so close to home. You can't point at it because it *is* the process of pointing. It is no-self. But without this no-thing, there is no beginning from which one can move forward.

Fascinated by the observing abilities of the ego, Freud did seem to sense that there was something special about this power:

> The ego is the subject par excellence: how can it become the object? There is no doubt, however, that it can. The ego can take itself as an object; it can treat itself like any other object, observe itself, criticize itself, do Heaven knows what besides with itself. (quoted in Sterba, 1934, p. 120)

Freud suggests that anything is possible, but he might have been surprised to hear that the ego, through observing, can transcend itself.

Although traditional Western psychology balks at the "transcendent" aspect of selfhood, it has made ample use of the idea of an observing self—as in the psychoanalytic concept of the observing ego. The absence or presence of observing self-awareness is often considered a primary diagnostic determinant of psychopathology. Borderline and psychotic patients typically lack this ability, whereas neurotic patients take a major step forward when their symptoms shift from being "ego syntonic" to the self-reflective condition of being "ego alien." Deikman believed that the progressive clarification and strengthening of the observing self has been the single most important contribution of Western psychotherapy. Through free association, self-observation, insight, and self-knowledge, psychotherapy leads to the freeing of the observing self from the pathogenic thoughts, emotions, conditioned perceptions, and habitual reactions that are engraved into the object self. By centering within the observing self and acquiring some distance from their symptomatic condition, patients attain autonomy and choice in the face of their conflicts: Activating the observing self frees the willing self. Even for highly functioning people, rallying the observing self can be therapeutic by liberating them from the cultural standards and biases that may distort, misdirect, or restrict their ability to engage experience. The observing self, according to Deikman (1982), can wake us up from the "trance of everyday life."

Deikman suggested also that we do not want to remain rigidly fixated on an observing self. Alluding to the necessary balance between an observing and experiencing ego, as postulated by psychoanalytic theory, he stated that the observing self must be flexible and yielding to the immediacy of experience. Heightening the observing self tends to minimize the intensity of affect and makes mastery of the experience and choice possible. But sometimes we need an immersion into the experience without the awkward baggage of an added-on observing awareness. Catching a falling spoon and orgasms do not require—and will even be hindered—by a superfluous observing mind. However, Deikman quickly pointed out that for most people, the immediacy of experience is less of a problem than a deficient observing self. The development of self-awareness falls along a continuum. Even when relatively healthy people have acquired some ability for self-reflection, they nevertheless may be underdeveloped in the higher-order dimensions of observing awareness. Psychotherapy rouses the more basic functions of the observing self, but the depth of the no-self realm may remain untouched.

At this point meditation can carry the person further along the path to the more pure observing awareness of no-self. This has been the longstanding goal of all spiritual meditative traditions. During insight meditation (similar to free association) one allows the mind to flow freely from one point of awareness to another. Ideas, feelings, and recollections drift into consciousness, but the meditator simply becomes aware of these impressions and then lets go of them without fixing attention on them. By simply observing and letting go of the contents of the object self, the meditator becomes centered in the observing self and gradually empties the stage of the object self or the self-as-structure that is the target of consciousness.

This process, simple to describe but difficult to achieve, triggers a process Deikman (1966b) called *deautomatization*. It involves an unraveling of the psychological operations that organize, limit, select, and interpret perceptual stimuli by reinvesting those operations with conscious awareness. It is an unraveling of the self and object representations of the self-as-structure. Deikman refers to the work of Hartmann (1939b) and Rapaport and Gill (1959), who define structures as configurations at a slow rate of change that are organized hierarchically, with higher-order, more complex structures founded upon more basic ones. Through the course of development, structures become "automatized," in that the mental operations or motor patterns controlled by those structures come to function independently, without requiring the cathexis of conscious awareness. Deautomatization, a concept first introduced by Gill and Brenman (1959), is a reversal of this process. By redirecting attention to a structure, its function becomes less automatic, less independent, more susceptible to a dissolution into the substratal structures that constitute it.

By progressively letting go of all targets of awareness, the meditator steps back from those experiences into a self that simply observes without clinging, thus freeing the mind from those experiences and opening up deeper, more elemental experiences that were previously unavailable to the observing self. Aspects and functions of self structure that were once regulated automatically, without conscious awareness or control, are now accessible to awareness. The hierarchical arrangement of the self-as-structure is reversed and unraveled, allowing observing awareness to penetrate to underlying, more fundamental aspects of the self. The meditator can be conscious not only of previously hidden self and object representations, but also the very psychological processes that contribute to the construction of self structure. By undoing and peeking below structure, the observing self can witness the activities of such basic psychological operations as memory, attention, and perception. Brown (1986) conceptualized this meditative path as the systematic deconstruction of all psychological structures and functions, beginning at most advanced levels and progressively working toward deeper, more elemental intrapsychic domains: from attitudes and behavioral schemes to thinking, to gross perceptions, to the self-system, and eventually to the time-space matrix.

Ultimately, as the process of deautomatization continues and the self-as-structure unravels toward and beyond its most elemental components, what is left? This is the question the Zen master posed to van de Wetering when he pointed to the piece of disintegrating cork in the stream. When there is no more object self, no more contents of consciousness, no more self-as-structure, there remains only no-self. It is the pure awareness and pristine consciousness that defies the Western phenomenological premise that consciousness is always conscious of something. The observing self witnesses nothing. It is empty. It is witnessed by emptiness. The distinction between the observer and the observed breaks down. This is the state of enlightenment, *satori*, or *nirvana*, to which Eastern traditions point—a paradoxical condition of selfhood that defies easy conceptualization.

There are a variety of reasons why we might object to the enhancement of an observing self. For instance, "observing" implies being evaluative, critical, analytic, or intellectualized. Indeed, in psychotherapy these qualities sometimes contaminate the observing self—but they are not intrinsic to it. In its purest, most elemental form, the observing self as no-self does not cling to judgments, intellectualizations, or evaluations. During meditation such acts become the objects of awareness, rather than features of bare awareness itself.

A more powerful criticism is that the observing self pulls people into a distant, detached position in relation to their experience. In its extreme form, it could encourage a schizoid split between experiences and an observing ego that defensively guards against involvement in those experiences (Guntrip, 1969). As mentioned earlier, Deikman (1982) himself took care to point out that we do not want to magnify the observing self to the exclusion of the experiencing self.

Does the observing self, in its purest form as no-self, involve any detachment at all? When there is no-self, there is no-other to be detached from. During meditation—as well as in the peak experiences as described by Maslow (1971)—the distinction between self and other disappears. There is no separation between the act of observing and the object observed. The observer and observed merge. Awareness encircles self, other, and awareness itself. Deikman (1982) alluded to this curious nondetached quality of the observing self when he described the "receptive" mode of being—a receptiveness to experience the environment rather than act upon it. He mentions the example of listening to music. In the receptive mode, the sense of self is less discrete and prominent, which permits the blurring of boundaries and the experience of connection or merging with the environment. Attention becomes diffuse. Past and future fall away. Sensations dominate over verbal meaning and analytic thought. The awareness of awareness becomes possible.

This awareness of awareness—an awareness within the immediate experience—is a direct, intuitive knowing. It is a knowing by being that which is known. The observing self is not a distant observer, but an observer within the experience itself. We *are* our awareness of the music; we *are* the music itself. Here we stumble upon the inadequacies of words and conceptualizations, for the meaning of "awareness" and "observing" now becomes unclear. Aren't we talking about the experiencing self rather than the observing self? Either the observing self, at some point, transforms into the experiencing self, or the distinction between the observing and experiencing self breaks down. Deikman (1982) seemed to be addressing this confusion when he introduced the analogy of a pond:

> Our awareness, the observing self, is the surface of the pond. Thoughts, feelings, and other mental activities are like splashes and ripples in the water, as if small stones were being tossed in from the shore. When such activity subsides, the pond is smooth, still, and reflective; at such times the observing self is enhanced, becomes prominent, and is the major dimension of consciousness. At other times, when thought has transformed the surface into a mass of waves and ripples, awareness seems to have vanished and consciousness contains only the patterns of disturbance in the water. In such a situation there is no need to postulate an outside observer to experience the stillness and the ripples. There need be no experiencing agency because the experience is the state of stillness or ripples, as the case may be. (pp. 103–104)

Following this analogy of the pond, we can think of the observing self, the no-self, as the formless context in which an experience occurs—a type of prepsychological "space" that enables the creation of the self-as-structure. The experience and the observing space in which it crystallizes are not separable. For example, Atwood & Stolorow (1984) reported a vivid case study of a patient who was fascinated by water and glass because she identified with their paradoxical quality of being both transparent and reflecting (an identification with the observing self). Within these elements she could both disappear and witness her own image. In one session she reports a dream in which she is consumed by fire at a train station; only her eyeballs survive the flames, and roll about in their attempt to glance at each other. Atwood and Stolorow point out the theme of self-disintegration and the last desperate attempts, symbolized by the eyeballs, to maintain self cohesion. But even if the eyeballs, too, were totally consumed, leaving nothing of the self-as-structure, there would still be the observing self's awareness of that event. There would still be the presence of the empty, boundaryless no-self that constitutes the space and context for the dream to form. The observing self enables and permeates the experience of the self's dream-image, including the experience of the self's negation.

No-Self as Spontaneity and Unity

As evident in the discussions so far, the further we probe into this self/no-self dilemma, the more complex and sometimes confusing the issues become. It is tempting to conclude that the true self, at its deepest level, is woven with such intricacy that volumes of analyses are required to penetrate it.

Zen would take a very different position. The true self, it would claim, is simple and straightforward. The great master Bashō stated that "Zen is one's everyday mind. When hungry, eat. When thirsty, drink." The actions of the self that functions in accord with its own internal design are spontaneous, fluid, unhampered by the machinations of thinking. The self moves with fully open awareness of its actions, but with no specific, focused consciousness of its own workings. It moves with unity and wholeness, functioning freely, easily, without, as Watts (1957) stated, the sensation of a second self, mind, or awareness standing over it with a club. According to the Taoist principle of *wu wei* (action through nonaction), one lets things happen of their own accord, without force or conscious intention. Any deliberate attempt to cultivate such action, using Chuang Tzu's analogies, would be like beating a drum while in search of a fugitive, or putting legs on a snake.

This unified spontaneity originates from a condition of unselfconsciousness, no-mind, no-self. Although its presence permeates the experience, the self is forgotten, and so recedes into the unnoticed background, where it functions quietly, efficiently. Perhaps we think of this spontaneity as the actions of the experiencing/willing self in its purest form. Or perhaps, in what is experienced as a condition of unbroken unity and wholeness, all the distinctions between the self as a willing, observing, experiencing, or structured entity merge, disappear, even become irrelevant.

In his final book, Kohut (1984) expressed similar ideas. The outcome of psychoanalytic treatment is a self that functions spontaneously, without the burden of superfluous thought and reflection. Although the analytic process consists of innumerable interpretations, experiences, and insights—events that pave the way to an integrated, harmonious self—the mind no longer has any use for them once therapy reaches its natural conclusion. The patient's memories of these analytic events sink into oblivion via processes unrelated to repression. The normal mental functionings of the self rest on seamless, silent, and smoothly interacting psychic processes. The self-as-structure exists not as a discrete collection of nuts-and-bolts parts tightened together, but as a blended system of enduring yet changing processes invisibly woven into each other. Kohut used the analogy of the pianist who plays without thinking about his or her fingers, similar to Bach's (1984) centipede that walks without thinking about its legs. These examples illustrate the self's intrinsic potential to function fluidly, spontaneously, in accord with its own design—provided it is not encumbered by the anxieties and defenses of overlaying selves. The great Zen master Dogen similarly stated that to study Zen is to study the self, and to study the self is to forget the self.

In his fascinating comparison of the statements of mystics and an ex-analytic patient, Fingarette (1958) described how both the mystic and the patient speak, in a seemingly contradictory fashion, about consciously acting, deciding, or feeling—but not really consciously doing so. Fully aware of themselves, they do not experience self-consciousness weighing down upon them. The self is both purposeful and self-forgetful. According to Fingarette, the self that is forgotten—the self that hampers spontaneity and intrapsychic fluidity—is the self-consciousness colored by conflict or anxiety. The person who is confident does not have a conscious feeling of confidence. The person who is wise does not think of her- or himself as wise. People who have such feelings or thoughts are troubled by anxiety and doubts that force them to reassure themselves.

When mystics speak about attaining no-self, they refer to the need to resolve/dissolve the introspected, self-conscious "I" that is saturated with a dominant affect derived from anxiety. It is a component of the self that has been warded off and acquires the characteristics of an undigested piece of beef that fragments the intrapsychic world and radiates tension into it. Borrowing a Buddhist concept, Fingarette (1958) suggested that therapy helps the patient to overcome "abiding" in the specific thoughts and affects of these conflicted spheres of the self. When the self becomes anxiety-free, we have the self-forgetfulness of no-self that allows us to act spontaneously, fully knowing we are acting, but not with the extra baggage of the anxiety-tinged self-consciousness. One eats or sleeps because one is hungry or tired, rather than because one needs to quell the anxieties and needs of defensively formed splinters of the self. To achieve enlightenment is to abolish the tension of the self-awareness that runs against the grain of intrapsychic fluidity. The death that leads to rebirth is the death of the subjectively experienced, anxiety-generated "self" perception. It leads to the freedom of introspective self-forget-fulness and a unified self.

This unified self contains no rigid or abrasive boundaries be-tween its intrapsychic components. Any conflict involves a tension between two or more opposing affects. Pathological self or object rep-resentations are pathological because they grate against other self or object representations. Repressive barriers between them prevent their being integrated or harmonized. In the spontaneity of no-self, all intrapsychic spheres are united seamlessly, effortlessly. Perhaps we can think of them as united by and within the superordinate self, the overarching condition of selfhood that embodies all psychic pro-cesses and structures. But subjectively, there is no experience of self. There is only no-self. This does not mean that intrapsychic distinc-tions are lost, dissolved into a condition of chaotic undifferentiation. Suzuki (1970) stated that "when it is day the night comes." Surely we know when it is day and when it is night, but the transition from one to the other is seamless, without boundaries. Day shades into night, and vice versa. One spontaneously brings the other; they are united in this spontaneous action. This is how the intrapsychic world func-tions in no-self.

Even thinking itself produces boundaries or spheres of tension within the internal world. The classic psychoanalytic theory of the ego's development, including thought and reason, is that it evolves as an intermediary between environmental stimulus and action. Thought is a cathexis of energy, of tension, that delays (for a practi-cal reason, one hopes) the expression of affect and the impulse to do. The Zen literature similarly describes thinking as lines of energy that create internal pressure (Sekida, 1975) or as "traces" that complicate and obstruct the mind (Suzuki, 1970). Although contemporary psy-choanalytic theory underplays the idea of intrapsychic energy, it would still conceptualize thought as schemata that create boundaries between intrapsychic structures and stand as intermediary represen-tations of the external world.

In the spontaneity of no-self one acts without thinking, even though the plan and precision of "thoughtfulness" remains. There are no boundaries, lines of pressure, traces, or intermediaries. When you first learn to play the piano, you have to think your fingers into position. But when this skill is mastered, the fingers play themselves, and, in fact, allow deeper layers of self-expression to emerge sponta-neously.

The seamless unity and spontaneity of no-self account for why Zen masters sometimes seem to possess, as Matthiessen (1987) puts it, a "transparent aura." When there are no grating or discrete boundaries between internal structures, no internal tensions between structural surfaces, the self appears invisible—not an insubstantial invisibility, but rather, a quiet, nonabrasive presence that nonintrusively captures the essence of things. One becomes like a lake that reflects the moon: The moon does not change the lake, and the lake does not change the moon. It is the blending of the experiencing and observing self into one pristine awareness. In the no-self, where anxious self-consciousness and the weighty burden of thinking have fallen away, one becomes empty, and through this perfect emptiness one experiences perfect form. On a clear day, Watts (1975b) noted, the air is unobstructed, and we see all things clearly. In psychoanalysis we might say that transferences and other parataxic distortions—the outgrowth of internally abrasive tensions—are gone.

My favorite Zen story about the unity and spontaneity of no-self was related by Watts (1957). An agitated, distraught man seeks out a Zen master. He wants to be shown his true self, but the master dodges his insistent questions. Finally giving up in frustration, the man turns to leave. At that moment the master calls out to him by name. "Yes," the man replies. "There it is!" says the master. Spontaneously and with complete internal unity, the man shows his true self. Obviously he is conscious of having replied to the master, but in that spontaneous moment he is unaware of having revealed his true self. I always imagine him responding to the master's "There it is!" with a perplexed, "What?"—to which the master casually answers, "Nothing." And he is right. It *is* nothing. It is no-self.

So, too, the patient approaches the analyst with questions, doubts, and anxieties stemming from the perspective of a split, fragmented, or distorted self in search of its core. But restricted within the structures of the false, defensively constructed self, there is no pathway to that source. Fostered by the empathic, intersubjective field, the true, nuclear self must unfold spontaneously, in accord with its own internal design.

The spontaneity and unity of no-self is not the exclusive possession of those who are enlightened or who successfully complete therapy. In the course of everyday life even "normal" people get a small taste of this no-self. In my undergraduate course on psychotherapy, when I introduce ideas from Eastern philosophy, students invariably respond with puzzled objections. "What do you mean by 'no-self'?" I ask them to imagine doing some chore or activity in their everyday life that typically makes them uncomfortable, anxious, or self-conscious. Then I ask them to imagine a time when they were involved in exactly the same activity, with all aspects of it being essentially the same—except at that time, for some reason, they no longer felt uncomfortable, anxious, self-conscious. They just did it—and as they look back on the experience, they can see that it happened easily, fluidly, all by itself. "That," I tell them, "is no-self."

With that remark, they all understand.

Perhaps the most fascinating account of how one realizes the spontaneity and unity of no-self is in Herrigel's (1971) classic story of learning archery from a Zen master. At a crucial point in his training, he struggles with the impossible dilemma of letting loose the arrow without deciding or intending to let it go. It must simply happen of its own accord, the master tells him. Herrigel comes to learn that it is ambition, conscious intention, even thinking itself that gets in the way:

> Man is a thinking reed but his great works are done when he is not calculating and thinking. "Childlikeness" has to be restored with long years of training in the art of self-forgetfulness. When this is attained, man thinks yet he does not think. He thinks like the showers coming down from the sky; he thinks like the waves rolling on the ocean; he thinks like the stars illuminating the nightly heavens; he thinks like the green foliage shooting forth in the relaxing spring breeze. Indeed, he is the showers, the ocean, the stars, the foliage. (p. viii)

Herrigel realizes the emptiness of no-self is the only possible source of the unity and free spontaneity he seeks. He quotes Takuan, a famous master of the sword:

> Perfection in the art of swordsmanship is reached, according to Takuan, when the heart is troubled by no more thought of I and You, of the opponent and his sword, of one's own sword and how to wield it—no more thought even of life and death. "All is emptiness: Your own self, the flashing sword, and the arms that wield it. Even the thought of emptiness is no longer there." From this absolute emptiness, states Takuan, "comes the most wondrous unfoldment of doing." (p. 85)

Although Zen speaks of the need to abandon all desires and aspirations to realize the no-self of selfhood, this does not necessarily contradict the idea in self psychology that ambitions and ideals are essential components of the core self. Ambitions and ideals that are in accord with one's internal, nuclear design are seamless, silently functioning facets of self structure. Like playing the piano without thinking about one's fingers, the inherent striving toward intrinsically felt ideals is spontaneous, unself-conscious. In Zen's paradoxical terms, it is to strive without striving. In Kohut's (1977) words, it is to joyfully experience the self as a center of initiative, "to experience the joy of existence" (p. 285)—the joy of the willing and experiencing self. Only ambitions and ideals born from pathological selfobject relationships—ambitions and ideals tinged with anxiety or guilt and usually imposed by the selfobject needs of the caretaker—violate the internal, nuclear plan, thereby disrupting the unity and spontaneity of the self.

Within this context, the significance of insight takes on a new meaning. "Looking into" and "understanding" the self are components of self-transformation in Zen and psychoanalysis, but not the ultimate objective. Insight implies a bifurcation in the self, a splitting between the subject that understands and an object self that is understood (the observing self and self-as-structure). It obstructs the final aim of self-unity. The kind of insight that is consistent with spontaneity and unity is a seamless, silently functioning awareness within the self that simultaneously is both subject and object, observer and observed structure, observing and experiencing self—a type of "experiential" or "affective" insight that defies the Western, rationalistic concept of knowing, but nevertheless is essential to both Zen and psychoanalysis (Fromm, Suzuki, & DeMartino, 1960). It is a "living within" the organization of self-as-structure that enhances the broadening and flexibility of self-experience.

Perhaps humankind's search for the self—for an insight into the "true" self—can be compared to a dog's relationship to its tail. One dog does not even know its tail is there and never bothers to look. Another dog gets a glimpse of it, snaps at it a few times, and realizes the impossibility of latching on. Still another chases it around and around in circles, perhaps playfully, perhaps filled with a desperation that ultimately leads to collapsing in exhaustion. Finally, perhaps some dog, fully sensing that its tail is there, just wags it.

The Developmental Path to No-Self

One way to solve the self/no-self dilemma is to place the attainment of self and no-self at different levels along a developmental path that marks the evolution of human consciousness. The most notable advocates of this developmental concept have been Engler, Wilber, and Brown (Engler, 1981; Wilber, 1977, 1980a, 1980b, 1981; Wilber, Engler,

& Brown, 1986). Drawing on his exceedingly comprehensive review of the literature on spirituality, psychology, and psychoanalysis, Wilber offered a thorough and complex model that depicts development as a nine-stage ladder (with subphases), where each rung or "fulcrum" marks a different structure of consciousness, eventually culminating in the ultimate condition of enlightenment (no-mind, no-self). This complex model can be broken down into three general phases: (1) the *pre-self phase,* as in early childhood, when the self-as-structure has not attained full cohesion and continuity, differentiations between self and object have not fully formed, and the observing self is still absent; (2) the *self and object phase,* where a cohesive self-as-structure has developed, including the differentiation between self and object representations and the capacity for observing self-awareness; and (3) the *trans-self (no-self) phase,* as in conditions of advanced spiritual development where the self and the distinctions between self and objects have been transcended. Other similar models have been proposed by Meissner (1978) and Fowler (1981).

How, exactly, does this developmental model address the apparent contrast between the West, which touts the need for an integrated self, and the East, which calls for the attainment of no-self? Put simply by Engler (1981), "You have to be somebody before you can be nobody." Attaining the spiritually enlightened conditions of no-self and no-mind is not possible without the prerequisite of a structuralized, integrated, and cohesive self. "Both a sense of self and a sense of no-self—in that order—are necessary to realize that state of optimal psychological well-being that Freud once described as an 'ideal fiction' and the Buddha long before described as 'the end of suffering'" (p. 65).

The advantage of this developmental model is that it unites ideas from the East and West, enriching each perspective where it has been deficient. Western psychology, particularly object relations theory and self psychology, has constructed a very elaborate developmental theory that accounts for how the individual evolves from the pre-self phases of infancy to the structuralized conditions of a cohesive self and object relations that mark adult normalcy. Engler (1981) pointed out that this developmental concept is lacking in the Eastern systems, which always assumed that people had a structuralized self and never fully explored the conditions of narcissistic deficiency that Western psychology describes as psychosis and borderline disorders. On the other hand, Western psychology always assumed that development ended with the structuralized self, and ignored the idea that selfhood is but another phase that one must pass through. Rigidly attaching to the self without progressing to higher stages in which the self is realized as transitory is a fixation in the developmental path, a blocking in the manifestation of no-self, which brings the fullest actualization of consciousness and well-being. Combining the developmental insights of both East and West, we arrive at a full-spectrum model of self development.

The advocates of this model point out that the conditions of the pre-self should not be confused with that of the trans-self. Wilber (1980b) stated that the confusion can run both ways. Some theorists may believe that individuals at the trans-self phase of development are in fact psychotic or borderline, i.e., they have regressed to functioning at a pathological pre-self level. On the other hand, Wilber stated, there also is a tendency to herald the experience of mindlessness and inner emptiness reported by schizophrenics and borderlines as evidence of the spiritually enlightened conditions of no-self. When one falls prey to these two types of errors in this "pre/trans fallacy," there is a "mixture and confusion of pre-egoic fantasy with trans-egoic vision, of pre-conceptual feelings with trans-conceptual insight, of prepersonal desires with transpersonal growth, of pre-egoic whoopee with trans-egoic liberation . . ." (Wilber, 1980b, p. 58).

The full-spectrum model also refutes the romanticized idea that enlightenment and the associated experience of no-self is actually a return to the precontaminated, idyllic experience of childhood perceptions and understandings. Although the nonrational, nondualistic consciousness of the child resembles the enlightened awareness of the spiritual master, the two are not identical. In his seminal article that anticipates a developmental model, Fromm (1959) addressed this point about enlightenment clearly:

> This new experience is a repetition of the pre-intellectual, immediate grasp of the child, but on a new level, that of the full development of man's reason, objectivity, individuality. While the child's experience, that of immediacy and oneness, lies *before* the experience of alienation and the subject-object split, the enlightenment experience lies after it. (p. 95)

Fromm emphasized the point that the unity experienced in enlightenment is not the regression to a preindividual, preconscious harmony of paradise. Instead, it is a unity that can be reached only after one has experienced separateness—after one has passed through a stage of alienation from the world and oneself. As a precondition of this religious awakening, reason must develop to its highest stage, in which it no longer separates oneself from an immediate, intuitive grasp of reality.

Although the developmental concept clarifies the juxtaposition of self and no-self in the ontogenic (and phylogenic) evolution of consciousness, it does not in itself describe exactly what is meant by "no-self." Engler and Brown (Engler, 1981; Wilber, Engler, & Brown, 1986) addressed this issue more specifically. Similar to Deikman's (1966b) idea about the deautomatization of the self-as-structure, Engler suggested that meditation involves a "return" (a Buddhist and Taoist term) to more basic levels of thinking and perceiving. Intrapsychic processes, including representational functions, are reversed or "retraversed." During meditation, as one observes the stream of consciousness, each mental event and physical sensation is witnessed as having an absolute beginning, a brief duration, and an absolute end. Each awareness arises only after the previous one disappears. By not attaching one's attention to any particular experience, by not clinging to evaluations of the experiences as positive or negative, the stream of consciousness literally breaks up, and self and object representations are discovered to be discontinuous events. These discontinuous packets of self and object representations themselves break down into the discrete units of sensation, perception, and feeling that comprise the representations. In this moment-to-moment awareness of things "coming to be and passing away," the meditator reverses the stages of the representational process, which reveals the separate self and object representations as the end products of a long, complex collection of intrapsychic functions. In this sense, Engler suggested, insight meditation is like psychoanalysis because both are designed to set ego and object relations in motion again from a point of arrest. In psychoanalysis this occurs through regression, which takes the form of transference, in which one undergoes a controlled and partial return to more elemental ways of thinking, feeling, and behaving. In meditation, the return involves a reactivation of elemental stages of internalized object relations.

Engler (1986) described this return as a controlled retracing of the stages in the representational process itself as it occurs moment by moment during meditation. Viewing forward, the meditator observes the perceptual, cognitive, and affective pathways by which the "self," "object" and the entire representational world are constructed. Viewing backward, the meditator watches the deconstruction or decompensation of "self" and "object" into their elementary components, processes, or events.

Where is the no-self in this meditative experience? Engler suggested that as the stream of consciousness breaks up, one loses the sense of being an independent observer. The sense of being a separate observer or experiencer behind one's observation or experiencing is discovered to be a perceptual illusion. In this state one disidentifies with the personal self and recognizes that the personal "I" was never a "doer," a causal agent, a willing self: The sense of the self as an agent/doer is realized as just another representation without inherent existence, a representation that unravels in meditation (Epstein, 1990a). All that is apparent is the simple process of knowing, the moment-to-moment awareness of events. The only reality is this flow of events. No enduring observing, experiencing, or willing self exists behind or apart from these moment-to-moment awarenesses. The self is not a fixed entity that exists continuously across time. It does not exist apart from its relation to the object in the moment-to-moment awareness. Self and object are discovered as always creating and re-creating each other in their moment-to-moment existence. The self is discovered to be no-self at all. Using "S" to symbolize "self" and "O" to symbolize "objects," Engler (1986) depicted this realization in the following diagram:

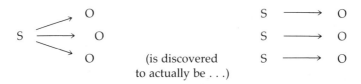

(is discovered
to actually be . . .)

Of course, the words "is discovered to actually be" present the old epistemological problem that forever plagues verbal attempts to describe no-self. As Zen would ask, who is it that does this discovering? Show us this self that realizes its own discontinuity and inevitable relationship to the object, that discovers itself as an illusion. Is this not the true self (no-self)?

If we set aside this persistent dilemma, we see that Engler's concept of no-self is a valuable contribution to the developmental model. Pathology at the pre-self level consists of deficient object relations and a poorly structuralized self. Pathology at the self level consists of the rigid attachment to fixed representations of "me" and "not me." In both cases the representational process is stymied and needs to be set back into motion. At the pre-self level it needs to regain its "upswing"; at the self level it needs to regain its "downswing." The ideal conditon of well-being is reached when the representational process is flexible, fluid, allowing the potential for both self and no-self.

One potential problem with the developmental model is the notion of linearity and stages (which is implied in many, if not all, developmental schemes). The idea of linear progress toward an ideal end state is a favorite in the Western world, and may have its roots in the eschatological theories of the soul's progression to an afterlife that dominate Western religions, particularly Christianity. Eastern religions, by contrast, often emphasize the circularity of phenomena: All things move in eternal cycles. Therefore, any theory that describes humankind as moving up a ladder (note the hint of Plato) toward conditions of enlightenment and no-self must be examined carefully for the effects of being colored by the values and perceptions of Western civilization. What appears as linearity and stages in the actualization of self and no-self may involve more complex and subtly intertwining rhythms of cyclical process. Taoism offers the additional complexity that such cycles also contain opposites that are embedded within each other. The seed of integrated selfhood exists within the heart of the child's pre-self or no-self (the "internal nuclear program," as described by self psychologists), just as the nucleus of no-self resides within the heart of the adult's integrated self.

Understanding the social-cultural contexts of the East and West also will help us examine some of the assumptions made about the pre-self/self/trans-self spectrum. Roland's (1988) psychoanalytic work with Indians and Japanese revealed that their sense of self is much more merged with others in a "we-self" that differs profoundly from the separate, autonomous "I-self" so typical of Westerners. Given this distinction, we can see why Western psychology typically emphasize the self phase of development, whereas Easterners, who intuitively are more familiar with states of merger, seem so adept at understanding the trans-self conditions. However, the developmental theorists sometimes make certain assumptions about how Easterners experience the self—assumptions that may be inaccurate. For example, one premise is that spiritual masters take for granted that an integrated, "normal" sense of self exists before students begin meditation practice. But what they know as a "normal" self is not what we Westerners know. Their normal experience of self roots more in merging self-object relationships than ours; it is not the separated and individuated self as Westerners know it.

Another questionable premise is that Eastern systems have not elaborated a developmental understanding of the pre-self phase of development. Although they may not have formulated as distinct a developmental model as Western theorists, their understanding of pre-self experiences may be profound on, at the very least, an intuitive level. Spiritual masters even may be more aware of narcissistic disorders than sometimes credited. The *I Ching*, for example, often describes people suffering from an "inner emptiness." Engler (1986) himself noted that the diagnostic paradigm in the Buddhist Abhidhamma describes problems in object relatedness (although he insists it still is not a developmental system). Engler even described the case of a meditation teacher who leads an anorectic woman, apparently suffering from a narcissistic disturbance, to a relief of her symptoms and then on to the preliminary stages of enlightenment over the course of a few months—a feat that points to the teacher's understanding of and ability to therapeutically correct self-disturbances.

The most important point is that any attempt to integrate Eastern and Western ideas (including this book) runs into a cross-cultural dilemma: On a fundamental, experiential level, the sense of "self"— the ordinary, day-to-day experience of self—is not the same in the West and the East.

Also, in the realm of metapsychology, the developmental stage model churns up some problems. There is a curious paradoxical flavor to it. Does it make sense to draw distinctions among various categories and stages in order to describe the progression toward no-self in which categories, concepts, and discriminations are realized as illusory? It's difficult to shape a wide-reaching vision using tools that have a narrow range of motion. An analogy might be the attempt to use Newtonian physics to explain relativity theory. In Chuang Tzu's words, it's like beating a drum while in search of a fugitive.

As pointed out by Wilber, Engler, and Brown (1986), many Buddhist texts do indeed describe stages in the attainment of enlightenment (e.g., Nyanamoli, 1976), so the concept obviously is not foreign to Asians. Brown and Engler's (1986) empirical research with the Rorschach administered to meditators also tends to corroborate the stages depicted in these texts. Yet not all Eastern spiritual leaders agree with the efforts to map out stages in spiritual development. In the Zen tradition, Suzuki (1970) insisted that such notions were introduced by later Zen teachers, and not intended by the original masters. He stated that when one sits to meditate, enlightenment is already present. There is nothing to attain. Conceptualizing, anticipating, and reaching for the next stage—as if it did not already exist—is just another manifestation of the ambitious, goal-seeking "monkey-mind" that invariably disrupts the meditation practice. Scholarly efforts to chart and catalog the path to enlightenment may also smack of this monkey-mind. Categories and distinctions tend to breed more categories and distinctions, which often culminate in a complex edifice where we tend to focus more on the edifice than on the insight that originally inspired it and transcends it.

Leaning on the concept of a linear progression from pre-self to self to trans-self, as postulated by the developmental model, may make us susceptible to fall into oversimplifications that do not hold up in reality. Working on the pre-self and self level with their patients, psychoanalytic clinicians are beginning to recognize that people do not function exclusively on one level or the other. All people, including neurotic and normal individuals, contain different mixtures of pre-oedipal and oedipal issues; object-related and selfobject dynamics can coexist and interact. The Mahlerian notion that there is a progressive push toward higher and higher states of individuation and separation is yielding to Kohut's insight that the need for selfobject ties exists and is necessary throughout life, along with the need for autonomy.

This type of coexistence and intermixing also may exist between the self and trans-self (no-self) dimensions. Recognizing this, Wilber, Engler, & Brown (1986) were careful not to overemphasize the linearity of their model. Wilber, for example, introduced Grof's (1975) concept of COEX systems, which are developmentally layered or onion-like complexes in the psyche. Maladaptive experiences at one level of development invade or contaminate the developmental process at higher levels. In the introduction to their book, Wilber, Engler, and Brown summarized their position:

> ". . . the contemplative stages of development are probably not parallel (or alternative) to the normal, typical, or conventional stages of development, but rather refer to different and higher stages of development altogether (although this by no means precludes very complex interactions between the two; a rigidly linear and unidirectional model is not at all what we have in mind). (p. 7)

Their parenthetical thinking deserves emphasis.We might consider the possibility that the self and trans-self (no-self) dimensions do exist at parallel, though interacting, planes. In psychoanalysis, an analogy is the realization that libidinal, ego, and object-relational functions may all follow distinct developmental lines. To this we may add the "spiritual" line of no-self dynamics. As noted by Rubin (1992a), the developmental concept implies that a person rides an elevator and gets off on only one floor that corresponds to his or her developmental level. Instead, he suggests, the individual may be a multifaceted "mosaic" that possesses many dimensions, including the spiritual/no-self dimension, which interact with each other in complex ways but exist on distinct developmental planes. Even the spiritual dimension itself can serve a multifaceted purpose in intrapsychic dynamics, at some levels enhancing psychological well-being, at other levels bolstering narcissistic or instinctual conflicts. At the 1990 Conference on Contemporary Psychoanalysis and Religion in Boston, Engler acknowledged the inaccuracies in his previously stated idea that "You have to be somebody before you can be nobody."

We also should be cautious about completely discrediting the no-self experiences of psychotic and borderline individuals. Although equating the schizophrenic with the enlightened master undoubtedly is a mistake, the spiritual insights proclaimed by psychotics may, in some regards, be genuine. Judging their no-self and no-mind experiences as strictly pathological and without any religious bearing, while praising the experiences of spiritual leaders, seems akin to allowing the poor to get poorer and the rich to get richer. In psychology there has been a longstanding fascination in the relationship between psychopathology and spiritual awareness. Jung, for example, took a keen interest in this topic. A general conclusion is that the cracked mind of "pathological" people may let in light to which the normal person is blind. This conclusion may be troubling to some theorists—including some developmental advocates who must face the task of deciphering how and why the stages at the end and the beginning of their spectrum have something in common.

Oscillations Between Self and No-Self

So far, this discussion has explored the various concepts of self and no-self, and of how the two are essential features of psychological functioning. One task that remains is to clarify exactly how these two conditions interact. Can we specify an intrapsychic process or mechanism by which they become related to each other? If they both contribute to psychological well-being, in what context do they coexist?

The attainment of the self (self-as-structure) relies on a process of integration. The attainment of no-self relies on deautomatization and retraversing—a process of disintegration. If we express the problem using these terms—integration and disintegration—we see that the psychoanalytic literature is filled with references to how the self and no-self as processes of integration and disintegration interact. Loewald (1960) described the patient's free association as mini-disintegration experiences and the analyst's interventions as a force toward new integrations. Winnicott (1971) believed that the patient's immersion into a "stage of hesitation"—a state of nonbeing and non-thought where nothing can be said or done—provides the catalyst for a breakthrough into new insights and subsequent new constructions of the self. The process is not unlike the oscillations between form and formlessness in the play of children, where the dips into unin-tegration allow access to a creative chaos that in turn enriches self ad-vancement. Borrowing Winnicott's idea of a stage of hesitation, Sloane (1986) suggested that delving into and tolerating states of in-trapsychic blankness, chaos, and void lead the analyst and patient to previously unseen realms of realization and change. Bion (1970), the great psychoanalytic mystic, spoke of the sturdy personality that ben-efits from its approach to "O," the archetypic condition of disintegra-tion and catastrophe that underlies being. Entering such states of formlessness marks an important stage in the act of creativity itself, as revealed in the psychoanalytic studies of art that point to an "uncon-scious undifferentiated ego matrix" and a "pregnant emptiness" as the realm of plenitude where old patterns dissolve, disappear, and re-shape into new ones (Ehrenzweig, 1971; Milner, 1957).

The disintegration/integration theme implicitly weaves through the basic premises of self psychology and intersubjectivity theory. Kohut (1984) believed that structure building occurs as a result of a temporary empathic failure on the part of the analyst. It is the "optimal frustration" of this break in the selfobject tie that stimulates patients to internalize the functions of the analyst and create intrapsy-chic structure "on their own." The underlying assumption in this idea of optimal frustration is that a phase of mini-self-disintegration accompanies the breaking of the selfobject tie and precedes the initia-tion of new structure building. In their description of obtaining "opti-mal structuralization" by widening the scope and flexibility of the patient's subjective field of experience, Atwood and Stolorow (1984) also implied the importance of a phase of disintegration: "As the ossi-fied, pathological forms that have heretofore structured the patient's experiences are progressively broken up and reorganized, a new and enriched reality opens up before him, made possible by the newly ex-panded and reflectively conscious structures of his subjective world" (p. 60).

In an early paper that anticipates some of the ideas of self psy-chology, van Dusen (1958) described the states of no-mind and void that appeared in his patients during the course of psychotherapy. Pa-tients often experienced this void as blankness, loss of memory, failures of concentration, or loss of meaning that felt like "holes" which threatened to engulf them. At first it seemed that these blank spaces were characteristic of schizophrenics only, but closer examination revealed that they appeared in all patients, to some extent. The patients feared these holes as a place of disintegration, loss of self, nothingness, and death. They struggled to avoid, fill up, or seal off these blank spaces with words, intellectualizations, and more symptoms. But van Dusen discovered that the feared place is a fertile void. Rather than being a condition of depletion and emptiness, the black hole was a rich, perhaps infinite condensation of meaning and affect. Exploring it proved to be a turning point in therapy. Believing the hole to be an expression of the Zen no-mind and no-self, van Dusen encouraged his patients to enter it in order to discover previously hidden aspects of self. For each person the void held different meanings. Entering it resulted in spontaneous, natural changes that seemed to be the result of an unlocking of the willing self.

What all these findings have in common is the idea that healthy psychological functioning depends on an oscillation or balance between integrating and disintegrating, between self and no-self. This idea bears similarities to the psychoanalytic concept of a "regression in service of the ego," also known as "adaptive regression" (Kris, 1952; Schafer, 1958). According to this concept, the temporary, controlled regression to primary process enables one to gain access to unconscious affects, fantasies, and unusual thought styles, which, when subsequently mastered by the logic and practicality of secondary process, results in the enhancement of psychological health. It is the oscillation between primary and secondary process that is the source of psychotherapeutic progress and also the fuel for creativity (Suler, 1980).

So, too, the oscillations between self and no-self advance psychological well-being. In fact, the shift to conditions of no-self, as described in the Zen literature, bears elements of primary process: the breakdown of habitual patterns of thinking and feeling, the reversing to more fundamental styles of perceiving, the suspension of time, the unflinching expression of contradictions, the simultaneous coexistence of opposites, and the mobile cathexes—the capacity for anything to symbolize or stand for anything else. These elements point to a unity of existence among things. Rutstein (1985) suggests that the shifts to and mastery of primary process can explain the unity/oneness experience of mystical traditions because it is a process that allows for a greatly expanded ability to sense relatedness beyond the usual personal boundaries. Krynicki (1980) similarly suggested that the ability of Zen meditators repeatedly to experience states of merging and oneness and return to states of autonomy and individuation therapeutically alleviated fears of both separation and symbiosis by strengthening psychic regulatory mechanisms for alternating between these two subjective conditions. Contrary to the traditional psychoanalytic labeling of these oscillations as a *regression* (even if adaptive), Rutstein described them as a *progression*—an idea endorsed by many East/West theorists.

Of course, primary process as traditionally conceptualized may not adequately cover the full meaning of no-self as proposed by Zen. Interpreted from the most radical perspective, the movement into no-self, in its purest form, requires an immersion into total disintegration, timelessness, chaos. It is the piece of cork disintegrating in the currents of the stream. It is a condition in which all identity is lost, in which all things become like all other things. But it also is a condition of complete possibility and potential. Because there is no identity, any identity is possible. Complete reorganization first requires complete disorganization, because chaos enables any and all things to be taken apart and rearranged. Anything can be discarded, and anything can start anew when complete openness is available. By immersing into this no-self, the self is highlighted; and by contacting the background of meaninglessness, meaning takes form. Ongoing oscillations between self and no-self give rise to the ongoing death and birth of all structures and functions of selfhood.

The references to death here are important. Death represents the existential inevitability of no-self as a phase juxtaposed with life. The self's impermanence often surfaces as a pivotal theme in both Zen and self psychology. In *The Restoration of the Self*, Kohut (1977) frequently mentions death anxiety while discussing the more general issue of disintegration anxiety. So, too, in Zen training, as revealed by Kapleau's (1980a) case studies, the fear of death and self-dissolution often becomes a primary concern. Narcissistic injuries arising from encounters with death or symbolically similar losses often precipitate the person's seeking Zen, just as they might lead a person to psychoanalytic treatment. In fact, Oremland (1985) suggested that the encounter with death may account for the implicit religiosity in Kohut's theory, i.e., the religious, even mystical notion of a teleological self moving toward preordained self-validations and self-realizations of a higher order and purpose. Kohut's theory may have been influenced by the fact that he was approaching the end of his life, that his views reflected the mourning for the loss of self, or perhaps the wisdom that comes when one realizes the true finiteness of life.

This wisdom may have been the recognition that the forces of self-integration and life affirmation counterpoise the forces of self-dissolution and death. Although Zen speaks of self-loss, and self psychology speaks of self-unification, both approaches implicitly point to an intimate balancing of integration and disintegration. Despite Kohut's emphasis on the developmental striving toward self-cohesion and unity, the psychological need to encompass the intrinsic and inevitable impermanence of the self also is a subtle but important theme in his work. In *The Restoration of the Self* (1977) he stated that optimal parents are people who, despite their competition with the rising generation, are sufficiently in touch with the "pulse of life" and accepting of themselves as "transient participants in the stream of life" that they can "experience the growth of the next generation with unforced, non-defensive joy" (p. 237). He also expressed his hope that the psychology of the self would someday be able to explain the fact that "some people regard the inevitability of death as proof that life is utterly meaningless . . . while others can accept death as an integral part of a meaningful life" (p. 242).

Because self structure is the organizational context that provides meaning to experience (Atwood & Stolorow, 1984; Stolorow, Brandchaft, & Atwood, 1987), the ability to accept death as an integral part of life indicates an ability to embody meaninglessness within meaning and the dissolution of self structure within self structure. Death may be understood as a metaphor for the disintegrating processes that break apart the self—processes that necessarily interact with and balance the integrative processes. The therapeutic reorganization and building of self structure necessitates stages of deorganizing and demolition, an idea reminiscent of Freud's dynamic between the life and death instincts. A theory that emphasizes only an intrinsic striving toward self-integration may be an unbalanced oversimplification.

Interpenetration of Self and No-Self

Near the beginning of this chapter, I speculated about how Zen masters might respond to the psychological concepts of selfhood. Perhaps they would say that the self is all these things and none of them—or, even more abstrusely, that the self neither is nor isn't any of these things. Such a reply would be more than a mere play on logic and words. We may not be able to know the self in its purest form, but only the manifestations it takes. As suggested by the Zen reply, the most primary manifestations express themselves in the form of dualities: apparently contradictory dualities of is and isn't, dualities couched in negation and paradox.

The theories about oscillations between self and no-self offer a useful, understandable explanation of how these conditions of self-hood interact. The theory fits neatly into a larger psychological framework, but it may be an oversimplification. The relationship between self and no-self may be more intimate, more intertwined than depicted in the notion of an oscillation between two distinct states of selfhood, or even in the idea of a balancing between two distinct processes. Some of the theorists who seem to emphasize the oscillation concept, in fact, touch on this insight. To say that the self is and isn't something, that it neither is nor isn't something, points to an intermeshing coexistence of self and no-self that is not readily captured by traditional psychological conceptualizations.

Zen states that "all form is emptiness and all emptiness is form." At the deepest level of the self, its primary, paradoxical manifestation embodies an *interpenetration* of structure and void, an identity of self and no-self. We can envision this interpenetration in a variety of ways. For example, the structures that constitute the self-as-structure actually are processes at a slow rate of change—but processes have no specific origin and no final form or content: Self and no-self are simultaneously interfused.We also have described the process of negating and deautomatizing the structures of the object self to free the observing self that is without form or boundaries; but the term "observing" is misleading because this self is not distant or isolated, but rather manifests itself within the object itself. Zen interprets this self as the void that is the "unconscious" (Fromm, Suzuki, & DeMartino, 1960)—not a static and lifeless void, but rather a void of infinite potential and possibility, a no-self, that interpenetrates and nourishes self structure. The observer and the observed give rise to and infuse each other. Finally, close inspection reveals that the processes of integration and disintegration do not simply work side by side, but actually interlace with each other, encompass and are encompassed by each other. All structures, including rocks, trees, and the psychological representations constituting the self, are wrapped in an ongoing process of simultaneously becoming and un-becoming. Any given thing, in the smallest fraction of time and space, exists—but only in that illusory, infinitesimal moment which is interpenetrated by the ongoing flux of change and transformation. The self is and isn't. The experience of selfhood exists interpenetrated with the experience of no-self. As Suzuki might say, the self and no-self are not two and not one; they are both one and two.

Of all psychoanalytic thinkers, perhaps Bion (1963, 1970) most closely approached this rather mystical vision. He describes the condition of "catastrophe," of nonbeing, that underlies existence—that is the very ground of existence. Ubiquitous, it cannot be named directly. We tend to ignore it, but its influence is felt everywhere. It is the primary binding force that holds the self together, a primordial source from which structure and function spring. The self-as-structure bathes in this infusing, ongoing catastrophe. From this sense of catastrophe arises the "faith" of the willing self that drives the creative act of doing and becoming.

Bion's ideas resemble those of the great existential thinkers, especially Nietzsche (1892–1954). Nietzsche envisioned the "eternal recurrence" as the chaotic flow of all things in which everything is identical to and joined with everything else. There is no identity, no meaning, no distinction among things. Everything simply and truly is. One belongs to the whole, one is the whole. This condition is the grounding in absolute being, the fertile source from which the resurrection of new life is possible. It is the void that exists in every moment, the center that is everywhere. The eternal presents itself in the here and now and is available at our fingertips at each and every turn. It infuses every step, every moment. Through the "will to power" one claims that moment and sets into motion the process of becoming.

Drawing on the ideas of Winnicott and Bion, Eigen (1986) similarly describes how conditions of nonbeing, chaos, emptiness, and catastrophe are the "zero point" that infuses and grounds the self. It constitutes the "psychotic core" that exists not just in schizophrenics, but within normal people as well.

> To speak of a zero point of mind takes us to the edge of meaning and perhaps over that edge. Yet the Zen master, as well as the psychotic, speaks of no-mind. Something very basic is meant when one speaks of nothingness. . . . It threatens to hurl the personality into an unimaginable abyss beyond oblivion, a horrific spacelessness in which there is no direction or valence other than horror itself. It fuses chaos and nothingness, scattered noise and blankness. This happens because the personality is in the process of disintegrating, experiencing and representing its disintegration, representing the disintegration of representations, and undoing itself and its representational capacity as far as inhumanly (yet all too humanly) possible. (p. 119)

Here Eigen depicts the horror of the experience of no-self—a theme reminiscent of the existentialists, such as Kierkegaard, Sartre, and Nietzsche, who portrayed the encounter with the nonbeing that soaks into being as a type of sickness, insanity, or nausea. Mystical traditions also speak of the dark night of the soul, or the Great Doubt in Zen, when the first engagement with no-self stirs anxiety about not simply the possibility of losing the self, but the realization that the self is already, essentially, lost. In both Taoism and Zen, great spiritual masters are often portrayed as fools or crazy people. Tapping both the self and no-self that inevitably constitute who they are, how could they be anything else but wise fools? For this reason, a simplified developmental perspective that places pathology at the pre-self phase and spiritual integrity at the trans-self phase may be overlooking the interpenetrating complexity of self and no-self, insight and insanity.

Likewise, it would be a mistake to conclude that the Zen experience is simply an immersion into prepsychological chaos comparable to early infancy, or that it strives for a state of self-disintegration comparable to the conditions of psychosis or severe narcissistic pathologies. In early infancy and severe pathology the integrated, cohesive self is absent or grossly disrupted. In the Zen experience it is not. Instead, the integrated self exists and thrives through its interpenetration with no-self. The full self is only realized and appreciated in the encounter with the interfusion of no-self. Speaking metaphorically, Suzuki (1970) stated that it is wrong thinking to believe that the self vanishes after death, just as it is wrong to think that it survives after death. Self and no-self are two interweaving sides of the same thing.

Perhaps different types of pathology may be understood as different disturbances in the interpenetration of self and no-self. In neurotic disorders, one clings to overly rigid, distorted self structures and tries to avoid any subjective experience of the underlying void. In the narcissistic disturbances, one senses the shifting sands of inner chaos and makes defensive, precarious attempts to build castles upon it. And the psychotic, as Eigen (1986) noted, may dive head first into the zero-point not as an act of renewal, but as a means of escaping the vulnerabilities of selfhood.

The presence of the analyst, like that of the Zen master, serves the selfobject function of sustaining the person through the realization of the no-self that interpenetrates the self. The analyst's presence is the intersubjective manifestation of self structure holding and embodying selflessness. Language and words, though not capturing the essence of this process, do enhance the intersubjective context that makes it possible. Although Zen ultimately attempts a deeper probing into the roots of no-self, not everyone can endure the full course of Zen meditation—just as some patients, though greatly benefiting from their treatment, cannot tolerate a full immersion into the prepsychological chaos underlying their core defects.

The ideas discussed in this section sometimes portray the no-self as intensely powerful and mysterious. But the Zen expression of the no-self takes a less dramatic, simpler form. The no-self is one's everyday mind. There is nothing to reach or attain. It is already present, even in the simplest events of everyday living, in the most ordinary, spontaneous actions of the willing self. The developmental theory suggests that you have to be somebody before you can be nobody. But you already are nobody. Perhaps, if there is anything at all to attain, it is the simple realization that there is nothing to attain because the no-self is already present. Perhaps the expression can be modified: "To realize fully that you are somebody is to realize that you are nobody."

Interpenetration of Self and Object

To explore the dynamics of no-self is to explore the relationship between self and object. Because the no-self entails an intertwining of being and not being a self, it also includes the experience of the object as being and not being a part of the self. When the self is and is not, objects are and are not. If the self/no-self duality is one primary manifestation of the self that is unknowable, a second manifestation is the duality between self and object.

A fundamental insight in Zen, and in all mystical traditions, is that the self and other cannot exist without each other. They are interdependent and, at the deepest level, one. Separateness is an illusion. In fact, some Zen masters (e.g., Suzuki, 1970) would state that self and other are not two and not one, suggesting that the very distinction between a self/other duality or unity is extraneous. This idea differs significantly from traditional Western psychology, which, according to Watts (1975a) has always suffered from the conceptual "cancer" of dividing the subject and object. Until recently, psychoanalysis often sided with the traditional camp. Developmental theory emphasized the maturational progression from states of oneness and symbiosis to separation and individuation. States of fusion were considered pathological or developmentally primitive—an idea rooted in the view of many psychoanalytic thinkers (Alexander, 1931; Fingarette, 1958; Freud, 1930; Horton, 1974; Jones, 1923; Lewin, 1950; Ross, 1975; Schroeder, 1922; Shafi, 1973) that mystical visions of oneness are a regression to the primal experience of oneness with the mother.

Kohut's (1984) concept of selfobject relationships offered a new perspective on separation and autonomy that was more resonant with the Zen insight that self and object are interdependent. He suggested that there is a symbiotic overlapping of psychic functions between self and object that enhances the cohesion and continuity of self structure. The intertwining of self and object (with separateness as a condition of this interdependence) is a natural aspect of the evolving integrity of self. From birth to death, self-selfobject relationships form the essence of psychological life. The move from dependence and symbiosis to independence and autonomy "is no more possible, let alone desirable, than a corresponding move from a life dependent on oxygen to a life independent of it . . ." (p. 47).

Developmental research (e.g., Beebe & Lachmann, 1988; Lichtenberg, 1983; Stern, 1985) seems to bear out this intertwining, interpenetrating relationship between self and object, which is present even at the earliest phases of development. The infant, rather than being a passive recipient, actively seeks out the caretaker's selfobject responses in what constitutes a complex, interweaving dance of selves as initiators/motivators (willing selves) and selves as evolving structures. As infancy turns to adulthood, the interpenetrating relationship does not end, but progresses to a level where the unity of self and object is in a new, developmentally advanced context. Like the analogy of needing oxygen to breathe, neither the infant nor the adult is usually aware of living within and around the sustaining, infusing presence of the selfobject. However, the aim of the Zen enlightenment is the direct experience of this reality, a simultaneous experiencing of union and separation—what Krynicki (1980) called the "double orientation of the ego." The traditional psychoanalytic view is that this simultaneous awareness of self and other as both one and two reaches its fullest form when experienced from the perspective of the adult, structuralized self.

The interpenetrating dynamic of self and other is a primary, seemingly paradoxical manifestation of the self. The self is and is not just itself. Winnicott (1967) noted that separation separates within a broader context of connection. It is the awareness of this interpenetration that makes separation tolerable. "This is the place that I have set to examine, the separation that is not a separation but a form of union" (p. 21). Resonating with Winnicott's vision of the basic inseparateness of self and object, Eigen (1986) suggested that psychotic and narcissistic disorders involve an attempt to break apart the paradoxical interweaving of union and distinction by escaping into states of selfless fusion or grandiose autonomy. But the contradiction remains at the root of the self. In summarizing Mahler's developmental concept of autism—in which a subject exists without an object, followed by symbiosis, in which subject and object are fused—Eigen revealed the paradox that surfaces when psychoanalysis explores the origin of self: "We begin as one within ourselves before we are and move to oneness with the other before it is" (p. 150). This paradoxical interweaving of self and other also is implicit in the attempts to define "selfobject" not as the caregivers themselves but as "a dimension of experiencing an object in which a specific bond is required for maintaining, restoring, or consolidating the organization of self-experience" (Stolorow, Brandchaft, & Atwood, 1987, pp. 16–17): The self, which is not differentiated from the other, contains within itself a dimension of experiencing the other as maintaining that self. Such statements bring to mind the Zen master Lin Chi's warning (see Watts, 1975a), "Make no mistake: There is nothing on the inside and, likewise, nothing on the outside that you can grasp."

In Eigen's (1986) fascinating review of the literature on ego and self boundaries (Balint, 1968; Elkin, 1958, 1972; Federn, 1926, 1952; Grotstein, 1980, 1981, 1982; Kohut, 1971; Mahler, 1968; Winnicott, 1958, 1971, 1974), he concludes that experiences of boundarylessness are indeed a hallmark of psychosis, but they also are integral to the normal experience of self. He points to the fundamental manifestation of the self as an interpenetration of self and object. Psychotics stumble on this complexity and are overwhelmed by it. They are mesmerzied by it. The extremes of psychosis present them with the paradoxical contradictions that must be taken into account in order to grasp human nature. It is too easy, Eigen stated, for unity to become obliterating fusion or separation to become autistic-paranoid isolation. Both tendencies operate in varying balances and intensities:

> Is boundlessness objectlessness? In my view, no. The self arises through the encompassing horizon of an infinite other. It exists in a bounded perceptual field permeated with a sense of boundless immateriality. How is this possible? We do not know. But both dimensions—boundedness and boundlessness—are given to us and give us ourselves. (Eigen, 1986, p. 166)

The paradoxical interpermeating of self and other is the essence of the transformational mergings generated through twinning relationships and empathy. A Zen story (see Van de Wetering, 1978) tells of a master whose first insight was his recognition of others: Everyone he met had his own face. So, too, during the empathic immersion into the patient's experience the analyst realizes the I in the You and the You in the I. Self psychology's term *empathic-introspection* connotes this paradoxical process of seeing into the other and into oneself simultaneously. In his discussion of Zen, Fromm (Fromm,

Suzuki, & DeMartino, 1960) described the productive relatedness between analyst and patient as the act of being fully open and responsive to the patient. One is "soaked" with the patient. It is a center-to-center relatedness that sets the essential conditions for psychoanalytic understanding and cure. "The analyst must become the patient, yet he must be himself; he must forget that he is the doctor, yet he must remain aware of it" (p. 112).

In his study of boundary formation, Meares (1988) suggested that empathy does not simply involve a merging of self and other. The analyst's empathic stance encourages the patient to observe his inner experience—to become a spectator of his or her thoughts and feelings through the activation of the observing self, as if the patient learns to see his or her experience projected onto a metaphoric screen. Empathic contact enhances the *intrapsychic* split between subject and object (i.e., between the observing self and self-as-structure). This awareness of an internal distinction between subject and object in turn enhances the awareness of the *interpersonal/external* distinction between the patient as subject and the analyst as object. Empathy thus stimulates the sense of "self" versus the "not-self," thereby creating a feeling of "innerness" that is the observing self.

Here again we see the paradoxical quality of empathy. The blending of boundaries coexists with the sense of "innerness." The analyst's empathic immersion into the patient's experience involves, at some level, a merging, union, or joining of awarenesses; yet it also facilitates the awareness of the inner, observing self as different from the interpersonal other, as well as the innerness of the observing self as different from the intrapsychic aspects of self-as-structure that are observed.

The target of empathic understanding is the content of the patient's self experience. This empathy is attained *through* the merging or unity of the patient's and analyst's observing selves—the joining of the analyst and patient into a united, observing subject who becomes aware of the patient's self-as-structure. This empathy is only possible once the analyst and patient position themselves within the innerness that, paradoxically, they share—when they both negate or "decenter" from the features of the self-as-structure that create the illusion of separateness. Kapleau (1980a) stated that in Zen, "The purpose is to wipe away from the mind these shadows or defilements so that one can intimately experience our solidarity with all life. Love and compassion then naturally and spontaneously flow forth" (p. 103).

In Zen, this solidarity with all life, which is in some respects analogous to a twinship experience, extends even beyond animate entities to inanimate objects. Enlightenment is to "be like a block of wood." At first glance, this may seem to violate self psychology's concept of twinning as a strictly human, interpersonal relationship. Yet selfobjects that sustain self-cohesion may also be things, events, and environments—as in transitional objects and phenomena. As the term implies, a selfobject can be an intertwining of self and object that gives meaning to the animate via the duality and interpenetration with the inanimate. One's world, one's entire culture, Kohut (1984) stated, constitutes a complex constellation of selfobjects that infuses and sustains the self. The selfobject environment becomes a kind of "cosmic narcissism" (Kohut, 1966). This idea is reminiscent of the Zen vision that the self and its world constitute an interdependent unity. The participation of the animate self within the inanimate not-self is but an extension of the paradoxical dualities of self/object and self/no-self.

The spiritual genius of the Zen masters was their ability to express these seemingly complex, abstruse insights in the simplest of everyday actions. Suzuki (1970) spoke of the Half Dipper Bridge near the Eiheiji monastery in Japan, where his thirteenth century dharma ancestor, Dogen, would drink from the river. Dogen sipped only half a dipperful, returning the remainder to the river by pouring the water toward rather than away from his body. By drinking, Dogen allowed the water to become inside as well as outside. By pouring back half a dipperful, he too became inside as well as outside the stream of water. Dogen and the river were interfused, both two and one.

4

Paradox

The Meanings of Paradox

A paradox is a statement or behavior that is seemingly inconsistent, absurd, or self-contradictory, yet in fact true. As a derivative of the Greek *para* (contrary) and *dokein* (think), it signifies a countering of reason. It thrusts one, literally, into "nonsense" by challenging common sense and violating one's basic assumptions about reality. Many paradoxes embody the self-contradiction that arises when a statement implicitly turns back and reflects on itself, asking whether or not it is to be taken as an example of the idea it proposes. The classic example is, "Everything I say is a lie." If the statement is an example of the idea it asserts, it negates itself as it affirms itself. Paradoxical injunctions such as, "Disobey me!" turn disobeying into obeying and obeying into disobeying when the command turns back and enlists itself as an example of its own directive.

This self-contradiction arising from the action of the self attempting to grasp or reflect on itself may take the form of a paradoxical conflict between different levels of self-examination. Hofstadter (Hofstadter & Dennett, 1981) gives the example of the statement, "This sentence contains one error." On a manifest level, it is incorrect because there are no errors—but on a deeper level it is correct because it is incorrect in the estimation of its error, which in turn shows that it is in error, and so on. It is simultaneously both correct and incorrect. The paradoxical self-contradiction is rooted in the interpenetrating opposition of self-representations. The existence of the paradox itself points to the existence of these different and disparate layers of self-representation.

Hofstadter suggests that paradoxes are the consequence of a long-recognized dilemma: An object bears a special and unique relationship to itself. It is restricted in its ability to act on itself in the way it acts upon all other objects. A pencil cannot write on itself; a fly swatter cannot swat itself; people cannot directly see their own faces. Hofstadter (Hofstadter & Dennett, 1981) concluded:

> We can come close to seeing and understanding ourselves objectively, but each of us is trapped inside a powerful system with a unique point of view—and that power is also a guarantor of limitedness. And this vulnerability—this self-hook—may also be the source of the ineradicable sense of "I." (p. 278)

In Zen Buddhist training, paradoxes know as *koans* are presented to students to stimulate their progress toward satori, the state of enlightenment. The student must produce a solution to the puzzle even though there seems to be no logical answer. Some koans are one-liner questions: What is the sound of one hand clapping? When the many are reduced to the one, to what is the one reduced? Without using your mouth, body, or mind, express yourself. Show me your face before your parents were born.

Other koans are presented as a paradoxical situation that challenges the student to determine its solution or meaning:

- A monk asks the master if a dog has a self. The master replies "Mu!" (which translates as "not" or "none," or perhaps more accurately as the prefix "un" or "non").
- A man dangles over a deep precipice, hanging only by his teeth that clench the root of a tree. A Zen master appears and asks, "What is your true self?"
- A master holds a staff above the head of his student. "If you say this is a staff I will strike you. If you say it isn't a staff I will strike you. If you say nothing I will strike you."
- A man grew a goose in a bottle until it became too big to stay inside. If the bottle is smashed it will kill the goose. If nothing is done, the goose will smother.

Psychotherapists in the West, particularly adherents of the strategic or paradoxical schools (e. g., Haley, 1963; Seltzer, 1986; Weeks, 1985), often cite Zen koans as an example of how immersing a person into paradox can culminate in therapeutic insight and relief from symptoms. Yet few studies have focused specifically on the application of the koan and the underlying Zen psychology of paradox as a model for understanding psychotherapy. Such a focus can reveal the various elements of paradoxical self-contradictions that underlie psychological transformations—including the shift in one's perspective of reality, the conflict of internal representations and levels of self, the interweaving of self-affirmation and negation, and the puzzling dynamics of the self that turns back to capture, understand, or reflect on itself.

Entering the Paradox

For no apparent reason, a bright student miserably fails an entrance exam into graduate school. A patient who frequently cancels sessions claims that her psychotherapy is not going deep enough, so she wants to come every other week. Like a character from a Woody Allen film, a lonely man states that he would never join any organization that would have him as a member. By pointing out these self-contradictory behaviors, the therapist presents to the patient a paradox that seems to violate logic and common sense. These patients are disputing themselves by presenting an idea and then countering that idea, all in one breath—as if they have taken both sides in an argument in which the distinction between the subject and object is unclear. Although it may disturb the person to realize he or she is knotted into a self-contradiction, this personal paradox, similar to the koan, entices curiosity, for the person realizes there is more going on below the surface than meets the eye. By stepping back into the observing self to see him- or herself entangled in paradox, the patient gets his or her first alluring scent of a dispute between different layers of selfhood. As Kapleau (1980a) stated, the koan is like candy to coax a reluctant child, to stimulate the thirst for realization. Observing the dilemma from an objective viewpoint allows the patient to feel its outer shape and texture, yet quickly realize that this approach is insufficient. To untangle the knot of self-contradiction, they must enter right into it.

The patient's initial advance on the paradox typically involves the attempt to unravel it intellectually. But the paradox ultimately frustrates and cracks open any rational attempt to resolve it, for the solution is not logical. The koan has no answer; the answer is to be something different. The solution is an experience. As sophisticated as the person's intellectualizations may be, they are an illusion, a defense. Rational explanations meet only silence or another question from the therapist and a nonsensical retort or flat-out rejection from the Zen master, as in the response, "Mu!" At first this situation amplifies the person's attempts to grip it logically, cognitively. The struggle for a solution becomes an ordeal of "figuring out," a crisis of thinking that lasts as long as the person persists in cogitating an answer. The teacher has led the student down a blind tunnel, to the edge of a precipice, where the realization that intellect will not suffice forces the student to make a quantum leap out of it. Consistent with the principle of both psychoanalysis and Eastern philosophy that "intellect is a good servant but a bad master" (Watts, 1958), the koan sets a trap that breaks the back of rationality. And, as Kopp (1976) stated, one cannot get out of a trap until one first gets into it.

The crisis generated by the paradox quickly spreads into other realms of one's personality other than the intellect. During the Zen student's meditation on a koan and the therapy patient's contemplation of a personal paradox, a variety of conflicting affects, ideas, and memories surface. The paradox is a digging, churning tool that penetrates directly into the roots of who we are. Multiple components of one's self structure are jostled, loosened, forced to the surface. During meditation, conflicting layers of self-representation often take the form of vivid, almost hallucinatory images known in Zen as *makyo*. The paradox becomes all-consuming; one's whole being enters it. The self is at war with itself as the conscious and unconscious realms clash. Even the koan, which started off as a benign brain teaser that seemed external to oneself, now becomes the center of a desperate struggle around personal issues. The sane and irrational reasons that led the student to Zen are uncovered and questioned. The problems of one's life are uncovered and questioned. The koan is a struggle for one's very existence. One becomes the self in contradiction with itself. "He feels like a man seeking something he has forgotten, something he has to remember at any cost, because his life depends on it" (Herrigel, 1960, p. 43).

The student has entered the stage of the Great Doubt, which corresponds to the dark nights of psychotherapy when despair, hopelessness, and exhaustion prevail. Kapleau (1980a) uses the analogy of taking away a blind man's staff and spinning him around. The person is confused by and doubts everything—her- or himself, the teacher, the validity of the learning process. As stated in Zen, "Rivers are no longer rivers; mountains no longer mountains."

One has reached an internal deadlock. The koan, according to Zen lore, becomes a "red hot iron ball stuck in one's throat." Like repeating the same word over and over again until it loses its meaning, this stage marks a satiation effect, where the prolonged focus on self-contradiction brings one to the brink of cognitive and perceptual freezing, disintegration, and reorganization (Kubose & Umemoto, 1980). Gestalt therapists called it the *impasse* (Perls, 1976), whereas psychoanalytic theorists described it as a form of nonbeing, a stage of hesitation, where patients block and there is nothing to be said or done (Bion, 1963; Winnicott, 1971). It is the condition of catastrophe and oblivion, the surfacing of the no-self that grounds existence. It is the intrapsychic tangle of doubt, confusion, and crisis that precedes the religious conversion experience. Watts (1975a) told the story of a psychiatrist who asked a Zen master how he deals with neurotic people. "I trap them," he said. "And how do you do that?" the psychiatrist replied. "I get them where they can't ask any more questions." Haidar Ansari spoke similarly of a voice in the night that whispered to him: "There is no such thing as a voice whispering in the night!"

From this deadlock of the Great Doubt springs a sudden insight that expands one's perspective of reality. The old assumptions and perceptions of oneself and the world—one's "old hometown" (Mountain, 1983)—are realized as illusions and are discarded. For the Zen student, it is a clearer, broader view of the ontology of self and other. So, too, it is for the psychotherapy patient, although the insight specifically reveals the unconscious transferential and parataxic distortions that warp one's day-to-day perceptions of self and other. The bright college student realizes he sabotaged his exam because he fears his success will enrage and destroy his father. The patient who wants more from therapy and cancels her sessions realizes she dreads where the therapy is leading her and how her therapist will react to what they discover. The man who rejects any organization that would have him as a member discovers that he really hates himself.

The self-contradiction that led to insight loses its grip. The double bind forces the person outside the previous frame of reference, expands the individual's model of the world, "decontextualizes" the seemingly paradoxical symptom (Osmer, 1981; Seltzer, 1986). The koan and the patient's personal paradox now can be left behind, like discarding a brick that was used to knock open a jammed door or a tissue that was used to blow one's nose and clear the head (Suzuki, 1956; van de Wetering, 1978). The paradox was a finger pointing to the moon. It indicated a direction; it motioned toward another, deeper level of the self, something unverbalizable. It pointed to the unconscious.

The cracking open of the double-binding self-contradiction and the insightful reframing of one's crisis can only occur if, in the words of Zen, one "lets go of the hold" which corresponds to the Taoist principle of *wu wei*. One must let things happen of their own accord. Theories about paradoxical therapy (Frankl, 1967; Haley, 1963; Seltzer, 1986; Weeks, 1985) have documented how a person's desperate attempts to control or eliminate a problematic behavior only perpetuate and exaggerate the symptom. The insomniac who tries to force himself to sleep never will; the phobic who worries about avoiding an anxiety attack inadvertently triggers it. The paradoxical intervention amplifies the problem until the person, reaching the limits of exhaustion and despair, finally lets go of it, allowing change to be spontaneous. Old concepts, rationalizations, and perspectives are swept away, creating space for a transformation.

So, too, the psychotherapy patient and the koan student are caught in a paradoxical dilemma: The harder they try for spontaneity, insight, or enlightenment, the less likely they will achieve it. Like the student who is confronted by the Zen master's staff, they are caught in *samsara*, the action of the grasping self that tries to get "one-up" (Watts, 1975a) on something that cannot be consciously grasped. When a martial arts student asked his *sensei* how long it would take for him to become a master, the *sensei* replied, "Ten years." The student seemed disturbed. "I can't wait that long. What if I work twice as hard, come to every class, and practice every day—how long then?" "Twenty years," the *sensei* replied.

Even the attempt not to grasp is just another form of grasping that blocks spontaneity and fulfillment. Compulsive people who force themselves to play never have fun. Meditators who try hard not to focus their attention on anything in particular are focusing their attention on not-focusing, resulting in poor meditation. Conscious attempts to let go and let things happen miss the mark of the spontaneous, willing self. As noted by James (1902) in his studies of religious conversion and by Kris (1952) in his work on the creative process, the final trigger for an experiential breakthrough is an unselfconscious self-surrender, a relinquishing of control to the unconscious, to something beyond the conscious self. The tendency to cling to one's illusions and symptoms because they are familiar, out of a fear of the unknown, must be bypassed. Desperately hanging on the edge of the precipice, one must simply let go. Paradoxically, losing oneself is finding oneself.

Paradoxes Within and Between

Similar to exploring the koan in Zen training, psychotherapy probes the paradoxes of human nature, although the insights usually center specifically on the paradoxical aspects of emotional disturbances and psychological change, rather than on the deeper ontological aspects of selfhood. As noted by the strategic therapists (Seltzer, 1986; Weeks, 1985) and by Freud in his concept of the neurotic paradox, attempts to cope with one's problems often perpetuate them through anticipatory anxiety and other cyclical, self-fulfilling mechanisms. A woman with an avoidant personality so desperately wants to be loved that she cannot tolerate the possibility of being rejected, so she avoids other people, which makes her even more lonely and desperate for love. Because a paranoid man thinks other people are out to hurt him, he acts critical and hostile, which makes others want to hurt him. Psychoanalytic theory also has clarified how symptoms are compromise formations that are both adaptive and maladaptive, that simultaneously reveal and disclose the unconscious, resulting in a paradoxical meshing of seemingly contradictory ideas and affects. Obsessive-compulsives are controlled by their desire not to be controlled; masochists use helplessness to be powerful. Haley (1963) suggested that determining who is responsible for these symptoms becomes a metaparadox atop the paradox of the symptom itself. Your parents may be blamed, but they couldn't help themselves; you, too, are not to blame because you also are driven by your unconscious— but in therapy you are expected to take control of it. A patient once complained that he was not responsible for his problems because it was his unconscious that caused them. Capturing the paradoxical essence of human nature, the therapist responded, "Whose unconscious is it, anyway?" Finally, consistent with Eastern philosophy, psychoanalysis reveals how even reality and fantasy are paradoxically intertwined, how a simple memory is both truth and self-deception.

Although these self-contradictions are relevant mostly to the psychotherapy context and may only be peripheral issues to the Zen student, they do tap the more fundamental paradox that is the essence of the koan and the underlying Taoist philosophy of yin and yang: that human nature, in fact all of nature, embodies the balance, inseparability, and interpenetration of opposites. This principle became a key feature of Jung's theory of personality and was also implied by Freud—as in, for instance, his concept of ambivalence, that contradictory emotions are two aspects of the same attachment to a significant other and therefore exist side by side in the unconscious. The personal paradox in psychotherapy is the self-contradiction resulting from only one side of the ambivalence being conscious, whereas the other remains unconscious, with the two disparate levels of self in conflict with each other. Within the intrapsychic world, A and not-A do not mutually exclude each other. Psychological dynamics violate Aristotelian logic, which is why the koan is designed to break intellectualization. Instead, human nature follows a form of "paradoxical logic" (Fromm, Suzuki, & DeMartino, 1960) or "dialectics" (Seltzer, 1986; Weeks, 1985) in which all ideas, affects, and behaviors generate their opposites and demand a resolution. The concept of the unconscious itself embodies paradox: Its very essence is the negation of consciousness ("un-conscious"), and yet, according to classical theory, the unconscious itself does not negate contradictions and does not even know of "no."

The self is a complex, changing constellation of forces, properties, and relationships. Paradoxes within it abound. The variety of interpretations and interventions that constitute psychotherapy—which often are forgotten by the patient, even though they were entirely effective—probe these various paradoxes within the realm of the individual's unique personality dynamics. Koans, which also are set aside once they have fulfilled their usefulness, reveal the underlying, more universal paradoxes within the ontological realm of self and other. But these realms of the personal and universal, following the course of the *yin* and *yang*, are intertwined. The individual personality is rooted in the deeper ontology of self, and the ontology of self achieves expression through the individual personality. Realization of paradox on one level invariably affects the other. Drawing on the works of Jung, Federn, Winnicott, and Bion, Eigen (1986) masterfully uncovered these paradoxes or "reversals," as he called them, which fuel the conflicts of the individual and sink to the deeper self/other ontology—paradoxes of hate and love, unity and chaos, boundaries and fusion. These are the paradoxes that spring from the "psychotic core" within everyone, the core touched by Zen training and intensive psychoanalysis.

The paradoxes within the individual dovetail into the paradoxes between self and other. People use symptoms to place others into self-contradictory double binds; they attempt to control or get "one up" on others without openly acknowledging the fact that they are attempting to control (Haley, 1963). These double binds often take the form of implicit or explicit demands for spontaneity and genuineness, such as, "You ought to love me," "Don't be so obedient," or "You should enjoy this" (Jichaku, Fujita, & Shapiro, 1984). In psychotherapy the person plays out these paradoxical strategies to control the therapeutic relationship, often placing the therapist in a damned-if-you-do/damned-if-you-don't, goose-in-the-bottle dilemma. For example, if the therapist agrees to the patient's request to come less often, she may feel rejected and quit therapy; if the therapist suggests that the patient come every week, she may feel pressured and quit therapy. Like the koan, interpreting this predicament points the patient to the unconscious, where deeper, conflicted aspects of self contradict the conscious mind and gave birth to the paradox.

In their relationship with patients, therapists amplify the paradoxes of control, spontaneity, and genuineness to the point where the patient relinquishes attempts to be one-up and discovers genuine spontaneity (Haley, 1963; Seltzer, 1986; Watts, 1975a).The therapeutic context creates a variety of such double binds. The clinician stands for autonomy, maturity, and independence, but encourages dependency and regression. Therapy is supposedly voluntary, but missed appointments are interpreted as resistance. The therapist directs the patient to control the therapy session, but makes it appear that he or she is not being directive at all and that everything is the patient's initiative. In fact, the therapist's attempts not to influence the person become a profound form of influence that invariably directs the patient into the unconscious. Most of these interpersonal double binds seem to apply specifically to psychoanalysis, although Seltzer suggests that elements of paradox exist in all therapies. Clinicians are both detached and intimate; they want to help patients change and accept them as they are; the path to cure requires the patient to express and sometimes exaggerate the symptom (the regression, in psychoanalysis, that is essential for progression). In their most intense form, the simultaneously frustrating and gratifying contradictions of the therapy context, which often occur on different levels of communication, cause a disruption of reality testing and create the feeling that one is losing one's mind, being destroyed, or being engulfed by the other (Searles, 1965).

The relationship between Zen student and master also captures these paradoxes about control, authority, and spontaneity. The student believes that the master is implicitly demanding, "Be enlightened!"—which is as paradoxical as the therapist apparently demanding, "Be genuine and spontaneous!" Like the therapist, the master refuses to give any answers and throws back the student's question with a terse, "Mu!"—which frustrates the student to the point of crisis and self-disintegration. And yet the master is also a reassuring presence, the authority whose very existence proves that an answer exists, who acts as a container and holding environment for the student's psychological and spiritual storm. The master is the teacher, but "Zen has nothing to teach." If the student says the staff is or is not a staff, or says nothing, the master will strike the student. What can the student do? The staff, the Zen symbol of control and authority, is elusive, unnameable. Who is responsible for one's situation in life, for one's psychological and spiritual problems? Who is responsible for having an insight? At the peak of this interpersonal paradox, if the student can let go of his illusions about self and other, about who controls whom and who gives insight to whom, then the source of spontaneity and genuineness is revealed.

The koan and the personal paradox in therapy are always a question. The student and patient look to the master and therapist for an answer. But the request is turned back. Asking the question implies that the person already has the answer. Turning back the question reveals its source: The source of the question is within the questioning—within the illusive, willing self. When the insight occurs, the person knows it with certainty; acknowledgment from the authority figure is superfluous. The issue of control and authority is largely superfluous. The Zen student could seize the staff from the master, affirming that he ultimately is the authority on himself and responsible for himself, his spontaneity, his insights. Although this is indeed true, the path of the koan runs even deeper than this.

Beyond Within and Between

Zen training points to a state of mind that transcends paradox, that is beyond the notions of "within" and "between" individuals. This state transcends the paradoxical futility of the self that attempts to step back and objectively grasp or gain insight into itself. It moves beyond the consciousness of a distinction between self and other. It is the conscious mind that has no object as the target of its awareness.

The koan moves one in this direction through the act of negation or renunciation. As a paradox, it both affirms and negates the affirmation. When asked if a dog has a self, the master's reply, "Mu!" undoes and negates the concepts of dog, true nature, and "having," as well as undoes or un-asks the question itself. It negates the questioner, just as the master turns away from the questions, ideas, feelings, and other bits of self that the student offers as a solution to the koan. The crisis through which the koan leads the person entails the stripping away, piece by piece, of the layers to the personality until one experiences a "dropping out of the bottom of the self" (Sato, 1968). The act of negating is the act of letting go of one's old ideas and attainments, a letting go of one's own identity.

Paradox is the fuel that drives the deautomatizing and retraversing of the self-as-structure through the activation of the observing self. In Zen training and psychotherapy, attaining insight is becoming aware of the various self-contradictory qualities of one's behavior, personality, defenses, thought patterns. In Zen one even becomes aware of the self-contradictory situation of knowing you are thinking, attending, and remembering without being able to know or grasp the "you" who is thinking, attending, and remembering. Stripping away each psychological and ontological layer, a string of paradoxes drives one deeper and deeper into the source of the self. One comes to recognize that all the features of the object self—including self and object representations, thoughts, attention, memory—are not the core self. Transcending these features of the self-as-structure is the observing self that is conscious of these features but which cannot be observed itself—the self that is featureless, without boundaries or content. Frankl (1967) described this phenomenon as the self that detaches from symptoms through the technique of paradoxical intention, that leaves the psychological plane and enters the "noological" space where new meanings and attitudes about one's symptoms can be chosen freely. To instruct the phobic patient to deliberately pump up an anxiety attack will pop him out of the anticipatory anxiety that created the symptom—will make him fail at the task and even laugh at himself as he steps back and, with a sigh of relief, observes his paradoxical dilemma. In psychoanalysis, the excitement and even elation that patients experience when they gain insight into their conflicts springs from the sense of freedom associated with the activation of the observing self. Paradox forces one to step back to a position of wider scope, like stepping out of a mud field to see where you are headed. Self-contradictory behaviors are seen in a new light, are reframed. From this new perspective, there no longer is the feeling that one is trapped within the paradox, but rather the sense that one has encompassed the paradox. Fresh, informed actions—free will—now seem possible. Centered within this illusive observing and willing self, one feels stabilized, unfettered. One experiences that distinctive yet ungraspable sense of "I-ness."

While clearing one's head through koans in Zen training and personal paradoxes in therapy, one encounters the same questions. Who is it that has this conflict, that symptom? Who is it that experiences this anxiety, this crisis, this paradox? Paradoxes point to deeper layers of the personality and highlight the opposing polarities of the self, but they also point to a place where one can be free from these aspects of the object self and live within the observing self that stands beyond the paradox. The observing self is the origin of the possibility for having a new perspective, of being able to see past the illusions and distortions of the object self. Zen compares this self to a mirror that reflects but is not altered by the act of reflecting. It is your face before your parents were born, your expression of who you are without using your mouth, body, or mind.

The final paradox in Zen, which points to the observing self in its purest form, is the state of mind in which the observing self observes itself, which cannot be observed. This is the consciousness of consciousness that has no content, the awakening in the unconscious, a consciousness of nothing, as occurs when two mirrors face each other and when the eye sees itself. It is the true self in its most pristine state—the no-self and no-mind, a state of emptiness, void, enlightenment that holds absolute freedom and is replete with possibility and potential. Total negation paradoxically leads to complete affirmation, for the chipping away of the self by the koan allows the koan to sink to the level of being and willing in the purest form. This true self that is no-self is a state of completeness, the sound of one hand clapping, the place to which the one returns that transcends all polarities, contradictions, and paradoxes of the self: good/bad, unity/disunity, assertion/denial, being/nonbeing. The goose is out of the bottle, and the bottle is unbroken.

This no-self also transcends the distinction between self and other that is the illusion of the rationalizing, discriminating mind. The koan reveals that the world is an interdependent whole, that the self is that whole, and that the self/other duality is an illusion. Separation is experienced within union and union within separation. This insight helps one transcend the crippling, paradoxical message imposed by society: You are independent, but you must not be so independent that you realize you are not independent (Watts, 1975a). The very act of resolving the koan forces the person to abandon the subject/object dichotomy. "The inability of the koan to be resolved as an object by the ego as subject is, in fact, precisely the inability of the ego as ego in its subject-object bifurcation to resolve the existential contradiction which is that bifurcation" (Fromm, Suzuki, & DeMartino, 1960). Only when the self becomes its innermost contradiction does it become subjectless and objectless. In a more down-to-earth style, Watts (1975b) framed the subject/object paradox in terms of the dilemma frequently experienced in science. As we study the world, we continually uncover more questions than we discover solutions—as if the world is running away from us. But what is it that always retreats when you try to pursue it? Yourself.

Expressed in classic Buddhist terms, this most basic paradox is the paradoxical inseparability of relative and absolute truths. Relative truth—the protocol of logic, distinctions, cause and effect—guides our everyday, conventional experience of ourselves and the world.

Relative truth is the life of the individual and the dynamics of the individual mind. Absolute truth is the vision of unity—of the emptiness—that binds the collection of relative truths. It is the universal mind that transcends cause and effect, conditions, and categories. However, even though the absolute transcends and contains the relative, the relative and absolute are identical; hence the paradox that arises when a class of things is equated with a thing that is a member of that class (Jichaku, Fujita, & Shapiro, 1984). The life of the individual is the life of the universal, as illustrated by Jung in his concept of the collective unconscious, or in the idea that ontological development recapitulates phylogenic development. The individual mind is the universal mind, the particular is the general. If not, how could psychoanalysis derive any "laws" of intrapsychic dynamics, or physics derive any laws of nature?

By emphasizing the no-self and the mystical union of self and other, Zen seems to depart from Western psychotherapy. Many writers have stated that psychotherapy is not designed to produce enlightenment. However, as discussed in Chapter 3, there are many indications that in-depth psychotherapy taps and utilizes the pregnant emptiness and self/other dissolution that is the state of no-self. Although they use a variety of technical and not-so-technical terms—such as unconscious, undifferentiated ego matrix; symbiotic oneness; fertile void; blanking out; or simply "holes"—many therapists describe how their patients often contact an inner emptiness, oblivion, or boundlessness. Dangling over the abyss, frightened by it, they may at first attempt to fill the void with talking, acting out, materialism, or more symptoms; but eventually they discover that the dive into this emptiness reveals it as the source of insight, possibility, and spontaneity. When asked to show your true self, giving the answer means letting go and falling into this emptiness.

As a state of mind in which the self/other barrier dissolves, boundlessness becomes the source of empathy and the transformational merging of patient and therapist. This is revealed in the story of the Zen master whose first insight was his recognition that everyone he met had his own face. So too the psychotherapy patient, during the moment of empathic merging with the therapist, realizes the I in the you and the you in the I. The therapist also, in making an empathic interpretation that is truly rooted in his own experience, transcends the paradox of simultaneously forgetting and being aware of himself, of being both the patient and therapist.

The resolution of the personal paradox, like that of the koan, springs from this condition of merging. One must enter that transitional space where separation is a form of union, where the subjective and objective are interpenetrated—an intermediate zone of me-and-not-me that encompasses both external reality and one's own internal capacity to create. Winnicott (1971) thought of this transitional phenomenon as a stepping stone to separation and individuation. The koan and the personal paradox in therapy are types of transitional objects that serve as stepping-stones in the opposite direction of separation and individuation. They lead to the no-self that counterpoises and highlights one's separation and individuation.

Like the koan, all forms of intensive psychotherapy deal directly or indirectly with the fear of the loss of self, whether it takes the form of anxiety about personal loss or injury, separation, or, ultimately, death. After all, the most basic paradox is that we are all born to die and that death gives life meaning. In his analysis of the existential therapies, Yalom (1980) discussed how death anxiety is a primary source of psychopathology and how "boundary" experiences, which involve the temporary loss of self, produce powerful psychological transformations. Paradoxically, psychological well-being and the integrity of self are generated from the oscillation and interpenetration of self and no-self. Through the act of negation, the crisis of self, and letting go, the paradox immerses the individual into this existential awareness. A Chinese allegory tells of a monk who embarks on a long pilgrimage to find the Buddha. After many years, he crosses a wide river to the land where the Buddha lives. There is a corpse floating on the water. It comes closer. The monk loses all control and wails, for he recognizes the corpse—it is his own. That moment is his liberation.

Here we return to the themes in Chapter 3, for the most fundamental, knowable manifestations of the self express themselves in paradox—the paradoxical dualities of self and no-self, self and other. Neither self nor no-self, self nor other, alone accounts for who we are. Zen is quick to point out that we are and aren't at the same time; that when we die we both die and don't die; that we are both two and one simultaneously. When we speak of the most basic, graspable expressions of the self, we must contradict ourselves. The mathematician Gödel once demonstrated that any sufficiently powerful logical system will eventually lead to a conclusion that cannot be proven true or false within that system, that will even violate the basic assumptions of the system (see Hofstadter, 1980). Self-contradiction is intrinsic to any and all entities, including intrapsychic systems and all facets of selfhood. The primary function of the paradox is to point to something that lies beyond that entity—something deeper, more fundamental, a wider frame of reference that includes and surpasses that entity—something that cannot be named. The paradoxical dualities of self/no-self and self/other are these pointing fingers that motion toward the "true" self that can be signified, but not comprehended directly. As Eigen (1986) stated, "I am but am not my I."

The Paradox of the Willing Self

As an undergraduate student, I attended a university in which the psychology program, a strong bastion of behaviorism, offered little in the way of psychodynamic or humanistic theory. To expand my education, I felt compelled to take courses in philosophy, sociology, and religious studies. One of these was an introductory religion course with Thomas Altizer, a scholar recognized in academia for his philosophy of Christian Atheism, and known by his students as eccentric and charismatic. With wild, fiery eyes and greying hair that always appeared windswept—as if he had just stepped in from a metaphysical storm—he gave me the impression that he had one foot in this world and the other in a reality that only he understood.

One afternoon I visited him during office hours to discuss my term paper. The discussion turned to Nietzsche, who, along with Kierkegaard, was his favorite philosopher. He talked of Nietzsche's vision of the "will to power" with a conviction and fervor that could inspire even the most stolid of skeptics. Nevertheless, I decided to raise a doubt. Drawing on my background as a psychology major, I mentioned the established fact that Nietzsche, toward the end of his life, became schizophrenic (the final outcome of general paresis, a prolonged, untreated syphilitic condition). How, I asked, could we reconcile Nietzsche's philosophy with this fact? How do we take into consideration his being completely mad?

Altizer looked me straight in the eye and replied, "Maybe he willed it."

What exactly did that mean? Isn't that like willing the fact that you have brown eyes, or that there's a tornado in the next county, or that you were born? It didn't make sense. Then again, somewhere in my head, maybe it did—because most things that don't make sense quickly slip away from memory, but this idea stuck with me.

Several years later, in graduate school and during my clinical internship, I learned how to do psychotherapy. My early psychoanalytic training impressed one fact upon me: My patients will do anything to prevent themselves from getting better. They benefit in some paradoxical way from their psychopathology—the phenomenon known as "secondary gain." When I told one supervisor about my difficulty in following what one of my patients talked about, he described how some people unconsciously break connections between their thoughts, causing their ideas to be disjointed, with no overall rhyme or reason to their story. How amazing, I thought at that time, are our patients' strategies to prevent us from understanding and helping them! Of course, such insights are basic tenets of traditional psychoanalysis. In fact, some analysts believe that the essence of treatment is the analysis of the resistance to therapeutic progress.

This philosophy is firmly rooted in Freud's classical model of intrapsychic determinism. All emotions, behaviors, and thoughts are vectors arising from the complex interaction of unconscious drives. They are locked into place. Psychological symptoms, the compromise formations of these dynamics, are also locked in. The person is locked into conflict. There is no free will, no agency in this intricate knot of intrapsychic forces. Only the analyst can untangle the binds and launch the patient toward a new, healthier equilibrium.

But psychoanalytic theory has changed since Freud's time. In object relations theory and especially self psychology, we no longer find this explicit assumption that people are passive victims of jammed, counterbalanced, and redirected intrapsychic energies. Theories that emphasize the self rather than drives as the cornerstone of psychological functioning have reopened the psychoanalytic world's eyes to the vicissitudes of inner agency and volition. Kohut (1977, 1984) described the self as a joyfully experienced, independent center of initiative, a developing, coordinating agent that is the superordinate dynamic of personality structure and functioning. He spoke of a tension arc between one's ambition and ideals—a teleological rather than biological energy that is the core of the self's propulsion through development. Predating Kohut, Rank (1945) labelled even more specifically this "cosmic primal force" that launches the person toward the actualization of autonomy, psychological well-being, and creativity. He called it "will."

The concept of will has a long history in the theories of personality and psychotherapy. Most notable are the works of Leslie Farber, Otto Rank, Rollo May, Viktor Frankl, Silvano Arieti, and Allen Wheelis. In his widely acclaimed book on existential psychotherapy, Yalom (1980) claims that the most basic goal of therapy is to liberate will, which brings choice and responsibility. It is the will to heal and develop, the will to find the meaning and purpose of one's existence. At the most basic level, it is the will to create one's identity: the willing of the self.

The psychoanalytic literature on object relations and self psychology are filled with descriptions of these vicissitudes of will. From his comprehensive research on infant development, Stern (1985) concluded that acquiring a sense of "agency" constitutes a fundamental step in building the core sense of self. In their pioneering work on infants, Mahler, Pine, and Bergman (1975) claimed that the child holds the "lion's share" of responsibility for moving through development. Although the parents' skills, or lack thereof, surely affect the child's evolving sense of self, some children are much stronger, more determined, or willful than others in seeking what they need, even from pathological caretakers. Kohut (1977) similarly noted how children, if thwarted or hurt by one parent in their attempt to develop a cohesive self, will bypass that person to connect to the other parent—and if that person fails, to aunts, uncles, neighbors, or any potentially significant other. Even much later in life, people will reopen old developmental lines and resume building neglected sectors of their self via relationships with new "father" or "mother" figures—a boss, teacher, father- or mother-in-law.

All these theories, implicitly or explicitly, share two basic assumptions about the nature of will. The willing self strives for the creation of a cohesive, harmonious, stable, and unified self structure. It also drives toward connectedness to what is not the self, to the other. Object relations theory and self psychology both maintain that the self's path toward cohesion and integration is achieved through this connectedness, through such processes as mirroring, idealizing, twinning, and internalization. In Plato's *Symposium,* Socrates, too, spoke of the life force, Eros, as the drive toward connectedness to the other—an always open-ended, searching energy that pushes toward higher and higher forms of connectedness, that is, the source of creativity and life.

Yet the path of the willing self is paradoxical. The willing of the self begins and ends at paradox. The intrinsic drive to develop the self, to find its origin, seems to originate from an ungraspable source, from the no-self. Ultimately, this drive leads to the transcendence of self, to the no-self. This movement from and to no-self also follows the paradoxical path of affirming the self via the process of negating it. By activating the observing self through the deautomatization of psychic structure and function, by canceling conscious overthought to actualize internal unity and spontaneity, the negation of self gives birth to its willful affirmation. The movement toward integration and connectedness necessarily entwines with the dimensions of no-self and not-self. At their frontiers contemporary psychoanalytic theory and self psychology have begun to probe this insight. These frontiers mark a transition between psychoanalysis and Eastern thought. The fulfilling of the self entails the opening to the interpenetrating action of no-self. To will the self is to will the negation and transcendence of self. The willing of connectedness culminates in the recognition that, from the start, there never was any disconnectedness.

To immerse oneself into no-self, one must relinquish conscious control of the self. Rooting into the no-self, attaining connectedness and unity with the other, require letting go. Willing the self is spontaneous, unself-conscious abdication. Willing embraces surrender. When you hang over a precipice, holding on only by a tree root clenched between your teeth, the will to speak of your true self is the will to let go of it. Farber (1966) spoke of the conscious experience of will in which we decide and act in the situation at hand, and contrasted this with the deeper, more fundamental realm of will that is unconscious, that we realize only after the act, that provides propulsion but eludes immediate, direct scrutiny. Paradoxically, this primary realm of will is a willing without conscious willing: One must surrender to its action.

> I can will knowledge, but not wisdom; going to bed, but not sleeping; eating, but not hunger; meekness, but not humility; scrupulosity, but not virtue; self-assertion or bravado, but not courage; lust, but not love; commiseration, but not sympathy; congratulations, but not admiration; religiosity, but not faith; reading, but not understanding. (Farber, 1966, p. 15)

Nietzsche's vision of the will to power also is a vision of paradox—the paradox of the self willing its own creation. To return to the source of self, to create the self from chaos and void, to will the self's continuing evolution, one simultaneously becomes both the creator and the created. The subject and object become one. This is the paradox embodied by the immersion into the not-self and no-self. To realize the interpenetration of self and no-self is to will the becoming and unbecoming of the self, and to be willed by that becoming and unbecoming. Ancient rituals embodied this paradox by allowing the participants to reenact the role of the gods who created humankind and world: simultaneously, the participants were both god and mortal, creator and created, self and world (Eliade, 1959, 1976). Zen meditators participate in this quintessential form of creativity each time they complete their meditation session, when they rediscover and recreate themselves by emerging from the no-self of *zazen* (Suzuki, 1970); during that moment of returning to their everyday self, they both create and are created. At this primary, paradoxical level of the will, the distinction between voluntary and involuntary collapses into the recognition that the two are really one. Willing seems to come from nowhere in particular, but its effects are witnessed everywhere. According to Watts (1975b), this realization is the essence of enlightenment:

> ... the difference between what you do and what happens to you, the voluntary and the involuntary, seems to disappear. This feeling may be interpreted as the sense that everything is voluntary—that the whole universe is your own action and will. But this can easily flip into the sense that everything is involuntary. The individual and the will are nothing, and everything that might be called "I" is as much beyond control as the spinning of the earth in its orbit. But from the Taoist standpoint these two views fall short. They are polar ways of seeing the same truth: That there is no ruler and nothing ruled. What goes on simply happens of itself without either push or pull, since every push is also a pull and every pull a push. . . . This is, again, the principle of "mutual arising." (p. 53)

This paradoxical vision of a willful creating that arises from nowhere, that fuses the creator and created, may seem far removed from our everyday experience. But, intuitively, we all recognize the manifestations of this paradox everywhere around us. We easily note the extraordinary examples, such as Viktor Frankl (1963), who, from his encounter with nihilism, torture, and death in a Nazi concentration camp, uncovered a joyful purpose in life—his "will to meaning." For those of us who are psychotherapists, we see people using their own bootstraps to climb out of symptoms and create a new sense of self. All of us see children willing their own becoming.

A few months ago I reread Kurt Vonnegut's *Breakfast of Champions* (1975). It's a story about the ordinary people of a small city who seem trapped by their own lives, filled with despair by a fate over which they have no control. A renowned artist who sells a painting to the city arrives for the dedication ceremonies. The painting, entitled *The Temptation of Saint Anthony*, consists of a single vertical stripe of day-glo orange reflecting tape on a background of avocado green. At first the people are outraged. That isn't art, they protest, a child could do it. The artist leaps to his own defense:

> I now give you my word of honor that the picture your city owns shows everything about life which truly matters, with nothing left out. It is a picture of the awareness of every animal—the "I am" to which all messages are sent. It is all that is alive in any of us . . . It is unwavering and pure, no matter what preposterous adventure may befall us. A sacred picture of Saint Anthony alone is one vertical, unwavering band of light . . . (p. 221)

He is a rip-off artist, but his point is well made. He points to awareness, consciousness—the immutable, ungraspable self that is the universal connectedness and union of all selves. No matter what befalls us, it is all that is alive; it is the source of becoming and will. Most important, the people immediately understand his point. The willing of the self is intuitively known to all.

Here Vonnegut draws us into the paradox of the willing self that is both the creator and the created. Can the characters of a novel truly understand the nature of their own will? After all, they are just created people in a created story. Vonnegut answers this question by placing himself into the storyline as himself, the writer, but just another character in his own story. As the master of the novel, he informs the protagonist that he created him, momentarily transports him to the surface of the sun as convincing evidence of this fact, and then, paradoxically, sets the protagonist "free." But as a character in his own novel, Vonnegut surprises himself when the plot takes "unpredicted" turns. A dog jumps out at him and scares him half to death. But didn't he create the dog and that scene? Why should it surprise and scare him? He is the novelist and the character, the creator and the created all at once.

Not unlike Nietzsche, who was mad, he wills the very predicament that befalls him. It is this willing ourselves into predicaments—and out of them—that is a primary concern of psychoanalysis and Zen.

The mystical qualities of paradox and the Zen koan may strike Westerners as bizarre, alien, irrelevant to their own lives. But once again we see that the final outcome of Zen is simple and familiar. Mountains are once again mountains, and rivers are once again rivers. Zen is one's everyday mind: You eat when you are hungry and sleep when tired. Similar to the outcome of psychotherapy, one lives in the spontaneity of the willing self and accepts one's predicaments and life rather than blaming oneself or others. The solution to the paradoxical problems that trouble our personal lives, as well as to the universal paradoxes of being human, is to see that they are not to be felt as problems. This simple realization is not unlike Freud's idea that psychoanalysis turns an extraordinary misery into an everyday suffering. As Watts (1975a) noted, The Zen master, too, has shortcomings, but has learned to accept them as perfectly and simply human, unlike people who are at odds with their humanity and are attempting to be angels or demons. The difficulty, according to Watts, is that self-acceptance can never be a deliberate act; it is as paradoxical as kissing one's own lips. The liberating realization is that one's self can only be genuine, spontaneous, and unfettered in its willfulness if one lets go of the struggles to own it as property. Like the solution to the koan, once grasped as ungraspable, the self becomes free to move on its own accord.

5

Grasping Reality: Words, Images, Things

Zen training, like many religious disciplines, Eastern and Western, strives for a spiritual transformation of the individual. According to Zen, this transformation blossoms in the experience of enlightenment called *satori* or *kensho,* which is an immersion into no-self. Zen claims that *satori* opens the mind to a direct, unbiased awareness of reality. *Kensho,* meaning "to see essence or nature" (Suzuki, 1956), is the pure perceiving into the intrinsic quality of things.

Although some Zen masters and other spiritual teachers may vigorously insist that this targeted spirituality transcends psychology, the path of spiritual development cannot be neatly excised from the cognitive, emotional, and social foundations of personality dynamics. Spiritual growth must entail psychological processes. The concepts of psychology, therefore, can be valuable instruments for investigating Zen training.

The history of psychological theorizing is particularly rich in research on how we perceive, process, and recall experience. The very origin of scientific psychology lies in the study of sensation, perception, memory, and the cognitive processing of experience. How can this knowledge be applied to understanding the Zen process and outcome? When the individual strives for the experience of enlightenment—the experience of no-self and the direct awareness of things—what are the psychological operations involved in the processing, assimilation, and remembering of that experience and the striving toward it?

The Representational Systems

To explore these questions, we can draw on a comprehensive theoretical framework about representational systems that has been formulated from the large body of research on memory and cognitive processes. Within psychoanalysis, this framework has been discussed by a variety of theorists interested in development, cognition, and emotion (e.g., Bonanno, 1990; Bruner, 1964; Horowitz, 1983; Stern, 1985). It proposes that the processing and memory of experience involves three distinct representational systems: *enactive, imagistic,* and *lexical.* An experience may be coded in any one of these systems, or in various combinations of them. Bruner concluded that the systems evolve in a developmental sequence.

Enactive representations, which are the first to emerge during early infancy, consist of memory encodings of one's motor actions and are derived from the activity of the body's muscle groups. Bruner (1964) described this early form of representing experience as an "action schema." These motoric codings of experience often are unconscious, existing outside the realm of abstract, rational thinking. The concept of this representational system may be expanded to include a variety of other physiological patterns, including gastrointestinal, vascular, respiratory, and cardiac activities. Enactive representations may be a component of a larger "somatic" representational system. Clinicians recognize these representations of experience in any of a variety of nonverbal expressions of unconscious meanings, such as acting out, compulsive behaviors, somatizations, facial and body gestures. On the widest scale, any routinized behavior, pathological or adaptive, may be conceived as an enactive representation that articulates an underlying constellation of subjective meaning. Such behaviors may include personal habits, culturally determined customs, and a variety of social and religious rituals.

Imagistic representations emerge next in the course of development, and are based on input from the sensory systems of the body. Mental images are sensory/perceptual experiences that occur in the absence of environmental stimulation. They include visual memories and imaginings—the so-called "pictures before the mind's eye"—as well as the other imagistic submodalities of auditory, tactile, olfactory, and gustatory sensations. Being holistic rather than linear expressions, images can depict simultaneously a variety of affects and ideations. As suggested by the aphorism "One picture is worth a thousand words," multiple cognitive and affective aspects of self and object relationships can be condensed into a single image. Images revive behavioral and psychophysiological processes, as well as store a complex array of emotions. They serve as internal reference points for the sense of continuity of one's experience of self and objects across time. The extensive literature on imagery has led to the conclusion that images readily access unconscious affect and are heavily influenced by primary process. The literature also suggests that different images may vary considerably in their "associative elaboration" (Suler, 1989a)—i.e., in the extent to which they are the recollection of a specific past event, a synthesis of several memories, and/or a symbolic expression of experience. Similar to Buddhist psychology, which states that the self is constructed from the synthesis of our images of the outer world (Engler, 1981), Western research also concludes that imagery is an organizer of experience and a supporting structural system for the sense of self.

Finally, as the course of development progresses, the lexical system emerges as the representational mode that involves an abstract, semantic coding of experience. Sometimes also described as the "conceptual" representational system (Bruner, 1964), it involves the creation of words and language as abstract signifiers for underlying experience. This system contains the mechanics of conscious, rational reasoning. Representations in this mode are coded linearly and are more heavily influenced by the reality-oriented demands of secondary process.

These three representational systems are alternate mechanisms for the organization of self structure (Suler, in press-a). They provide different pathways for the "concretization" of experience (Atwood & Stolorow, 1984) and for organizing the subjective experience of self and object that constitutes the intrapsychic reality of one's "representational world" (Sandler & Rosenblatt, 1962). In normal functioning, all three systems operate as an integrated network, providing a cross-coding and confirmation of subjective experience that results in enhanced coherence of self structure. Exactly how these representational systems interact with each other while they process the "it-ness" of experience is one of the oldest issues in psychology and philosophy. As Bugelski (1970) suggested, one of our central concerns is the dynamic relationship among words, images, and "things."

Using this formulation about the tripartite representational structure of the self, we can investigate the path and outcome of the self's transformation during Zen training—including the experience of no-self and the direct knowing of reality that Zen attributes to *satori*.

The Word

Traditionally, Zen has emphasized how words, language, and the conceptual systems that they support cannot capture the essence or totality of enlightenment. Language and its abstractions act as filters that confine and distort the direct experience of reality for which Zen strives. They freeze the continual flux that is reality into categories and concepts that we substitute for reality. All experience becomes reified to the point that an experience will not even come into awareness if language provides no word for it. The world vibrates with a vast array of changing "things" and "its" for which our vocabulary gives us limited views. The representational map is not the terrain itself; eating a menu cannot substitute for a full-course meal. The nonverbal reality that is experienced through Zen training lies beyond the arrest by words. It is for this reason that Lao Tzu begins his *Tao Te Ching,* the classic Taoist text, with the warning that "The Tao which can be named is not the eternal Tao."

The Zen master Phillip Kapleau (1980b) described verbal explanations and descriptions as mere peepholes into a limitless universe. Like magic tricks, words and concepts will bewilder you unless you have seen what lies behind them. Kapleau cites Chuang-tzu: "Words exist for meaning, but once you understand the meaning you can throw away the words. But where can I find a man with whom I can converse without words?" (p. 20). Like many Zen teachers, Kapleau even underplayed the importance of the cherished sutras of Buddhism. They are "the entombed words of the Buddha" (p. 123) that point to the truth but must not be mistaken for it. Zen does not denigrate the sutras, he suggested, but simply warns that they are only a finger pointing to the moon (no-self) and not the moon itself. They are "sketches of the infinitely extensible IT" (p. 137). That is why Zen, in its purest form, does not base itself on any scripture.

Kapleau added that on the level of words, it is easy to confuse enlightenment with megalomania or narcissism. To speak of being one with the universe, or identifying oneself *as* the universe, is verbiage that sounds more like egotistical self-preoccupation than the enlightened awareness which may exist behind the statement.

To trigger an uncontaminated, direct awareness of reality, Zen training works diligently at deconstructing one's representational mockup of reality. This deconstructing process is the purpose of intense, prolonged meditation. Deikman (1966b) described the process as the "deautomatization" of intrapsychic structures. Engler (Wilber, Engler, & Brown, 1986) called it the "retraversing" of representational operations. One of the first components of the representational world to become deconstructed is the lexical system of words and language that feeds the conceptual concoctions of the intellect.

In addition to meditation as a means to break the back of words and abstractions, Zen may advocate a vow of silence. For Mountain (1983), the vow took control of her, rather than she consciously choosing it. One day during her training she simply stopped talking and did not speak again for eight months. She discovered that "cutting off one's tongue" (p. 188) was the severing of the part of one's body most closely associated with the conscious sense of self. Silence amputates the linguistic/conceptual home of selfhood and leaves it to wither and die. At the same time, silence points one inward toward deeper dimensions of the self that cannot be expressed in words. As in psychoanalytic treatment, silence creates a transitional space in which previously undetected perceptions of self and object crystallize. Silence clears the air to allow fresh, unobstructed awareness. It also allows the realization of an interconnection to the other than runs deeper than that experienced through verbal interchange alone. The interpenetration between self and other that one experiences during the empathic encounter is most powerful during the moment of silence. Linguistic operations that mechanically separate subject, object, and action into the word-strings of sentences only blow smoke screens that tend to obliterate this realization.

As convincing as these arguments may seem, there is something curiously contradictory about the world of Zen. Considering that masters advocate the demolition of verbal/conceptual speculations and discourse, Zen people seem to be doing quite a bit of writing and discussing on the topic. Books, articles, presentations, and workshops proliferate. This apparent violation of the Zen spirit may simply be a symptom of the West's intellectual efforts to grasp the Eastern teachings. But writing about and discussing Zen is not alien to Eastern cultures. Even in many traditional monasteries, Zen masters offer daily orations (called *teisho*) to assist their students in their training. D. T. Suzuki (1949, 1956, 1960), perhaps the most renowned Japanese Zen scholar, was a master of intellectual analysis. The universal need to apprehend Zen through words and concepts reflects something important about the functions of the mind in how it encounters experience.

During his Zen training, Matthiessen (1987), a writer by profession, struggled with this dilemma. In the eyes of his teachers, his literary endeavors placed him in the most hopeless category of Zen student. He cited Muso Soseki, a fourteenth century master, who claimed that those who "devote their efforts to literary endeavors are nothing but shaven-headed laymen and are not fit to be classed even with those of the lowest grade" (p. 188). Matthiessen rationalized Muso's warning by suggesting that Muso perhaps railed at dilettantes, not true poets. But even in the case of the dilettante, Matthiessen added, the literary endeavor is an expression of one's Buddha nature—an expression of the inner self that a psychoanalytic self psychologist might describe as one's "nuclear program." Humans, by their very nature, are word-and-idea-tinkering beings. Matthiessen concluded that since Zen is the manifestation of life itself, neither murderers nor poets can be excluded.

Dogen, a radical thirteenth century Zen master, directly challenged the traditional teaching that talk which can be grasped by thought is not true Zen. Instead, he argued against the stale, mechanical readings and recitations of the scriptures that lacked insightful penetration to their inner meaning. Matthiessen enlisted Dogen's ideas in defense of writing about Zen. For those who are skilled enough to create them and for those who are prepared to understand, word representations *can* accurately reflect the Zen experience. There would be no haiku if this were not the case. A similar situation arises in the psychoanalytic arguments about whether language can accurately capture the affective and ideational complexities and nuances of unconscious primary process. Clearly, some literary forms, such as poetry, can capture even the most esoteric unconscious plays on time, affect, and symbolism. This is also true of the spoken word. In psychoanalytic treatment, the clinician listens to the patient's verbal free associations as echoes of underlying unconscious dynamics, just as the Zen student listens to the master's *teisho* for flashes of insight into the nature of reality and mind.

The psychoanalytic literature contains many debates about the value of verbalizations in the psychotherapeutic process. Without doubt, powerful intrapsychic transformations can take place on preverbal dimensions. Damage to self structure at the earliest stages of development is usually repaired first in the form of selfobject functions that are experienced by the patient at a preverbal level. However, those selfobject functions are mediated through a verbal interchange, or, more accurately, through the dynamic polarity of silence and words. And during the most advanced stages of psychotherapeutic progress, even the most primitive or preverbal sectors of memory and affect are understood, mastered, and assimilated by verbalizing them. Psychoanalysis is, after all, a talking cure. The cure that is the Zen path does stretch into the realm of a wordless knowing of reality, but it ultimately returns to one's everyday social life, in which one continues to work through and apply that knowing. The cure must be experienced and shared in the social exchange (including words) with others.

Despite the shunning of words by Zen, talking, writing, and reading will continue to be an essential component of the Zen process. As wordless as the experience of enlightenment may be, the compelling need to try to describe it reflects the need to assimilate that experience. Like psychotherapy patients who struggle to describe their illusive feelings, Zen students who grapple with language to speak of their evolving awareness are attempting to consolidate their evolving self-transformation. Words and concepts are structures through which underlying experience manifests itself. Experience penetrates through the word representation. The inexpressible penetrates through the expressible. Formlessness and form, no-self and self, are two sides of the same coin. Through their interpenetrated relationship they give expression to one another.

Imaging and Un-Imaging the Self

Although the contemplative goal of deconstructing the representational world is profound, the instructions for Zen meditation (*zazen*) are deceptively simple: while sitting, with eyes slightly open, allow the mind to focus on nothing in particular. Ideas, feelings, and recollections will drift into the field of awareness, but do not let attention attach to them. Empty the mind by letting go of all targets of consciousness. Although it sounds simple, beginners often find that they last a minute or less before they realize their meditation has been punctured by a nagging thought, a worry from the past, a plan for the future, or any of a variety of mental conversations with oneself. Hungry for something, anything, on which to affix its attention, the beginner's mind only occasionally slips into periods of no-thought.

With practice, the distractions are overcome and the upper conceptual/verbal layers of the mind become still. At this point, when the meditation deepens, the person often experiences vivid imagistic sensations known as *makyo* (see Luk, 1960; Suler, 1990b). Kapleau (1980b) stated that they are most intense during the third day of sustained *zazen*, and are a sign of progress, of a ripening mind. These imagistic experiences include a variety of sensory impressions—sounds, smells, tastes, bodily sensations, and visual images, sometimes hallucinatory in quality. Meditators have reported hearing musical instruments such as flutes and pianos, feeling insects crawling over them, believing that their bodies were levitating or floating. The sound of a nearby bell ringing may be experienced visually as waves of light. One meditator reported to me that he saw faces in the patterns of a rug—animals, people, the face of a baby that turned into an old man, an angel that became a demon. *Makyo* may take the form of childhood memories—pleasant, painful, or mundane—

sometimes so vivid that meditators believe they are actually reliving those events. Crying, depression, elation, or other intense affects may accompany these experiences. For some meditators, *makyo* triggers important personal insights and beneficial changes in psychological health. For others, it is a disorienting, disturbing encounter.

The meditative process of *zazen* can be conceptualized as a relaxing of conscious mental activity, which then penetrates to and loosens repressive barriers. By "letting go" of any thought that enters their mind, meditators immerse themselves into a form of free association (as in psychoanalytic therapy) resulting in a drifting of attention beyond the habitual censoring and regulatory restraints of intrapsychic functioning and into previously unconscious realms of self-experience. As a result, pieces of self structure that were previously hidden or warded off rise to the quieted surface of the mind in the imagistic form of *makyo*. Even when they are apparently simple or mundane images, *makyo* may contain highly compacted expressions of multiple unconscious affects and ideations. Sometimes they are dissociated memories or conglomerations of dissociated memories. Sometimes they are more symbolic expressions of self and object representations that have been denied integration into the main body of self structure.

Consider the following Zen story. A student comes to his master, troubled by a vision that appears to him during *zazen*—a vision of a large, menacing spider. The hallucinatory image is so real and threatening that the student insists on bringing a knife to his next sitting. He intends to stab the insect when it again appears. Calmly, the master tells the student not to take a knife but rather a piece of chalk. He tells him that when he sees the spider, he should mark an X on its belly. The next day the student returns to the master and informs him that the spider did return, and that he marked it with the chalk as instructed. In reply, the master tells the student to lift up his shirt. There, on his stomach, is the X.

This story, itself an imagistic depiction, points to multiple insights into the nature of *zazen* and *makyo*. Borrowing classic psychoanalytic symbolism, the image of the spider may be the toxic introject or object representation of the pathological mother who narcissistically ensnares, poisons, and devours the child. It may be the representation of the feared and hated aspects of oneself. Based on religious symbolism, it may represent the student's concept of evil—or, in a Dostoyevskian fashion, his concept of God. Whatever the subjective meaning of this hallucination, it is the projection into an external perception of something that is fundamentally a component of self structure. It is an intrapsychic attempt to concretely objectify a subjective experience. As Kapleau (1980a) stated, *makyo* is a condensation of *ma* (devil) and *kyo* (objective world). The meditator must recognize these imagistic experiences as devils of the objective world that only derive power from their roots in subjective meaning. The Zen master understands this. It is his lesson to his student.

From a psychological perspective, personal insights and improvements in mental health after experiencing *makyo* may be the result of identifying, detoxifying, and assimilating these previously split off and isolated aspects of experience. One critical therapeutic effect may be the modulation and integration of affect that had been locked into these repressed representations. While participating in a clinical research group for studying mental imagery in psychoanalytic treatment, I once described *makyo,* wondering whether this phenomenon was related to psychoanalytic therapy. Lloyd Silverman, the leader of the group, offered the suggestion that *makyo* were forms of implosive imagery which tapped and assimilated reservoirs of warded-off affect that were derived from trauma or unconscious fantasy. This idea is similar to how Silverman (1987) conceptualized the role of imagery in psychotherapy. Kapleau (1980a, 1980b), a noted American Zen master, similarly described *makyo* as a type of dredging and cleansing process that releases stressful experiences embedded in deep layers of the mind. In the case of meditators who react to *makyo* with excessive disorientation and a prolonged pathological disruption of psychological functioning, the integration of self structure may have been unstable prior to Zen training and deficient in the resiliency to endure *zazen*. As Kapleau states, *zazen* is not beneficial for everyone.

These ideas about *makyo* uncovering problematic aspects of self structure, accompanied by the assimilation of affect encapsulated in those structures, parallels basic psychoanalytic concepts about the beneficial effects of images experienced in psychotherapy (Suler, 1989a, in press-a). However, this seems to be only a partial explanation of *makyo*. Not all of these imagistic experiences are psychologically toxic, nor do they all bear any obvious psychological meaning or symbolism. Although Zen masters would agree that *makyo* can lead to personal insights and psychological growth, they nevertheless insist that the path of *zazen* necessitates going beyond *makyo*. As holds true for any experiences that enter consciousness during meditation, one must not dwell on them. One must let go.

Moving down through the layers of lexical and imagistic representations on the path to no-self, self structure progressively unravels during *zazen*. The images of *makyo* are bits and pieces of self structure that break away and "disappear." Once having been habitual and often rigid patterns that existed outside awareness, imagistic self and object representations lose their inflexible automation, surface into consciousness, and disintegrate into more basic patterns of affect and perception. Deikman (1982) attributed this unraveling and deautomatization of self structure to the meditator's activation of the observing self. By relinquishing all targets of awareness, the meditator steps back from experience into a self that simply observes without cleaving to the experience. Unfettered from attachments, the mind unfolds to other, more elemental, patterns of experience that previously were beyond the range of the observing self. Intrapsychic functions that were once regulated automatically, without conscious intervention, are now opened to awareness. Proceeding beyond the awareness of imagistic representations of self and object, the meditator may become aware of the more basic psychological processes that contribute to the construction of self structure. The observing self can "see" in process the activities of memory, attention, and perception. Often the awareness of these functions takes the form of imagistic experiences of light. For example, Deikman suggested that meditators who report seeing shifting movements of light patterns actually may be observing the process of attention moving from one thought content to another, or from one representational feature of self structure to another. The experience of waves of light concordant with the ringing of a nearby bell actually may be the observation of the sensory-perceptual processes associated with that sound. Deikman thought that the meditator may even be experiencing the imagistic counterpart of the neural activity itself.

Ultimately, in the process of deautomatization and destructuring, the observing self lets go of *makyo*, the imagistic operations that create *makyo*, and the surrounding psychological activities that support those operations. The outcome is no-self, the "pure awareness" (Brown, 1986) that is freed from structure. Liberated from the words and images that filter, color, and distort perceptions, awareness of reality is clean and direct.

Consider the following analogy. Imagine a person sitting in a movie theater, watching images being projected onto the screen before her. The person, who represents the observing self, is the spectator of the images of *makyo* that move across the surface screen of the mind. If she follows the instructions for *zazen*, she will let go of each image, allowing it to pass away, perhaps to be replaced by another image. By gradually freeing herself from all the projected images, she also frees herself to observe the outline of the screen itself, the walls of the theater, and the projector that casts the images onto the screen—just as the meditator can observe the psychological structures and mechanisms that produce and contain *makyo* or any other content of conscious thought.

Yet the observing self is not limited to this scenario, for now imagine that the person can step back from the theater to observe herself sitting in the theater, watching the screen. Or imagine the next step, that the observing self moves even further away, to observe the person observing the person in the movie theater. We can imagine the observing self, *ad infinitum,* stepping further and further back, observing the observing of observing, to a point where the movie theater and the screen images dissolve into the background—the point where all that remains is observing.

So, too, the meditator steps back from experience into the process of the observing self. By letting go of the images of *makyo* and all contents of objective awareness, by stepping back from the act of seeing, the meditator attempts to root himself into the very source of the act of imaging and seeing. The observing self ultimately seeks the ground from which the image springs, and when that goal is attained, the duality between the imager and the imaged, observer and observed, subject and object, dissolves. We often speak of "images before the mind's eye," a metaphor that parallels the analogy of the person watching the images on the theater screen. Zen also speaks of the "eye that sees itself," capturing the paradox of the observing self observing its own act of observing—which is the folding of observing into itself, or, more accurately, the return of awareness to its own essence. In that state of awareness, self structure dissolves, just as the features of the movie theater fade away somewhere along that chain of watching the watching of the person in the theater. It is the enlightened condition of a pure awareness that lies beyond psychological structures.

This dissolution of the structures of the self is accompanied by the release of intrapsychic energy that was infused into those structures, which perhaps accounts for the sensation of a diffuse, boundless light as reported by experienced meditators (Deikman, 1982). In electronics, an analogous situation arises when a video camera, connected directly to a TV monitor, is pointed into the screen of that monitor. When the camera is tilted on a slight angle as it points into the monitor, on the screen appears an infinite regression of monitors, ending in a bright, white light. When the camera is pointed directly, head on, into the monitor—when the camera is "seeing" purely and only the very act of its own "seeing"—the regression of monitors disappears, leaving only the glow of white light.

Passing beyond self-images and immersing into the pure awareness of no-self is not the final outcome of Zen. The culmination is the realization of the balanced interpenetrating relationship between pure awareness and structure, between no-self and self. This interpenetration is the source of the fluidity and flexibility of the self. It facilitates the oscillation of self structure between the polarity of dissolution and reintegration—the polarity that is the source of the self's harmony and cohesion.

In his research on the "stein image," Ahsen (1987) poetically captured this dynamic by describing the intertwining relationship between focus and periphery, recall and forgetting, vividness and unvividness. Subjects could easily focus on a clear, crisp picture of a colorful stein that had been placed before them. At first, they do not attend to the background on which the image is drawn. But over time, they begin to realize that the background is not a static, monolithic plane. Not as easily noticed or identified, the field that surrounds the stein image appears to contain vague, implicit life. When the subjects delve into that realm of unvividness, they discover that it is a mythological sea of previously undetected sensations, emotions, and imaginings. Unlike the focused image of the stein, which appears stark, rigid, and bound, the periphery feels magical, free, mysterious, as having a hidden strategy or intentionality. By being fluidly amorphous and accommodating, the periphery nourishes the center stein image. The center focus arises from the fertile ground of the periphery; it is a manifestation and a condensation of the periphery; it expands into the periphery. The vivid and the unvivid are interdependent. In the terms of psychoanalysis, the bold relief of an imaged self or object representation flows from and dissolves into the multiple self and object images that seep through the peripheral realms of self structure.

In *zazen*, the meditator's mind wanders between focus and periphery, vivid and unvivid, allowing new representations to emerge, crystalize, coalesce with other representations, and recede to the background. *Makyo* are rigid points of focus that highlight reified aspects of self structure. They are objectified aspects of self that may refuse to yield to the periphery. They may become, as Ahsen (1987) would say, a form of torture that conforms to the objective world's demand for specificity and clarity. But ultimately, when *zazen* progresses, the images of *makyo* dissolve into the peripheral ground from which they came. So too, the focus of the mind's observing eye on the center image dissolves into the background and periphery of the image, and finally, into the brimming emptiness of no-mind to which the periphery itself fades.

Realizing the emptiness upon which psychological structures are built brings new vitality and definition to those structures. That emptiness serves as a reference point, a center, a grounding for those structures—just as an image arises from and is supported by the vague periphery and seemingly blank background upon which it is built. In its statement, "All emptiness is form and all form is emptiness," Zen points to this inextricable intertwining of psychological structures and the experiential void that underlies them—not a void that is stagnant and dead, but rather vibrant and intentional. The ultimate goal of Zen training is the enhancement of the flow between these two polarities. The images of *makyo* serve as waystations in this process, as stepping stones or imagistic roadsigns of self-experience along that path between self and no-self.

In his analysis of dreams, Freud (1900) hinted at this vision of the intertwining of form and formlessness. As a result of the mechanisms of condensation, displacement, and symbolism, any single dream contains a multitude of affects and ideations. During the course of an entire psychoanalytic treatment, the patient may return again and again to the same dream, each time unpacking new meaning, as if there were no end to the chain of associations linked to the image. Freud suggested that, indeed, there may be no limit to the network of affect and ideation contained within the dream. At its deepest level, the dream image fans out into a boundless array of intrapsychic dynamics. Multiple determination is infinite determination. The structural form of a single dream image arises from a formless domain of immeasurable potential; and it is a complete, encapsulated expression of that domain.

Enacting the Inner Meaning

Enactments are a favored mode of expression in Zen. Stylized behaviors, rituals, gestures, mannerisms, and even the activities of everyday life can articulate meaning in the concrete form of behaviors within the moment. A parable describes how the Buddha once stood up before a group assembled to hear him speak, but rather than using words to convey his lesson, he simply held up a flower. No one understood, except one especially wise disciple who just smiled to the Buddha to show his appreciation. A variety of artistic methods in Japan and China have evolved from this Zen emphasis on the need to enact the essential meaning of things: flower arrangement, the tea ceremony, calligraphy, the No play, and the martial arts.

Using subtle, nonverbal behavior to communicate is a cultural hallmark of Japanese life. Morsbach (1973) relates the story of an American professor with an excellent command of the Japanese language who attended a faculty meeting at a Japanese university. On leaving the meeting, he spoke to his Japanese colleague about the decision the faculty had reached. He recalled how all the professors had spoken in favor of the decision. His colleague agreed with his observations, but finally remarked, "All this may be so, but you are still mistaken. The meeting arrived at the opposite conclusion: You have correctly understood all the words spoken, but you didn't understand the silences between them" (pp. 276–277). How similar this situation is to psychotherapy, in which the clinician must learn to read the nuances of silent, nonverbal behavior to detect the inner meanings that often contradict the spoken word.

Roshi Kapleau (1980b) and his students relied strictly on an enactment to educate a group of psychoanalysts about Zen. After being introduced by the institute director, the Roshi came before the group and sat down on a cushion placed upon the floor. A student entered, prostrated before the Roshi, and seated himself on another cushion, about a foot away, facing Kapleau. "What is Zen?" the student asked. Roshi produced a banana, peeled it, and began eating. "Is that all? Can't you show me anything else?" the student replied. "Come closer, please," the Roshi answered. The student moved in and Roshi waved the remaining portion of the banana before the student's face. The student prostrated and left.

A second student rose to address the audience. "Do you all understand?" When there was no response, the student added, "You have just witnessed a first-rate demonstration of Zen. Are there any questions?" After a long silence, someone spoke up. "Roshi, I am not satisfied with your demonstration. You have shown us something that I am not sure I understand. It must be possible to *tell* us what Zen is." Kapleau's reply was simple. "If you must insist on words, Zen is an elephant copulating with a flea" (pp. 8–9).

Suzuki (1970) clearly illustrated the power of physical postures and even simple bodily processes as enactments of the profound, underlying meaning to which Zen points. In the lotus position, the historically traditional posture for meditating, the left foot is placed on the right thigh and the right foot on the left thigh. Even though we have a right leg and a left leg, Suzuki explains, they feel as one. The position expresses the oneness of duality: not one, not two. Body and mind, self and no-self, self and other, are not one and not two. They are interpenetrated in both dependence and independence. So, too, the simple act of breathing during meditation conveys an essential meaning about the self. Inhaling and exhaling, in and out, enacts the essence of the "I," which is nothing more than a swinging door between the internal and external worlds.

Clinicians have also recognized the powerful condensation of meaning that may be embodied even in the simplest of behavioral patterns and somatic reactions. A fleeting facial expression, a quirky hand movement, a yawn, blushing, or an unexpected tightening of the throat muscles—all may be enactive pathways to unconscious realms of memory, thought, and affect. They are hints of the underlying, essential meaning. The psychotherapy patient must develop a conscious awareness of that meaning; whereas the Zen practitioner, understanding the signification, chooses to enact the meaning spontaneously, without the burden of conscious overthought.

Despite Zen's predilection for enactments, they too, like words and images, succumb to the process of deconstruction during meditation. At advanced stages of contemplative consciousness, awareness passes beyond its attachment to the body, as well as to thoughts, concepts, and imagery. Zen masters refer to this as a "falling away of mind and body." Tai Chi Chuan, a Chinese martial art derived from Taoism and Chan, involves the slow, meditative repetition of a "form" or sequence of postures, each one possessing spiritually symbolic as well as practical (martial) significance. For advanced practitioners, the enactive exercise, like meditation, uncovers repressed memories and affects that were embedded in the somatic representational system, often resulting in unexpected bouts of crying, joy, or anger. As the practice of the form continues, these memories and affects fall away. Eventually, at the highest level of Tai Chi development, even the postures of the form are destructured and disappear. The ultimate form is formless movement.

As is true of words and images, the structure of the enactment rises from and intertwines with the unbounded, hence formless realm of meaning that it signifies. Eating a banana could signify a sexual activity, the partaking of a forbidden fruit, the peeling of a secret, or any or all of an infinite variety of things. And sometimes a banana is just a banana. The just-plain banana is interpenetrated with all these meanings. In the practice of Tai Chi, the practitioner maintains the awareness that any of an infinite number of poses may occur at the next moment, even though the next standardized posture in the sequence is always followed. As a result, each movement is fresh,

spontaneous, and interpenetrated with the formlessness of all possible movements. Without this connection to the underlying realm of
multitudinous meanings—this connection to the infinite—stylized
enactments and rituals lose their vitality and decay into stale, rigid
deportments. Psychotherapy patients who have cut themselves off
from the unconscious meanings of their behavior fall prey to the inflexible pathological enactments that are their compulsions. When the
underlying meanings are tapped, the patients become free to abandon the enactment or transform it into an adaptive, enlivening behavior. Both Zen and psychoanalysis open a path to the limitless realm of
underlying meanings, not for the purpose of wallowing in that realm,
but rather to revitalize the customs and habits of everyday living.

Grasping the Thing

For all three representational systems—lexical, imagistic, and enactive—the process of Zen training is essentially the same. The deconstructing of intrapsychic structures is not, in itself, the goal; but
rather, the realization of the mutually arising and inseparable relationship between structure and structurelessness, self and no-self.
The structures that are the expressed word, image, and enactment are
all inseparable from the formless "thing" that cannot be expressed.
This means more than saying that words, images, and enactments are
parts of the elephant which we grasp in the dark. As indicated in
Buddhist philosophy, the universal expresses itself through the particular, such that the two are identical.

Psychoanalysis speaks of the need to "assimilate" experience.
Giving form to formlessness and expressing formlessness through
form is the essence of assimilation. One uses words, images, or enactments to digest and absorb the raw "thingness" of an affective
experience. At the same time, the word, image, and enactment can allow the affect to be expressed and experienced more fully. Finding
the right way to describe or portray what one has felt or sensed arises
with and is inseparable from the blossoming of the emotion or the
sensation.

Perhaps the most powerful way to grasp the "thingness" of experience is through a combination of lexical, imagistic, and enactive
representations. Psychoanalytic research suggests that affect is most
effectively integrated when it is cross-coded in the form of verbal
concepts, images, and behaviors (Bruner, 1964; Horowitz, 1983). Met-
aphors are particularly useful in psychotherapy because they are
multimodal, and thereby enable the translation and mastery of expe-

rience across the three representational systems (Bonanno, 1990). Oriental thinkers were familiar with the vigor of such multimodal depictions. The *I Ching,* one of the basic texts of Taoism, consists of 64 images known as "hexagrams," each one portraying a specific physical and/or natural activity, and each accompanied by a verbal interpretation. The Chinese language itself consists of ideograms that are imagistic representations, rather than abstract characters. And haiku, like any good poetry, uses words to create images and render actions that express underlying meaning.

When we examine the results of assimilating experience across the three representational systems, we discover some important insights into the nature of intrapsychic "structure." For example, when an image (e.g., a visual memory) surfaces in psychotherapy, extensive verbal interpretative work that uncovers its underlying meanings ultimately leads to the disappearance of the image. It is as if, Breuer and Freud (1895, p. 280) suggested, "the picture vanished like a ghost that had been laid to rest." Kohut (1984) believed that this image evaporation was the result of a developmental course that had reached its completion. The mind has no use for such images, and so they dissolve via processes that are unrelated to repression. Kohut noted that this is similar to how, at the end of a successful analysis, patients no longer remember the numerous verbal interventions and discussions that helped them resolve their conflicts or attain self-cohesion.

Images—as well as words, concepts, and enactments—may not be "structures" per se, but rather the precursors, reflections, or signifiers of structure. It is the *integration* of the three representation systems that culminates in a cohesive and harmonious self. This higher-order, unitary structure is sustained by the three representational systems, yet transcends them. Attempting to define "structure" at this deep level, as Kohut (1977) and Schafer (1968) suggested, runs us into troublesome tautologies and metapsychological dilemmas. Kohut believed it was the final bedrock through which psychoanalysis could not pass. Perhaps this structure, being the very basis of subjective experience, cannot be labelled, reified, or grasped, but only alluded to, reminiscent of how Zen likens itself to a finger that points to the moon. Perhaps, paradoxically, these structures may be best described as structureless.

One important issue remains concerning this discussion of representational systems and Zen training. Will psychoanalysis accept Zen's claim that words, concepts, and images can be dissolved so that one reaches a direct, uncontaminated knowing of reality? Many psy-

choanalytic theorists would refute the idea that understanding a patient can stand completely free from one's theoretical concepts and
one's own personality structure. Our representational world always
colors our perceptions and conclusions. Yet would it be possible for
the individual clinician to advance his or her skills, or for the art of
psychotherapy as a whole to advance, if we were not capable of even
brief, momentary breakthroughs into direct knowing? Borrowing Atwood & Stolorow's (1984) term, we could claim that "decentering"
from one's subjective structures is the essence of the unbiased understanding which we call empathy.

Our subjective structures only distort our perceptions when we
are not aware of them as structures. When we realize our own representational world, we can entertain the possibility of another world
within the patient. Knowing the "I" points to the realization of the
"not-I." To be aware of the form of our own structures enables the
momentary excursion into the realm of formlessness in which our
awareness of the patient's structures can crystallize.

6

Meditative Consciousness

The one aspect of Asian traditions that has most consistently captured the interest of Westerners has been meditation. The literature in psychology alone abounds with studies of this ancient practice from a variety of clinical, cognitive, and biopsychological perspectives. Most inquiries from the psychoanalytic standpoint have similarly concentrated on this facet of the Eastern disciplines. That meditation has attracted such widespread attention may be attributed to its central position in the various schools of Buddhism and Taoism. *Zen*—derived from the Chinese *chan* and the Sanskrit *dhyana*—means "to meditate." As a tangible adjunct to the sometimes elusive speculations of Eastern philosophizing, meditation is a distinct experiential practice with explicit techniques and identifiable intrapsychic processes that are readily amenable to psychological research. Psychoanalysis, by its very nature, has been drawn to the art and science of a kindred discipline that advocates the mind turning inward to understand its own workings.

The psychoanalytic literature contains many wide-ranging, complex analyses of meditation and meditative states of consciousness. Here I would like to highlight the overarching issues that have surfaced in these discussions: What are the intrapsychic mechanisms involved in the different types of meditative experiences? What are the detrimental and psychotherapeutic effects of meditation? Can meditation training benefit the clinician? What is the importance of the life context surrounding meditation practice? Finally, how should we study meditative states of consciousness?

The Intrapsychic Mechanisms and Types of Meditation

Psychoanalytic speculations about the intrapsychic processes involved in meditation have revolved around four basic themes. These themes roughly follow the major theoretical orientations in psychoanalysis (drive theory, ego psychology, object relations, and self psychology).

1. As originally viewed by Freud, meditation is primarily a *maladaptive regression* to infantile states of merger with the mother, or to even earlier biopsychological experiences of "oneness."
2. Meditation is a *specialized ego function*—for example, involving a "regression in service of the ego" in which the ego voluntarily reverts to unconscious processes and merger experiences for the ultimate purpose of advancing psychological health (Allison, 1968; Maupin, 1965; Shafi, 1973); or a "double orientation" of an ego that is therapeutically balanced between regressive oneness and separation anxiety (Krynicki, 1980); or a "spreading" of the ego, as described by Federn (1952), in which the ego's inner boundary that is turned toward the intrapsychic world and its outer boundary that is turned to the external world become flexibly permeable, resulting in altered states of experience (Werman, 1986).
3. Meditation is a *transitional space* where inner and outer realities creatively blend, which allows for the exorcism of toxic introjects, the internalization of adaptive psychological functions, and the strengthening of self structure (Finn, 1992; Horton, 1974).
4. Meditation is a *destructuring process* in which the framework of the self and its underlying intrapsychic processes are unraveled, expanded, and ultimately enriched by broadening the awareness of the observing self (Deikman, 1982; Engler, 1986; Wilber, Engler, & Brown, 1986).

These four approaches are not mutually exclusive. Common to all of them is the attempt to explain the paradoxical dynamics of self and no-self. How is it that an apparently healthy, integrated personality willingly yields or deconstructs itself into a condition of primary unity? Psychoanalysts have been fascinated, puzzled, even annoyed by these Eastern ideas about mystical oneness. They have been hard-pressed to provide an explanation. At the core of the debates is whether meditation entails a regression or a progression. The answer may be that it involves both, or neither. Personality is a multifaceted structure in which various sectors may be "regressing" or "progressing" and interacting with other sectors simultaneously. Setting aside the ideas about linear development that are implicit in the regression/progression distinction (and adopting a more Taoist model of change) we may discard the distinction altogether in order to conceptualize meditation as an uncovering of the intrinsic, circular rhythms of oneness/separateness and of intrapsychic processes in general.

Although many psychoanalytic studies attempt to unravel the meditative experience of the self/no-self interpenetration, they do not always distinguish this as a specifically advanced level of meditation. With the notable exception of Wilber, Engler, and Brown (1986), few investigations have clarified the differences among the complex series of meditative stages. The distinction between the preliminary and advanced stages may be an especially important one to psychoanalytic research. Similar to patients entering psychotherapy, beginning meditators are learning how to enter the stream of intrapsychic experience. For those who are unfamiliar with the internal world, they may be captivated and/or frightened by this new realm that is opening up to them. Also similar to psychotherapy, the early phases of meditation entail a process of uncovering and destructuring that triggers insights into previously unconscious components of self structure— what Engler (1986) labeled as the " psychodynamic" level of meditation. This level differs from the more advanced stages in which the meditator becomes aware of the underlying intrapsychic mechanisms that lead to self structure and that constitute the basic functions of memory and perception. The distinction is between *meditating on intrapsychic content* of the representational world and *meditating on intrapsychic processes or functions* that culminate in representational structures. Of course, these contrasts, again, are based on notions of linearity, stage development, and a dichotomy between structure and process, all of which may be questioned from a Taoist perspective, which emphasizes the circularity and interpenetration of opposites.

Epstein (1990a) warned psychoanalytic researchers to heed the distinction between the two basic types of meditation: *concentration* and *insight* (also called "mindfulness") practice. In the concentration method, the meditator allows the mind to remain focused, without wavering, on a single object such as a sound, sensation (often breathing), image, or thought. In insight practice (*vipassana* in Buddhism or *shikan taza* in Zen), meditators allow their attention to drift from one target of awareness to another without attaching to anything in particular. Concentration practice is sometimes used as preliminary training to prepare meditators for the more difficult insight approach. Epstein noted that most psychoanalytic studies have centered their investigations on the concentration method. Because this meditative style culminates in profound feelings of tranquility, bliss, and a merged absorption in the object of concentration, these researchers were led to the conclusion that meditation involved a narcissistic immersion into the experience of "oneness." Researchers have tended to overlook the insight practice, according to Epstein, which does not dwell on states of undifferentiated merger and union, but instead moves toward the realization that the "I" as a "doer" is just another self-representation that has no permanence or inherent existence. Discovering the insubstantiality of the cherished image of a doing self may be more anxiety-provoking than tranquil or blissful.

Although this argument has validity, we should not overemphasize the distinction between concentration and insight meditation. The attempt to dichotomize into categories will eventually uncover an intertwining of the dichotomies that confuses the categories. As with insight meditation, "merging" with an object during concentration practice can lead to the realization that the distinction between knower and known, doer and done, is illusory. Insight practice also entails a distinct form of concentrated awareness, paradoxically, without concentrating on anything in particular. This is why concentration practice may be used as a prelude to insight practice. In an earlier paper, Epstein (1986), as well as Speeth (1982), noted that various styles of Buddhist meditation demand a delicate interplay and integration of the two methods. Focusing and unfocusing, convergence and divergence, interpenetrate each other. Most important, the essential intrapsychic process in the two meditative styles may be the same. The deautomatizing and retraversing of psychic functions, which Engler (1986) considered the basis of the insight method, occurs similarly during concentration approaches. In his groundbreaking experimental studies, Deikman (1963, 1966a) found that even beginning meditators who focused on a blue vase experienced a variety of hierarchical shifts in perceptual, cognitive, and reality-testing functions. For these reasons, an overly strict contrast between concentration and insight methods may whitewash the intrinsic similarities and intertwining dynamics between the two.

Meditation is but one type of altered state of consciousness among a wide range of types. It may be a more disciplined, studied method of altering intrapsychic processes, but it would be a mistake to conclude that it is qualitatively different from others. Hypnosis, sensory deprivation, dreams, peak experiences, drug-induced states, creative reveries, and moments of inspiration—all may bear some similarities to the various states of mind triggered by meditation practice, including the process of deautomatization and the unity experience. Everyday life itself is far from being a monolithic line of consciousness. Instead, it is peppered with an assortment of significant, though perhaps momentary, dips into meditative states. The Asian discipline of meditation is the art and science of cultivating the seedlings that already exist within the intrapsychic sphere of everyday consciousness.

The Liabilities of Meditation

As a process of systematically deautomatizing and destructuring the self, meditation may pose some threats to psychological health. According to Epstein (1981, 1990b; Epstein & Lieff, 1986), the problems may change according to the level or intensity of the meditative practice. During the early psychodynamic phases, when unconscious content is first being uncovered, there may be restlessness, anxiety, depressive episodes, depersonalization, derealization, or other dissociative symptoms triggered by being a detached observer. On occasion, psychotic episodes during intense meditation retreats have been reported. At deeper levels of practice, when the powers of concentration improve and shift from intrapsychic content to process, meditators may experience grandiose feelings of accomplishment and an anxiously compulsive preoccupation with their practice (in Zen called the "Zen sickness"). Such symptoms may reflect narcissistic pathology. The sustained destructuring of the intrapsychic world that fades the self into no-self ultimately leads to the spiritual crisis of some meditators known as the "great terror" or "great doubt." At this stage the solid aspects of personality structure drop away, pulling the ground out from under the meditator, leaving the meditator with the frightening realization that the "self" is an illusion. For other meditators, the prospect of losing the self reinforces their pathological need to merge with the idealized other and/or to abandon the fears associated with having a self. Epstein (1990a) noted that meditation practice poses dangers when it reifies either of the two poles of narcissism: the fear/desire to fuse in oneness with the perfect other and the fear/desire to isolate oneself in an emptiness that is independent and separated from others.

The motivations to become a meditator and the reactions to the practice are determined by the individual's personality dynamics. The stability of self structure, the capacity to tolerate derepression, the type of neurotic or narcissistic pathology—all are important variables that determine whether the person can endure the meditative process and what reactions will ensue. Such issues are discussed further in Chapter 7.

The Therapeutics of Meditation

Despite the possible drawbacks to meditation, most psychological research has been devoted to understanding its therapeutic qualities. The field is not free of debate. Whereas some studies support a wide variety of hypotheses about meditation's salutary influences, others claim that beneficial outcomes may be attributed to the effects of expectation or simply resting, and not meditation per se. Considering that meditative disciplines predate psychology by some 3000 years, that they have evolved into highly complex systems that Westerners are just beginning to understand, and that meditation is perhaps the most ubiquitous health practice in the world, we may regard contemporary psychological research as still preliminary in its development.

Like clinical research as a whole, psychoanalytic investigations indicate that meditation has diverse therapeutic repercussions. As a process of uncovering unconscious content, the early stages of insight meditation bear some resemblance to psychodynamic therapy, traditionally conceptualized as a method of facilitating derepression and insight. Engler (1986) suggested that meditation employs four technical procedures which resemble those used in psychoanalysis. The process is *technically neutral* in that attention is kept "bare"; mental and physical events are observed as they are, without injecting emotional reactions. If such reactions do occur, they in turn become the object of bare attention. Simply observing thoughts, feelings, and sensations without discrimination or selection requires a *removal of censorship* that resembles the basic rule of free association in psychoanalysis. The meditator also follows the *rule of abstinence* while observing events, because wishes, impulses, desires, and strivings that may be stimulated are not acted upon, but delayed in being gratified for the sake of attaining deeper insight. Finally, being able to detach oneself from thoughts and feelings and step back to objectively observe them entails a *therapeutic split in the ego*. Curiously, advanced meditators, as compared to inexperienced ones, do not show a decreased level of conflict on the Rorschach, but rather a nondefensive awareness and acceptance of those conflicts (Brown & Engler, 1986). This is similar to the outcome of psychotherapy. Following Zen philosophy, we may consider it evidence of the return to "everyday mind."

Other ways of conceptualizing the therapeutic benefits of meditation focus less on its ability to stimulate insight through the derepression of unconscious content, and more on its reparative influences on the self and narcissistic dynamics. Meditation may lead to a stronger, more flexible self structure that can balance states of merger and separation, as well as effectively integrate potentially destabilizing experiences (Krynicki, 1980; Epstein, 1988a). It may also help alleviate the infantile narcissistic investment in an ideal self that is cherished as an omnipotent and perfect entity unto itself (Epstein, 1986). By facilitating the oscillations between the raveling and unraveling of both intrapsychic content and function, meditation invigorates the cohesion, continuity, and affective coloring of the self.

If meditation is similar to psychotherapy, is there resistance to meditation as there sometimes is in psychotherapy? The concept of 'resistance to meditation' has been proposed by Rubin (1992b). Meditators go through periods when they neglect their practice, sometimes having reasonable explanations, sometimes not. When they do sit, they may find themselves unable to deepen their practice. The same paradox originally discovered by Freud also arises in meditation: Why does the process become subverted if it is potentially therapeutic? The possible unconscious sources of such resistance can be identified by adapting the criteria proposed by Greenson (1967) for psychoanalysis. The need to defend against regression and overwhelming internal experiences may block one's "attendance" at the meditation session or wholehearted immersion into the process. Resistance to delving deeper into the practice may surface in the disguise of restlessness, boredom, or drowsiness. Meditators may be afraid to discover something about themselves that they previously did not know, or the resistance may be fueled by the basic narcissistic need to avert, at all costs, any threat to the stability of self structure. They may be unwilling to give up the secondary gain from their symptoms—symptoms that meditation offers to alleviate. Their superego guilt may force them to abandon any attempts to improve themselves through practice. Clinging to the familiarity of their personal status quo, they may fear the unknown and the possibility of change, especially when impending reality factors indicate that their current life situation and relationships will indeed change if they persist in their practice. In what may be a "resistance against resistance," obsessed meditators may throw themselves into fanatical bouts of practice, which reflects underlying narcissistic or compulsive needs that they are defending against.

Comparing meditation to psychotherapy begs the question of its relative effectiveness. Is it more powerful than psychodynamic treatment? Less powerful? Is it psychotherapy? There are several ways to view the correspondence between the two.

Meditation as Metatherapy

This position holds that meditation includes and surpasses the benefits derived from psychotherapy. The early phases of meditation uncover unconscious content, as does psychoanalytic treatment, but in the more advanced stages one transcends this psychodynamic work by uncovering the depths of intrapsychic process. This leads to insight into the essence of how the mind works, the nature of reality, and the relief of all suffering created by the mind's grasp of reality.

Besides being a blatantly Orientocentric position that idealizes meditation and devalues psychotherapy, this view presents other obvious problems. The traditional instructions for meditation encourage people not to dwell on the early psychodynamic phases. The meditator tries not to attach attention to any mental content. Therefore, covering this psychodynamic ground is not nearly as thorough, focused, or systematic as in psychoanalytic treatment. As compared to clinicians, meditation teachers usually offer little in the way of interpreting or working through the dreams, repressed affects, and unconscious memories that surface. They are not trained to do so. A large portion of the therapeutic effect at this psychodynamic level perhaps entails a cathartic or abreactive process, which, as Freud discovered early, is necessary but often not sufficient. Some of the writers who marvel at meditation's psychodynamic impact are clinicians themselves. Being skilled in self-analysis, they probably sift more therapeutic benefits out of this phase of meditation than does the average meditator. Perhaps meditation is more powerful in its therapeutic selfobject influence on the self and narcissistic dynamics. Yet most clinicians would agree that such therapeutic effects only fully blossom when interpreted and worked through on a verbal level—a process at which psychoanalysis excels. Although meditation may shine at revealing how the mind intersects with reality, as a substitute for psychoanalytic treatment it is less than ideal.

Meditation as a Sequel to Psychotherapy

This position recognizes that meditation does not excel at the psychodynamic level. At that tier, psychoanalytic treatment prepares the individual for the more "advanced" contemplative work of exploring the deeper processes of how the mind works. Psychotherapy is critical for those individuals whose self structure is so fragile, and narcissistic pathology so severe, that they could not engage meditation without fragmenting and spinning off into maladaptive, narcissistic reactions. This position rests on the developmental model, which claims that you have to have a self before you can transcend it; but this model may be flawed in its emphasis on linear progression (see Chapter 3). Orientocentric tendencies also are evident in this position, although they are not as severe as in the first. To assume that meditation works at a more advanced or deeper level smacks of idealization. Whether uncovering unconscious content, or the mind's underlying process is more therapeutic in alleviating human suffering remains an open question.

Meditation as an Adjunct to Psychotherapy

As a supplement or support to psychotherapy, meditation has much to offer patients. It is an excellent exercise in helping them learn how to free-associate and attend to their internal, subjective world. Between therapy sessions, it may help trigger new associations, thereby helping to fill out the analytic work. In the absence of the clinician, it can provide self-soothing functions through the reduction of anxiety and the taming of affect. Because it is a powerful method for stimulating imagistic experiences, it also may help revive and internalize memories of the therapeutic selfobject relationship with the clinician.

Relegating meditation to a supportive role regarding therapy tends to underestimate its unique characteristics, particularly its skill in revealing the mind's process and its impact as a "spiritual" discipline. The view of meditation as an adjunct to therapy easily tips over into Eurocentrism. It may tend to value the psychodynamic level of meditation, and overlook meditating on intrapsychic process. Some teachers question whether meditation on unconscious content is really insight meditation at all. Some meditators who become fascinated by the early psychodynamic phase dwell on exploring the memories and affects that emerge. They never progress to the latter stages. Engler (1986) cites an Asian teacher who stated, "Many Western students do not meditate. They do therapy. They do not go deep with mindfulness" (p. 29).

Whereas eclectic psychotherapists have experimented with meditative techniques in their work, psychoanalytic clinicians may be more reluctant. Since the idea of 'parameters' (Eissler, 1953) first cracked open the strict rules and conservativism of the traditional analytic method, clinicians have tried other styles of intervention. Often, their excursions are tentative, dressed with apologies, or carried out in secret. For some, acknowledging that meditation can enrich therapy may be a narcissistic injury. For others, news of such experiments may threaten the selfobject tie to a professional community that is not ready for such alterations.

Meditation and Psychotherapy in Complementarity

Perhaps the most accurate assumption is that meditation and psychotherapy overlap, but differ in emphasis by concentrating on adjoining sectors of human development. Meditation is therapeutic in some ways similar to psychotherapy, but it is not psychotherapy. Psychoanalytic treatment focuses on ideational and affective content for the purpose of stimulating beneficial behavioral and emotional changes. It leads to the enhanced awareness of one's personality dynamics, the enrichment of social relationships, and feelings of a vital personal self. Insight meditation entails an analysis of both mental content and functions—ideational, affective, and perceptual—although these operations become objects of, not vehicles for, insight. Meditation is primarily an exploration of how the mind constructs reality and how ignorance of perceptual processes contributes to human suffering. It leads to the wisdom and sense of liberation arising from "true" perception. Because these goals of psychotherapy and meditation intersect at various levels, they support each other. Because they approach, by different angles, the common goal of alleviating human suffering, they are complementary in design.

Rubin's (1992b) psychoanalytic treatment of a Buddhist meditator clearly demonstrates this potentially synergistic complementarity between psychotherapy and meditation. This synergy rests partly on the fact that meditation can be simultaneously curative and pathological. All behaviors are multiply determined. Psychotherapy can free up and amplify the beneficial outcomes of meditation by revealing and alleviating its harmful effects. In his case study, Rubin outlined six functions that revealed the constructive and defensive aspects of his patient's meditation practice which both enriched and limited his life. On the constructive side, meditation improved the patient's *cultivation of self-observational capacities*. By learning to attend to his internal flow of experience, and by *deautomizing thought and action*, he felt an increased sense of freedom from habitual, usually unconscious patterns of thinking and behaving. The chances of being an acting-out, out-of-control "animal" (like his father) were minimized. Observing his internal world impartially through meditation gradually replaced his perfectionistic father's criticalness, which led to his feeling more patient and compassionate, and to a *reduction of his self-recriminative tendencies*. Simultaneously, however, meditation also served as a *ratio-*

nale for self-punishment when the patient's unconscious guilt caused him to embrace practice as an ascetic withdrawal from the world. As his disposition to punish and criticize himself faded, the patient experienced less depressive affect and a clearer sense of his own ideas, feelings, and goals, all of which improved his *self-demarcation and affect regulation*. Combining both injurious and restorative effects, his meditation became an *expression of urgent wishes and ideals*. It was a symptom of his hungry need to identify with exemplary figures and exalted theories—a hunger stemming from his distant father, who was an inadequate role model. Although meditation was partially restitutive by offering him a substitute set of ideals and values, it also became an acting out, rather than an understanding of his need to win his father's approval by striving for perfected self-purification.

An important question remains regarding the therapeutics of meditation. Is meditation necessary? Of course, we must ask, "Necessary for what?" Rather than replying directly, we can pose another, related question: Is psychotherapy necessary? We would be hard-pressed to claim that it is a requirement for leading a happy, fulfilling existence or attaining self-knowledge. There are many lives that prove the contrary. There also are many life experiences other than psychotherapy that are highly therapeutic. Similarly, meditation is not an absolute prerequisite for either psychological or spiritual well-being, or even for penetrating to the essence of mind and reality. Religious insights, as William James (1902) demonstrated, come in all shapes and sizes besides meditation practice. Even some Zen masters have favored the "direct pointing" into enlightenment through question-and-answer dialogues with students, rather than the "aching legs" method of meditation (Watts, 1975b). And contradicting the notion that enlightenment is a hard-earned prize, James described the "once-born" people who received no special religious training, never worked through any religious crises, or experienced a marvelous transformation. From the start, they were compassionate, at peace, and in tune with the oneness of things. James offered Walt Whitman as a example. While tending to wounded soldiers during the horrors of the Civil War, Whitman stated, in what matches the insight of any Zen master, "What is called good is perfect, and what is called bad is just as perfect."

Both meditation and psychotherapy may be reparative for developmental operations that have gone awry. They may both accelerate normal development through its series of up-and-down cycles. In either case, they are formalized, systematic disciplines for addressing processes that occur "naturally" in the human psyche.

The Clinician's Contemplative Experience

Although, as evident in the psychoanalytic literature, clinicians rarely seem to encourage their patients to meditate, they more frequently endorse this practice for themselves. A number of writers (Epstein, 1984, 1988b; Rubin, 1985; Silverberg, 1988; Speeth, 1982) have called for an enhancement of the clinician's capacity for contemplative listening and advocated meditative training as a means to achieve this goal.

Most psychoanalytic clinicians writing on this topic revolve their arguments around Freud's (1912) recommendations for "evenly hovering attention." Freud suggested that the clinician, paralleling the patient's free associations, simply attend to all elements of the patient's stream of thought without selecting, concentrating, or consciously attempting to understand its elements. The therapist suspends all judgment and critical analyses in order to allow impartial, evenly distributed attention to everything that occurs within the analytic field. This style of listening opens the therapist to the unconscious dimensions of the patient's ideational flow. Following Freud, the literature rapidly grew with descriptions and analyses of the clinician's state of mind during the analytic hour. As detailed and sophisticated as these discussions have been, clinicians experienced in meditation—the refined art of evenly hovering attention—have pinpointed flaws and shortcomings.

Rubin (1985) stated that even though evenly hovering attention has been unanimously accepted as the cornerstone of psychoanalytic listening, the most crucial pragmatic problem is that the literature does not clarify how to cultivate it. The experience of free associating during one's training analysis helps, but is far from sufficient. According to Rubin, Freud and other theorists failed to see how evenly hovering attention, which corresponds to insight meditative awareness, can be effectively developed from preliminary training in concentration practice, when one cultivates the "one-pointedness" of attention that sets the stage for clear, unified, penetrative awareness. Also, by warning clinicians to suppress critical faculties and deliberate attempts to analyze, Freud clarified what to avoid, what *not* to do; but he did not specifically explain what positive steps they must take to develop effective listening. Rubin similarly criticizes Bion (1970), whose words of advice about forsaking "memory, desire, and understanding," which tend to distort and selectively filter the clinician's awareness of the patient, have become a battle cry for some therapists. Like Freud, Bion describes what not to do, but not what to do.

He suggested that one can drive out the three culprits by suppression and disciplined denial. His proposal, Rubin points out, is flawed because attempting to control the mind does not lead to open, evenly suspended awareness. Experienced meditators know that trying to control the mind, trying to stop any of its various activities, only fills it up with the effort to control and stop. The desire to have no desires is just another desire that does not free the mind, but instead occupies it. The art of meditation—and of psychoanalytic listening—is developing the ability to allow evenly suspended awareness to appear spontaneously on its own. It is more an expertise in "letting go" into contemplative attention than wrestling it into place. Perhaps the inability of Freud, Bion, and others to describe what to do stems partly from the paradoxical fact that the idea of "doing" meditative awareness is incompatible with meditative awareness.

Epstein (1984, 1988b) pointed out how theorists have tended to abandon the ideal of evenly suspended attention as originally proposed by Freud. Beginning with Reik (1948), a number of analysts rejected the idea that the clinician should maintain an evenly distributed awareness of all phenomena during the therapy session. Instead, they claimed, the clinician oscillates between receptive listening and intrapsychic reorganizing of the material for the purpose of making an interpretation. There is a rhythm between open-ended, evenly hovering attention, when selection and judgment are suspended, and the subsequent cognitive processing and restructuring of the insight that was attained through hovering attention. However, Epstein argued, it is not necessary to postulate a distinct cognitive mode for the conscious analyzing and reformulating of the insight. When correctly understood from the perspective of Buddhist meditation, evenly suspended attention does not preclude active, logical, discursive thought. It allows such thought to occur, pays close attention to it, and treats it as yet another phenomenon that provides a piece of information about the truth. It promotes the ability to observe, with detached awareness, the mechanics of formulating an interpretation. Evenly suspended attention includes within its domain the activities of intellectual processing. Because what is truly important will fully and continually present itself to the clinician's receptive listening, the clinician will know when it is time to make an intervention by this clear awareness of the essential information.

Epstein's argument points to important issues about the nature of interpretations and interventions in psychoanalytic treatment. Is the best interpretation or intervention one that springs spontaneously, unconsciously, from the soil of evenly hovering attention?

How much conscious analysis and restructuring is needed before the clinician decides to speak? The clinician's state of mind during the therapy hour incorporates contemplative elements, but it is not meditation per se. Through evenly suspended attention, some insights quickly crystallize in the therapist's mind and lead to spontaneous, un-thought-out interpretations that are highly effective. However, other insights may require sustained, conscious analysis, during or after the session, that does not follow the contemplative path. If one heeds the principles of insight meditation, one does not pursue the line of thought—the sustained attaching of attention to mental content—that may be necessary for clinicians in some psychotherapeutic scenarios. The basic meditation instruction to "let go" of elements in the stream of thought forecloses on the possibility of extended conscious evaluations. A great deal of powerful analytic work can occur within the realm of evenly hovering attention, but some work falls outside that range.

We may also question the assumption that clinicians, immersed in evenly hovering attention, engage a mental state that resembles insight meditation. Is it true that their attention is evenly distributed across all phenomena? Are the sensation in one's toe, the ticking of the clock, a breeze through the window, as well as the patient's clenched fist and her story about her saintly mother, all equally attended to? We could make the argument that psychoanalytic evenly hovering attention actually is a variant of concentration, not insight, meditation. The therapist is focused on the patient, or, on a wider level, the intersubjective field between patient and therapist. The ticking of the clock and the breeze across one's face may be discarded, consciously or unconsciously, as irrelevant phenomena. Although clinicians must inspect fluctuations in their desire to help the patient as important analytic data, they are molded by their desire to help—and by their professional obligation to help—into an implicit structure of concentration in which their body resides in a chair, their attention on the patient, and their objectives on reaching a cure.

Although clinicians may only rarely step into a truly insight-meditative mode, momentary excursions into this state of mind can be remarkably productive. The breeze and the ticking of the clock may be very relevant. The intersubjective field between patient and therapist may be wider than we realize. During long bouts of silence with a young schizoid man, I found my hovering attention drawn to the sound of a bird chirping in the distance. At first discarding the distraction as irrelevant, I finally decided to remark, matter-of-factly, that there was a bird chirping outside. The patient acknowledged that he, too, was listening to it, that he wanted to be outside—that, actually, he wanted to dive through the window! His fear of being trapped in therapy, of being exposed and made vulnerable, quickly surfaced as topics of discussion. During another prolonged silence, I found my attention drifting to the wall, where there hung a painting of a house. When I asked him what he thought of the picture, he responded, somewhat surprised by my question, that it bothered him that the door to the house was partly hidden from view by a tree. After some thought, I suggested that this was not unlike his situation—an interpretation that led to our exploring his ambivalence about letting me in.

Dips into the truly nonattaching mind of insight meditation may lead the clinician to a variety of creative, productive, and perhaps unorthodox interventions. One's attention may let go of any number of ideas about the process and boundaries of doing psychotherapy: I should be listening, the hour is up, he owes me money, this patient is neurotic, psychotherapy works. The possibilities open to evenly hovering attention at its meditative peak are infinite. Of course, there also may be many dangers to acting on such contemplative visions. The relaxed, freely hovering awareness that opens to a limitless array of possibilities is balanced by the disciplined mastery of theory and technique. For many clinicians, therapeutic contemplative awareness rests on hard-earned knowledge. As two sides of the same coin, the structurelessness of evenly suspended attention and the structure of one's conceptual framework give rise to, interpenetrate, and enrich each other.

The benefits the clinician can derive from meditative consciousness extend beyond receptive listening as a source of data about the patient. In her comprehensive paper, Speeth (1982) outlined an assortment of therapeutic gains: the ability to tolerate regression, regulate emotional withdrawal and independence, free oneself from theory, attend to oneself, avoid self-criticism, and accept oneself. Meditation can be an effective tool for the clinician's self-analysis, including the uncovering and probing of countertransference. Similar to how Kohut (1977) conceptualized empathy, Silverberg (1988) described the clinician's use of contemplative silence as a "therapeutic resonance" with the patient that is curative in and of itself.

Psychoanalytic clinicians often argue about how much the clinician should control patients while directing them into the unconscious: when and how to interpret, whether to give information and advice, when to simply listen. Suzuki (1970) offered an intriguing analogy about the contemplative mind that is relevant to these debates. The best way to control a sheep or cow, he suggested, is to provide it a large, spacious meadow and simply observe it. This is "control" in its widest sense. When absorbed in meditative awareness, the psychotherapist controls the patient and himself to the extent that he gives both the widest intersubjective field for wandering.

Meditation in Life Context

Classical psychoanalysts assumed that human nature could be fully explained by analyzing the intrapsychic world as if it were an entity unto itself. They were wrong. If there is any single impetus behind the progression of psychoanalytic theory, it is the recognition that the human psyche is entwined with the fabric of its surroundings. Recognizing this fact, we can see that meditation practice as an intrapsychic event never occurs in isolation from outside influences. It is embedded in a hierarchy of personal, social, and cultural contexts. Some meditators belong to a community of meditators, which, like any social organization, runs on a system of implicit and explicit norms, values, and doctrines. Those meditators outside such communities, consciously or unconsciously, inlay their practice into the mosaic of beliefs and behaviors that is each one's life. Within the widest environmental context, no one escapes the influences of his or her culture, which bathes everything we do, think, and feel.

People who enter meditation practice are not unlike people who enter psychotherapy. Before this decision is even reached, they may have already undergone a transformation in their personal philosophy. They realize either that something is wrong or something more is needed. They accept the fact that remedying the situation will require a change in their life context. If they venture the process of meditation or psychotherapy seriously, the effects reverberate throughout their personal and social spheres. They must reshape their daily routines in order to meditate or attend therapy; they must adopt an ideology to explain the meaning of this change to themselves and others; they shift their viewpoints and behaviors as they become acculturated to these new environments.

The reciprocal process is equally important. Their prior life context molds their new undertaking. The ways in which people engage meditation and psychotherapy reflects the power of their intrapsychic, social, and cultural dynamics. Does she cram 30 minutes of meditation somewhere into her hectic day? Does she liberally plan time around her sacrosanct therapy hour so she can make the most of it? Does he meditate one, two, five hours at a time? Does he frequently skip therapy sessions? Do they talk about, read about, write academic papers about, create poetry about their experiences or keep it to themselves? Do they try to convert others?

People often adopt meditation practice along with an accompanying Eastern philosophy of life (Buddhism, Zen, Taoism, etc.). They may swallow the philosophy and the lifestyle it endorses as an introjective whole; they may selectively adopt bits and pieces of it either to act out or remedy specific psychological problems; they may gradually sift through its complexities, thoughtfully digesting some components and internalizing them in an integrated self structure, while discarding others. When studying meditation, it may be difficult to separate out the beneficial effects of the meditation practice from the effects of the life philosophy as a therapeutic ideological agent.

Engler (1986) pointed out that meditation, in being transplanted to the West, was plucked out of its larger cultural context, in which Buddhist philosophy regarded it as a part of a total system of training, as well as a way of life. Buddhism advocates an extensive program of preliminary practices before one even attempts formal insight meditation. This "moral training," which is based on the Buddhist Eightfold Path, contains an elaborate set of instructions for changing attitudes about oneself and the world. It is a moral and ethical doctrine that outlines how one should think, perceive, and behave. Deikman (1966b) also described how some meditative traditions rest on a philosophy of "renunciation," in which one leads a life of silence, poverty, chastity, and solitude. To fully understand the impact of meditation on a Westerner's life, we must take into consideration the extent to which the person practices it within or isolated from such philosophical and cultural contexts.

From his detailed analysis of several different meditative traditions, Brown (1986) concluded that there are distinct stages in meditation that are cross-cultural and universal. However, what people experience as they progress through these stages will vary according to the philosophical/ideological perspective that colors their interpretation of their practice. These different perspectives also shape the various subjective meanings that are infused into the experience of contemplative climax, what is called "enlightenment." Similar to psychotherapy, the transformative process of meditation is a blending in which the universal and the particular give expression and contour to each other.

Epistemological Approaches

More so than any other point of contact between psychoanalysis and Eastern thought, meditation can be studied from a number of epistemological perspectives. So far, the psychoanalytic literature mostly has offered theoretical works. Many of these papers deal with

an analysis of the "oneness" experience, perhaps because psychoanalytic thinkers have been both fascinated and perplexed by this
phenomenon that seemingly flies in the face of traditional analytic
concepts about mental health. Some of these papers contain anecdotal accounts of meditation.

More than this is needed.

Psychoanalysis has raised the case-study method to both an art
and science. Unfortunately, with a few rare exceptions (e.g., Rubin,
1992b), it has not applied these exemplary methods to investigating
meditators. As long as we keep in mind the possibility that, due to
self-selection, meditators who are in therapy differ from those who
are not, we can learn a great deal from this epistemological approach,
especially about the interaction between meditative practice and personality dynamics. Biographical analyses of important figures in the
history of meditation can supplement this research, but they are no
substitute for "real time" case studies. Ideally, comprehensive studies
based on interviews and projective testing will be conducted with
nontherapy populations. Researchers will find it incrementally more
difficult to obtain subjects who are beginning, intermediate, and
moderately advanced in their skills. Although it is critical, especially
in fully understanding the implications of the unity experience, it will
be most difficult to recruit recognized masters.

Quantitative empirical work is also warranted. Brown and Engler's (1986) comprehensive Rorschach study of meditators at various
levels of development (including masters) was an invaluable contribution, as were earlier laboratory studies of novice meditators (e.g.,
Deikman, 1963; Maupin, 1965). Researchers might consider reviving
the methods and findings of the introspectionist school of psychology
that flourished in the late nineteenth century. To allow for greater
control and precision in hypothesis testing, traditional experimental
methods will be helpful. Such research will be most effective in understanding the experiences of beginning meditators, especially their
encounter with the early, psychodynamic phase of meditation practice. More than ever before, contemporary psychoanalytic research
(e.g., developmental research) is evolving in the direction of hard-
core experimental sophistication. Standing on the same ground with
other disciplines in scientific psychology, psychoanalysis can draw on
the findings from these other areas; psychoanalytic research on meditation should not lag behind. Brown and Engler, for instance, have
clearly confirmed the utility of concepts from cognitive psychology.
There is also a growing body of experimental research on the psychophysiological, affective, and personality changes associated with
meditation.

Does this raise an epistemological dilemma? Can objective and experimental methods capture the meaning of meditation as the art of delving inward to grasp the inner workings of the mind? Can the subjectivity of consciousness, in its purest sense, be understood objectively? The same sorts of questions have been tossed into the arena of psychoanalysis as a method of self-exploration. Can objective, quantitative research truly illuminate the subjectivity and intersubjectivity of the psychotherapy process? On such issues, psychoanalysis and meditation are uneasy companions.

If we accept the Taoist vision that opposites give rise to and interpenetrate each other, we can no more discard objectivity in pursuing subjectivity than we can discard day in understanding night. They are synergistic and mutually indispensable. Perhaps by holding "objective" investigations in one hand and "subjective" insights in the other, we will walk with greater balance toward the higher knowledge that transcends such distinctions.

7

Students, Teachers, and Their Relationships

Zen students are people. Zen teachers are people. Regardless of whether Eastern disciplines strive for "transcendental" realms, this fact cannot be ignored. Attempts to understand any type of spiritual training will be incomplete and inaccurate without taking into account the personality dynamics of those who pursue the training and those who conduct it, as well as the interpersonal dynamics between them. Overlooking, perhaps naively, these dynamics will deter the effectiveness of the instruction. Blatant attempts to ignore them can be disastrous.

Understanding personal and interpersonal processes is the specialty of psychoanalysis. A valuable contribution psychoanalysis has to offer the Eastern disciplines is its skill at evaluating the psychology of the student, the teacher, and their relationship. As an extremely sensitive instrument for detecting pathology, psychoanalysis can be especially useful for uncovering what leads students, teachers, and spiritual communities astray.

Hidden Motives of the Student

Unlike traditional psychoanalytic theory, which attributed most pathology to the repression of sexual and aggressive drives and the conflicts associated with them, contemporary object-relations theory and self psychology discovered that some psychological disturbances arise from disruptions in the self, e.g., the "narcissistic" and "borderline" disorders. The self may be poorly differentiated from others or lack cohesion in structure and continuity over time. Subjectively, in their experience of their own selfhood, such people feel inwardly fragile, depleted, hollow, empty, or evil. They are acutely vulnerable to social threats—especially intimate relationships—that may challenge, undermine, or overwhelm their sense of self. Any of a number of compensatory and defensive strategies may be employed to protect their narcissistic deficiencies. They may pump up their grandiosity and exhibitionism in order to disguise and offset their inner defects. In their "idealizing" and "mirroring" transferences, they may desperately seek out highly admired others with whom they can merge, or others who will reflect and affirm their omnipotence and grandeur. Through the defensive process of "splitting," they may break perceptions of themselves and others into discrete categories of "good" and "bad" in which they are perfect and others are flawed (or vice versa, for those who cling to masochistic self-perceptions). They may develop addictive and compulsive behaviors as a desperate attempt to shore up a precarious self structure. These strategies are designed to conceal from themselves and others the recognition of their internal fragility, and to prevent any further collapse of the self.

People suffering from such narcissistic and borderline disturbances may be attracted to the Eastern philosophical and meditative disciplines. As people who, unconsciously, are preoccupied with the problems of lacking an integrated self structure, they are especially enticed by the doctrine of "no-self." By accepting this doctrine as an ideal, they rationalize and justify their own inner emptiness. They consider themselves just and holy in their pursuit of enlightenment, whereas they regard others as lost and sullied. To them, attaining this purified no-self means they have reached a condition of perfection, invulnerability, and self-sufficiency. Everything bad has been purged from them. They launch themselves into their Eastern practice as spiritual junkies who use their compulsive, addictive devotion to bolster their fragile identity. While interpreting the Buddhist philosophy of non-attachment as a rationalization for avoiding intimacy with peers or as a justification for their inability to do so, they merge with the spiritual master, whom they have raised to idealized heights of perfection, and bask their weakened self in his divine acceptance of them.

Engler (1986), who pointed out many of these dynamics, described a student in one of his courses on Buddhism at the University of California at Santa Cruz. The student could not understand any difference between his own state of mind and that of enlightenment. He insisted that he already lived in a continual state of egolessness, so why bother to meditate? Suffering from an obvious narcissistic disturbance, the student oscillated between idealizing and devaluing Engler. In one class Engler was an all-knowing teacher who recognized the student's passion and genius; in the next he was just another uncaring person who did not appreciate his insights and originality. He either clung to Engler, or, with airs of superiority, rejected him. The classes were as unpredictable and turbulent as the student's changing perceptions. From such experiences as a teacher of meditation, Engler concluded that two major aspects of Buddhism attracted people suffering from borderline and narcissistic disorders: the grandiose perfection they attribute to the state of "no-self," and the hope of a mirroring and/or idealizing transferential relationship with a powerful, admired teacher. Unfortunately, he also pointed out, meditative practice often causes such people more harm than good by unraveling an already weak self structure. Following the principles of a developmental model, as discussed in Chapter 3, Engler believed that such people need first to create an integrated self before they can pursue the Buddhist path to no-self.

We should recognize, parenthetically, that these dynamics are not limited to Eastern disciplines. Narcissistic pathology runs rampant in many religions. Quests for perfection by pursuing the divine, for merging with or being mirrored by an idealized leader, for propping up an enfeebled self by clinging to devotional practices are universal religious phenomena (Finn & Gartner, 1992; Rubin & Suler, 1992). With its emphasis on no-self and nonattachment, Eastern philosophies may give these dynamics an added spin.

As contemporary psychoanalytic theory advanced, it recognized that narcissistic disorders of the self cannot be cleanly separated from pathology that stems from repression of sexual and aggressive instincts and the resulting neurotic conflicts, particularly oedipal conflicts. Within people who obviously suffer from narcissistic pathology, there often are oedipal themes. Within neurotically repressed and even "normal" people—who, theoretically, have an intact self—there often are traces of narcissistic problems. The dynamics of conflict and self, drives and narcissistic defects, interact in complex ways.

Like any behavior, the pursuit of an Eastern practice is multiply determined. For some people, the influence of narcissistic pathology will be blatant. For others, their predilection for Asian ideas may stem from complex mixtures of intrapsychic conflict and subtle narcissistic processes. Even normal people studying Buddhism, Taoism, or Zen may show shades of neurotic defenses, conflict, narcissism, oedipal and pre-oedipal issues intermixed. Psychodynamic analyses have revealed a variety of such personality dynamics that underlie some Westerners' preoccupation with Eastern disciplines (Engler, 1986; Epstein, 1986, 1990b; Fauteux, 1987; Hendlin, 1983; Rubin, 1992b). With the exception of Rubin's intensive case study and Fauteux's journey to the Orient to formally interview Westerners who became Buddhist monks, the findings of these studies are based mostly on the researchers' anecdotal accounts as clinicians and/or members of Buddhist communities. Many of the personality dynamics that draw people to the East interlock with the doctrine of no-self and the quest for the oneness experience; they revolve around the meanings related to having or not having an autonomous self. Some personality dynamics resonate with other themes in Eastern philosophy, such as nonattachment, intuition, irrationality, and equanimity. The descriptions of ten psychodynamic issues that follow overlap. They form clusters of maladaptive personality traits or are related facets of the maladaptive personality structures that may incline a person toward Eastern thought.

1. Fear of Autonomy

The search for enlightenment and the unity experience may be motivated by a fear of being a separate, autonomous person. To be autonomous is to be responsible, self-sufficient, assertive, competent in handling life tasks, and optimally independent from others. Some Eastern students may lack the conviction or the ability to live their own lives and make their own choices. The fears, conflicts, and deficiencies surrounding such issues can be escaped by defensively pursuing the idealized condition of "egolessness." If Buddhism demands that one should only strive to abandon the self, these people falsely believe, then working toward an independent, autonomous identity is an irrelevant, even poisonous, endeavor.

2. Refusal to Assume Responsibility

The fear of taking charge of oneself is an especially important nucleus within the fear of autonomy. The no-self philosophy may become a justification for detaching oneself from responsibility for one's own life or the world in which one lives. The Buddhist goal of freeing oneself from egocentric needs and desires becomes an excuse to avoid the anxiety of making difficult decisions and taking responsibility for them. One might make a mistake, feel inadequate, be rejected by others if an action is taken. Being detached from the accountability to oneself and the world hides an underlying self-doubt and lack of self-worth. In defense of themselves, some Western Buddhist monks interviewed by Fauteux (1987) presented a hypothetical dilemma to him. Would he help a man who had been hit by a car? If Fauteux saved him, the man might subsequently lead a life in which he was miserable and inflicted pain on others. These consequences would be the responsibility of Fauteux, who myopically interfered with a natural course of events—a death in an accident.

3. Withdrawal from Relationships

The Buddhist philosophy of nonattachment may reinforce needs to avoid social involvement. Mature relationships can be both demanding and risky. The Eastern student may dodge an assortment of anxieties associated with the possibility of being intimately involved with another—fear of being exposed, vulnerable, humiliated, hurt, rejected, abandoned, misunderstood, engulfed, defeated, used. Some of the well-known biographical accounts of Westerners-turned-Zennists are suspiciously sparse in the authors' descriptions of their families and love relationships. Some students find in the Buddhist philosophy a viable explanation for their alienation and loneliness. Schizoids may use it as an excuse to withdraw into their internal world rather than engage others. Other devotees may specifically target the spiritual ideal of detaching oneself from possessive cravings and desires as a means to absolve themselves of sexual fears. When Fauteux (1987) asked one monk why he avoided women, the monk explained that they evoked lust, a mental state that interfered with the stilling of his mind in meditation. Fauteux found that the monastery lifestyle may turn the flight from women into a virtue. The creed of detachment created an atmosphere where feelings and needs were isolated from others, where sexual tensions evaporated.

4. Grief and Mourning

The search for enlightenment may serve as a substitute for the grief and mourning process. For many students, a significant personal loss precipitates their enterprise into Eastern practice. Some Buddhist and Zen teachers deliberately accentuate issues about death and dying to motivate their students—for example, meditating on the image of a decaying corpse. Matthiessen (1987) described a Zen retreat in which the master provoked the meditating students into deeper practice by reminding them of the recent death of one of their friends. "Who among you will be next?" he asked. "Now sit!" (p. 25). Although the confrontation with death may be a powerful means to stimulate progress in spiritual practice, it may also drive students to use their practice as a defensive avoidance of the personal issues surrounding real loss. The social withdrawal that typically occurs after experiencing a loss may be acted out through the Buddhist doctrine of detachment. Students may try to eschew the anger, confusion, and depression of the mourning process by reaching for deliverance into no-self. They may try to quell their longing for a reunion with the lost person by using the quest for spiritual unity as a substitute.

5. Avoidance of Emotions

Any anxiety-arousing affect can be defensively evaded through the quest for nonattachment and selflessness. Disciples may interpret the mythical equanimity of the Buddha as a sign that one should be devoid of any disturbing feeling. Anger often is considered one of the primary culprits. Many Buddhists believe they should never show or feel hostility toward others. Fears of being punished or retaliated against, losing control of oneself, destroying or driving off others, jeopardizing a fantasized fusion with others may all be quelled by the self-hypnotic conviction that one can transcend rage and its many devious derivatives. Instead of developing the psychological strengths to control aggression, students may simply try to divert themselves from being consciously aware of it. In the transcendental experience of no-self, they may seek "oneness with the all" in which the tension between self and other, need and frustration, is magically erased.

6. Passivity and Dependence

Struggles against one's anger, competitiveness, and self-assertion may lead to a passive-dependent style. Buddhist philosophy can be misinterpreted to cultivate such maladaptive traits. In the name of egolessness and detachment from desires, students may shun any behavior that smacks of competition, slip off into amotivational lassitude, and dependently bend to the will of others rather than assert their own wants or needs. Such people may have difficulty feeling grounded. They may appear "spaced out." A passive-dependent style may make the student especially susceptible to the powers of the charismatic spiritual leader.

7. Self-punitive Guilt

Some students may quickly decipher Buddhism and Zen as an ascetic practice. They boycott their desires and attachments as a forum for acting out their self-punitive need and the guilt that underlies it. Depriving oneself may express a variety of self-punitive and masochistic issues stretched along the entire developmental spectrum: identifying with the aggressor or depriving other (and, simultaneously, with the person being abused or deprived); playing out one's self-representation of being "bad" and worthy of nothing; abandoning oneself before being abandoned; clinging to the moral superiority that arises from the conviction that one is enduring a hardship or performing a difficult, self-sacrificing task; aborting one's desires and ambitions to avoid the possibility of a success that will destroy a selfobject tie or symbolize a guilt-inducing oedipal victory.

8. Competitiveness and the Quest for Perfection

For some students, enlightenment symbolizes a state of personal perfection. The quest for this condition satisfies the narcissistic need to rid oneself of faults and placate the grandiose self. It may become a forum for oedipal strivings and sibling rivalry. By working toward enlightenment, one becomes better than the non-Buddhist. One is filled with elitist pride and self-righteousness. Comparisons and competitions exist even within the Buddhist or Zen community. Who is at a higher plane than whom on the ladder of spiritual development? Who has solved the most koans, traveled to Asia, studied with the best masters, written the most books, or given the most prestigious workshops on spirituality? Buddhist or Zen training turns into a game of spiritual materialism or "spiritual yuppyism," as Jeffrey Rubin (personal communication) called it—a game in which Westerners, while chasing the idealized condition of no-self, seem to be crying out, "I'm the best at being nobody!"

9. The Devaluing of Reason and Intellect

The emphasis on intuition, paradox, and irrationality in Zen offers a style of thinking that lures many personality types. Obsessive-compulsive tendencies can be buried beneath the (sometimes compulsive) preoccupation with ontological, metaphysical, and spiritual conundrums of Eastern philosophy. The histrionic flair for vague, impressionistic perceptions and "intuitive" actions (which mostly serve as a defense against the unconscious) may slip comfortably into the Zen knack for nonrational mentation; one wants to have experiences, not explain or analyze them. Just as clinicians are sometimes guilty of adopting the "therapist's defense" by answering a question with a question, eastern students may be guilty of the "Zen defense." With their back to the wall on a sensitive issue, they may resort to the elusive explanation that both X and not-X are true, or that neither is true. The truth of the matter—how one thinks, feels, or behaves—cannot be explained, because words and logic will not suffice. Everything is intuitive. One should not, as Zen states, even specifically identify oneself as a Buddhist or, for that matter, as anything else. The truth of one's identity and personal experience cannot be fully appreciated or understood by others: it is too subjective, elusive, transcendental. The Zen defense may actually be a type of narcissistic defense in which one protects the inner, vulnerable self from any threatening exposure. To preserve their fragile sense of having a unique identity, some people may need to feel that others cannot grasp them by understanding them.

10. Escape from Intrapsychic Experience

On the broadest scale, the Eastern doctrine of no-self and egolessness can be used as a rationalization to escape any unconscious fear, wish, fantasy, memory, or trauma. By striving for the abandonment of all aspects of selfhood, one can justify the "letting go"—the denial, suppression, or repression—of any anxiety-arousing insecurity. The Zen philosophy may become a dissociated womb in which one hides from oneself and any element in the world that has the potential to awaken insight into oneself; being "blanked out" or "spaced out" is mistaken for the unity experience. Epstein (1990b) suggested that Easternizing Westerners may dissociate themselves from anything unwholesome they perceive in themselves, and consequently find themselves irresistibly attracted to a powerful spiritual leader who contains the attributes which they try to disavow. Engler (1986) noted that two distinct populations in particular tend to become attracted to Buddhism and often appear at meditation retreats: those in late adolescence, making a transition to adulthood, and those passing through the midlife crisis. They attempt to use Buddhism as a short-cut to bypass the challenges they must confront at their stage of development. Misinterpreting the Buddhist teachings about no-self, they believe they can sidestep the whole array of issues concerning identity formation that stand before them.

The Student's Strengths

Under ideal circumstances, Buddhist and Zen practice can remedy some of these maladaptive dynamics. Many of them arise from a misinterpretation, rather than an accurate understanding, of Eastern philosophy. They all involve a clinging attachment. To fully apply the doctrine of nonattachment, one develops the ability to let go of fears about autonomy, responsibility, intimacy; to let go of guilt, self-punishment, passivity, dependence, withdrawal, narcissistic pride, competition, and the quest for personal perfection; to let go of denial, suppression, repression. When fully extended, this ability to detach opens the person to new dimensions and possibilities within the intrapsychic world, rather than locking the person into a rigid, maladaptive set of dynamics. It is an exercise in enhancing the fluidity of self-awareness and subjective meaning. Even the narcissistic and neurotic components of trying to be a "good" Buddhist, Zennist, or Taoist unravel, because one must also let go of the inflexible attachment to Eastern practice, including meditation and the quest for enlightenment. Paradoxically, one must even let go of the doctrine of letting go. An old Buddhist story tells of two traveling monks who met a woman at a river crossing. One shied away; the other helped her across. As the two monks continued on their journey, the first confronted the other. "You know we are not supposed even to look at women, and you carried one across the water!" The second monk replied, "This is true, but I put her down on the other side, whereas you are still carrying her in your mind."

Suzuki (1970) was fond of the Zen saying, "By pulling out the weeds, we give nourishment to the plant." When weeds are uprooted, they should not be thrown away; rather, they are placed next to the plant as a source of nourishment. In meditation, one detaches from the waves of mental distractions, but then learns how to use the "energy" of those waves to enrich the contemplative process. In the Zen training of detachment, one's maladaptive personality traits are not tossed away by repression or denial; they are observed for what they are and used as self-nourishment. When uprooted by the observing self, pathological patterns, once maladaptive, can now destructure into subcomponent clusters of affect and subjective meanings—the new, self-nourishing "fertilizer" that one can adaptively access, reorganize, and assimilate.

The Buddhist or Zen student's strength rests on the ability to undertake the wide-sweeping process of nonclinging and the deep spiraling into the intrapsychic realm that is stimulated by nonclinging. It also rests on the ability to utilize what is found there. Whether or not we regard meditation or Buddhist practice in general as a "regression," the personality and psychodynamic factors that facilitate a "regression in service of the ego" apply also to the student who pursues these Eastern practices.

Schafer (1958) described six such factors that facilitate productive excursions into the unconscious. First, the person must possess a *well-developed set of affect signals*. When the dive into the unconscious threatens to get out of hand—when it comes too close to drives, affects, and fantasies not assimilable in consciousness—appropriate signals must trigger the search for defensive disguises of content or a reversal of the entire process. One must have confidence in these signals. Second, one must possess a *secure sense of self* and a stable identity that can tolerate momentary blurring or loss of boundaries (an idea also expressed by the developmentalists, as described in Chapter 3). Third, there must be a *relative mastery of early traumata*. This mastery implies that the crises and crucial experiences of early development have not been completely sealed off from the development of the total personality, but have been given a place in it and have undergone some measure of transformation and working through. It also allows the person to experience how it once felt to have been a child, or to have felt receptive, helpless, omnipotent, and fluid in internal state and object relations. Fourth, the person must possess *moderateness of superego pressures*, rather than archaic severity, in close correlation with this internal fluidity. One must be able to let go of defenses and "play" intrapsychically, without severe anxiety and guilt. Fifth, a *history of adequate trust and mutuality in interpersonal relations* supports the feeling that the outcomes of the process will be empathically acknowledged, rather than responded to with panic, withdrawal, or punishment. Finally, *self-awareness and personal and effective communication to others* guarantees that the person will strive to integrate the outcomes meaningfully into the culture of the surrounding community. One attempts to use the unique experience of the unconscious to further one's social adaptation and impact, rather than withdraw into dissociation, self-restriction, or negative identity.

There is another intrapsychic strength that may be a prerequisite for the Buddhist, Zen, or Taoist student. At a deep intrapsychic level, the ability to undertake the all-encompassing process of detaching may require the ability to mourn. By letting go of all thoughts, feelings, and perceptions, one realizes, as described in Buddhist philosophy, "the arising and passing away of all things"—a realization that penetrates to a profound grief over the loss of the world and oneself. Aberbach (1987), in fact, suggested that mysticism and grief are parallel processes. Withdrawal from the world after a personal loss is comparable to the detachment in mystical traditions that drives the person inward. Yearning and internally searching for the lost person resembles the yearning and searching for the oneness experience. The anger, confusion, and depression that emerge in grief parallel the mystical "dark night of the soul" and the Zen Great Doubt. Union with the lost person by internalizing his or her presence is the unity experience of enlightenment in which self and object are realized as interpenetrating each other. In both grief and mysticism, this culmination of the mourning process transforms the individual, and finally leads one back to normal social life. The whole process, as Nietzsche suggested, is driven by the possession of "will." Ultimately, the detachment from and negation of all things leads to the willful affirmation of life.

The Teacher: Quirks, Pathology, and Crazy Wisdom

Sooner or later, many philosophical and autobiographical accounts of Eastern practices stumble on the unsettling fact that enlightened masters don't always look so enlightened. Like anyone else, they have their idiosyncracies, insecurities, and neurotic hang-ups. Suzuki (1970) described the hermit Zen master who could be found in his wilderness hut talking to and answering himself. Van de Wetering (1978) mentioned his Japanese roshi, who hated dentists, loved to watch baseball and movies about Africa, and avoided middle-aged ladies who came to ask questions. He also recalled an incident with his American teacher, who drove his truck into a ditch. Refusing to believe he couldn't drive it back out, despite van de Wetering's persistent advice, he tried over and over again until the engine was exhausted. While mentioning Zen masters who tended to lose their tempers, chase women, or became preoccupied with worldly ambitions, Matthiessen (1987) concluded that flaws in character prevent great teachings from taking healthy root. Are there any teachers who are not flawed? Tetsugen, Matthiessen's American Zen roshi, replied, "Such masters are very rare" (p. 228).

Unfortunately, the character defects are sometimes far from innocuous. Zen legends tell of competing masters who tried to assassinate each other (and in some cases succeeded). In more contemporary times, recognized Zen teachers have been accused and proven guilty of a number of outright pathological conducts. On several occasions, Japanese and American Zen masters, some of them married, were charged with seducing emotionally vulnerable students or carrying out long-term, secret affairs with students. In some cases the accusations were denied, in some not. The successor to an American Zen abbot, after being robbed at knifepoint, was arrested for brandishing in public an unloaded pistol that he had taken from the body of a suicide victim he had previously discovered in a park. A widely respected Tibetan Buddhist master suffered from chronic alcoholism. He drank gin while delivering public speeches, which were considered brilliant, powerful, and compassionate. In the end, surrounded by an inner circle of students who alone knew of his disease, he lay dying in bed, hallucinating, incontinent, his body eaten away by alcohol. In an incident that brought American Buddhism to the heights of scandal, the administrators of one community went public with the confession that their regent had been infected with AIDS for nearly three years; fully aware of his condition, he had neither taken precautions to protect his sexual partners nor informed them of the truth.

Buddha stated that enlightenment frees one from personal desires, brings an end to all suffering, and creates genuine compassion, an emancipation that, seemingly, should dissolve pathological behaviors. Why, then, do teachers who are supposedly enlightened display such obvious psychological problems? There are a variety of possible explanations.

One is that these teachers are not fully enlightened. Some may say that they have achieved only *partial enlightenment*. The Buddhist literature describes pre-enlightenment experiences that sometimes are mistaken for the real thing. One Zen school of thought stresses that a person works gradually toward full enlightenment, as opposed to those schools which insist that full enlightenment is always spontaneous and sudden. The Zen "Oxherding Pictures" portray a series of steps leading through brief glimpses, first encounters, the full-blown immersion into the oneness experience, and the eventual return to everyday life. Some masters claim that pre-enlightenment experiences produce powerful, beneficial changes in personality, but that these changes eventually revert to the status quo. At the "highest" level of enlightenment, the transformation of the person is permanent. Masters who have not attained this level are still vulnerable to their character defects. This line of reasoning can sound like a rationalization, but it bears some similarities to the kind of thinking evident in psychoanalytic discussions about whether or not someone is "fully analyzed."

There also may be *false enlightenment*. Spiritual teachers and psychoanalytic thinkers alike have speculated about oneness and no-self experiences that are not just preliminary versions of true enlightenment, but qualitatively different and pathological, as compared to the genuine state. Excursions into these states, though sometimes interpreted as enlightenment experiences, may actually reinforce, rather than alleviate, a spiritual teacher's psychological deficiencies. Some teachers, because of their character flaws, may be more susceptible to these states in the first place. In his review of the literature, Rutstein (1985) highlighted the distinction between the oneness experience in which there is a loss of self, when fusion with the other results in anxiety and identity confusion, and the expansion of the self, when unity with the other embodies a simultaneous experience of separateness and oneness. Epstein (1989) described various forms of emptiness that could be mistaken for oneness: emptiness as the internalized remnant of emotional sustenance not given; as a more tolerable substitution for rage or self-hatred; as an inability to integrate self and object representations; as the feelings of unreality and estrangement resulting from idealized images of the self that are not matched by actual experience; as the internal void in the representational world resulting from the constant devaluation of others; as a schizoid defense against feeling and attachments to others. Hendlin (1983) also outlined an assortment of "pernicious oneness" experiences, including states of dissociation, existential vacuum, and moments of "confluence."

Even when the oneness experience is genuine, it may need to be worked through. This idea is implied in the Zen schools that emphasize a gradual progression toward enlightenment. Some Zen masters believe that *satori*, even of the "sudden" type, does not automatically produce permanent changes, that the experience must be cultivated and integrated into everyday life—not unlike the psychoanalytic process of working through one's insight into unconscious dynamics. They claim that the enlightenment experience itself will eventually fade in its effects if it is not continually rejuvenated (psychoanalysts similarly speak of "tune-up" analyses). Essentially, according to this view, *unassimilated enlightenment* wears off. In the case of psychologically impaired teachers, this drops them back into susceptibility to pathological behaviors.

The position that enlightenment needs to be worked through suggests that its effects are felt primarily within limited zones of the personality and not immediately throughout the entire personality structure. Encouraged by Anna Freud (1963), contemporary psychoanalytic theory recognizes that there are different developmental lines for various sectors of intrapsychic functions. To this collection some theorists may wish to add the "spiritual" function or sector. Although the various sectors interact, development may be relatively more advanced in some than in others. Therefore, enlightened Zen masters may have blossomed in one target zone of their internal world, but other areas may remain unaffected. "Working through" means integrating the oneness experience into and using it to transform the other developmental realms. The Zen teacher Philip Kapleau (1980b) insisted that enlightenment does not clear up personality flaws, but rather highlights them. Before awakening, one can easily ignore personal imperfections. Afterwards, they are painfully obvious. Only continuous training after enlightenment, Kapleau stated, can purify so that one's behaviors are in accord with one's understandings. Muzika (1990) added that misguided enlightenment experiences may result in a detaching from the personal self in preference for transcendental flights. No longer caring about one's personality, one makes no attempt to change, and pathological traits continue to fester. Withdrawal from social relationships—a feature of some "enlightened" people and an obvious sign of deficient object relations—may make an individual especially susceptible to stagnation.

At a think-tank session held in Washington, DC in 1988, several noted authorities on Eastern practice and psychotherapy addressed the issue of why spiritual groups go awry and spiritual teachers become pathological (see Sanders, 1990). Jack Engler, one of the participants, used the analogy of trying to carry a golden egg through life without dropping it. Of course, in reality, one is always stumbling, dropping, and retrieving the egg or getting a new one. The spiritual process necessarily involves dropping the egg. Zen, Mountain (1983) concluded, is the art of failure. The most important aspect of working through enlightenment (not unlike working through insight in psychoanalysis) may be the encounter and mastery of failures in using enlightenment to transform the deficiencies in one's personality. An important trait in this process—perhaps a line of development in itself that overlaps with superego functions—is what the participants at the conference called "virtue," the strength of character, as defined in Buddhist tradition, that inclines one toward ethical and moral concerns. Without it, the supposedly enlightened person may simply become a loose cannon.

All the votes are not in regarding the notion of a "spiritual" sector or function within personality structure. Exactly what constitutes this spiritual sector, how it differs from the other sectors, and how the enlightenment experience is assimilated into and transforms these other lines of development are all issues that remain to be clarified.

The enlightened master is not an intrapsychic island isolated from outside influences. The oneness experience occurs in a social, cultural, and historical context. In the Eastern disciplines, the teachers, knowingly or unknowingly, train their students within this context. If characterological defects linger in a spiritual leader who has attained enlightenment, the surrounding social and institutional structure, with its complex system of norms and sanctions, may help regulate the teacher's behavior, perhaps by reinforcing the moral/ethical dimensions of object relational intrapsychic functions. How students react to the teacher's pathological influence—whether they reinforce or deter it—is also influenced by the social and cultural context. The various scandals in American Buddhist communities may be explained, in part, by a *contextually misplaced enlightenment;* removed from an appropriate governing environment that checks behaviors, the master runs amuck.

In her review of these scandals, Butler (1990) cited several noted authorities who described a variety of social and cultural factors that influence the spiritual teacher's behavior. In Asia, monasteries run on a strict moral code that demands chastity, abstinence, and duty to the monastery, as well as the surrounding community. Importing Buddhist teachers without the surrounding institutional structure may release them from these influential restraints, thus allowing pathological defects to surface. Asian students also approach teachers in a more subtle way than do Americans. Bound by cultural demands to respect authority, Asian students openly show deference to the pathological teacher, but within their highly interiorized "private self," as described by Roland (1988), they may reserve judgment and silently withdraw affection, respect, and willingness to internalize the teacher. On the other hand, because of a widespread cultural neglect of spirituality, some Americans are hungry for Eastern religions, a bit naive in discerning healthy from flawed teachers, and willing to introject immediately whatever comes their way. They cannot openly show deference for someone whom inwardly they no longer respect, without feeling hypocritical. To avoid cognitive dissonance, some abandon the teacher, whereas others defend against their inner feelings. As compared to Asians, American students may be better self-objects for supporting and perpetuating the master's pathological dynamics. In his cross-cultural analysis of Asians, Roland mentioned that it is the inferior person's duty to be dependent on his or her superiors as a way to idealize them and boost their self-regard; but in return, it is the superior's duty to be attuned to and satisfy the subordinate's needs. A deemphasis in the West on this reciprocity of obligations may release spiritual teachers from empathic attunement to their students and clear the way for their pathology to flourish.

The contextual misplacement of enlightened masters that contributed to the scandals in American Buddhism was compounded by deficiencies in the cross-cultural interface between East and West. When spiritual leaders in Asia were confronted about the behaviors of their representatives in the West, they resorted to cultural tendencies toward face-saving, avoiding conflict, and safeguarding hierarchies. Arnold Cooper, a Zen student interviewed by Butler (1990), suggested that the Japanese have no notion of hypocrisy, as Westerners do, and consider it noble to withhold their feelings in order to preserve group harmony. But when this attitude is transplanted to the West under the banner of enlightenment, Cooper stated, the results can be cultish and bizarre.

On a smaller social scale, pathological dynamics within the social structure surrounding the teacher may interlock with and perpetuate the teacher's pathology. Several of the authorities cited by Butler (1990) described how the dynamics in the spiritual community paralleled those in dysfunctional families, especially families involving alcoholism and sexual abuse. Serving as narcissistic extensions of spiritual leaders and as selfobjects for reinforcing their grandiose-exhibitionist selves, many students become "enablers" who assist the leaders' pathologies. They reenact, rather than understand and re-solve, the pathological dynamics of addiction, incest, and emotional abuse within their own families of origin. They idealize and become clones of the teacher in the hope of receiving a healing transforma-tion. One student, who had watched her own father die of alcohol-ism, admitted that she served a glass of gin every morning to her Tibetan teacher. Entire Buddhist communities may engage in massive denial and rationalizations of the teacher's addictions, sexual impro-prieties, and unempathic acting out. Holding tight to their need to idealize the master, the entourage of the Tibetan teacher believed he might be immune to alcoholism because of his spiritual powers. Even on his deathbed, when he was overcome by alcoholic dementia, some students interpreted his incoherence and hallucinations as evidence of a spiritually enlightened condition. The entire range of a teacher's suspect behaviors, from minor quirks and indiscretions to gross viola-tions of human decency, may be interpreted as spiritual "lessons." The students believe that the master is acting from knowledge that far exceeds their understanding—what the Tibetan teacher called "crazy wisdom." Their faith leads them to the heights of spiritual overdeter-mination: they attribute everything the teacher says and does to his godlike wisdom.

At this point in the discussion, it is difficult to consider the pos-sibility that "crazy wisdom" exists. However, the Eastern spiritual literature is filled with reverent stories of what may be called *idiosyn-cratic expressions of enlightenment*. In using the term *crazy wisdom*, the Tibetan teacher was referring to a minor but authentic tradition of ec-centric Tibetan yogis who used unusual methods to train their stu-dents. Zen legends tell of masters who twist disciples' noses, launch surprise attacks with sticks, and cut off fingers. Sadistic by Western standards, these masters, according to the legend, successfully trig-gered enlightenment in their students—for which the students were eternally grateful. Taoist myths often portray the sage as a fool. Even in the West, the notion of the insane genius or the spiritually insight-ful lunatic has widespread appeal. For one of his parables, Nietzsche, the existential mystic, picked a "madman," found wandering in the graveyard, to proclaim the vision of oneness and eternal recurrence to the townspeople, who failed to understand his ravings.

In his analysis, Podvoll (1979) concluded that psychosis and mysticism bear many similarities. For shorter or longer periods, they converge on the same path that is a part of everyone, regardless of health or illness: they both are attempts at self-transformation. On the other hand, Buckley (1981) delineated the various differences between mysticism and the pathology that is psychosis. Our understanding of the relationship between gifted spiritual insight and psychological disturbance is muddied both by our needs to idealize and our limitations in fully comprehending "enlightenment," which very few people experience. It is possible that the destructuring of self and world in Eastern practices opens the spiritual master's eyes to realms of disarray and emptiness not understood by others; that it forces some masters to use controversial disorienting and depatterning techniques to convey this understanding; that it adversely affects the psychological health of some masters, perhaps tipping them over into madness. Some masters may intentionally use their own personality quirks and flaws in healthy service of their teaching, which, in psychoanalytic ego psychology, could be described as the ability to separate behaviors from their pathological roots and move them into a more adaptive position of "secondary autonomy."

But, in some cases, it is obvious that pathological teachers are simply pathological, that their outlandish behavior expresses no crazy wisdom that is of any healthy use to anyone. At best, it expresses only the "wisdom" of their unconscious as it struggles with the subjective meanings of their troubled lives intersecting with some type of "oneness" experience.

Finally, to explain why some teachers appear pathological, we may conclude that "true" enlightenment does not exist at all. We may regard *enlightenment as an unattainable ideal.* Perhaps it is part of human nature to wish for, and come to believe in, some state of perfection in which personal defects fall away, suffering vanishes, and contentment reigns. Out of that need, some people may catapult spiritual leaders to fantasized heights of purity, even though they are still human, with human frailties. Students project their own visions of an ideal self onto the leader, a vision that varies from person to person. The process may degenerate into an acting out of pathological dynamics, but in some cases it can be beneficial. The idealized condition called "enlightenment," interpreted subjectively and differently by each person, can serve as a fuel and a template for the self's healthy strivings to correct its developmental derailments and to actualize its nuclear design.

The issue of why some enlightened teachers suffer from ordinary flaws boils down to one of the oldest, most basic of theological debates: How can the divine manifest itself in this often imperfect world? How can it appear in human form? It is the paradox of the interpenetration between the absolute and the relative, no-self and self. On the psychological level, the spiritual master's ability to be "fully" enlightened or to completely "work through" enlightenment corresponds with the ability to understand this interpenetration of the universal and the individual—to understand how the absolute is expressed through one's particular subjective world (including one's shortcomings) and how the meanings of one's subjective world come to be expressed through the absolute.

The Student-Teacher Relationship

Many studies of the Eastern disciplines tend to concentrate on the internal changes within the student while overlooking the interpersonal context in which those changes occur. The relationship between the student and teacher is emotionally charged, reciprocally impactful, and probably one of the most important catalysts in the transformation process. For our knowledge of Eastern disciplines to be complete, a two-person psychology must supplement the more typical one-person psychology: the intersubjective field between teacher and student cannot be neglected, especially while examining training methods such as Zen that specialize in triggering the purest realization of "subjectivity."

Psychoanalysis has long recognized the power of the bipersonal context, and has developed to a fine art the appraisal and orchestration of this context for the purpose of facilitating therapeutic change. Transference and countertransference have been its two frontline, carefully tuned instruments for working in the dyadic field. Because the Eastern teacher's expertise with these concepts, by comparison, is less developed, psychoanalysis has much to offer. Drawing a comparison to neglectful psychotherapists, Engler (1986) noted the heavy price paid by meditation teachers who tend to ignore the transferential aspects of their relationship with students. Students become pseudosubmissive, while keeping the therapeutic process split off from their deeper thoughts and feelings about the teacher. Outside the formal boundaries of the training, they act out those reactions— which, Engler noted, may partially account for the orgies (sometimes literally) of sensual gratification that occur after and between meditation retreats. Consequently, the transformational process intended by the training becomes shallow and stalemated.

Students' reaction to the Eastern teacher often takes the shape of the selfobject transferences described by Kohut (1977). In the hope of sustaining their identity, they seek out a mirroring of their needs and ambitions from powerful authority figures. They may also attempt to merge with the idealized leaders in order to participate in their perceived qualities of strength, calmness, and wisdom. As evident by the scandals in several American Buddhist communities, the pathological consequences of this idealizing transference, for both the student and teacher, can easily get out of hand when it goes unrecognized. In some cases the idealizing of the teacher oscillates with unrealistic, intense devaluing that is triggered by disappointments and frustrations. Because the Zen or Buddhist student is concerned (at least consciously) with spiritual issues, the mirroring and idealizing reactions may take on a special quality that is reminiscent of the "ultimate rescuer fantasy" described by Yalom (1980). Students pine for an infallible, all-knowing being to protect and rescue them from all the existential travails of being human: fears of responsibility, isolation, meaninglessness, and death. They seek the ultimate, healing transformation that will give their life purpose and direction without suffering.

Robert, a 45-year-old psychologist, came to me for therapy because he had heard of my interests in Eastern philosophy. During the first hour, I learned of his long-standing devotion to spiritual development—how he frequently attended workshops, lectures, and retreats concerning spirituality and Eastern religions, read widely on these topics, and had established a series of somewhat loose ties with teachers of various spiritual and religious persuasions. He had also been in therapy—including a two-year Jungian analysis—several times. In each relationship, however, he felt the spiritual work never progressed deep enough, so he typically left after a few meetings. In our work together he preferred not to dwell on his past—particularly on his relationship with his cold, critical, unempathic mother, which he felt he had already analyzed thoroughly in his previous treatments. Instead, he preferred to understand how his life "related to the cosmos," mostly, he hoped, by exploring his dreams, of which he reported many, usually centering on themes of going on a trip, being kidnapped and controlled, and being visited by a benign celestial being. This last dream was particularly important to him, since he felt he was searching for a spiritual "guide."

Within a few sessions, his devaluing of me quickly set in. He was not sure that I was experienced enough in spiritual matters. I seemed distant, sometimes "too clinical." I sensed that he was preparing to move on to the next ultimate rescuer. Walking a thin line between mirroring his spiritual needs and trying to understand their underlying psychological determinants, I attempted to interpret (sometimes by adapting Zen sayings and anecdotes) the dynamics that seemed to be quickly subverting our work together: his fear of being neglected and hurt as his mother had done to him; his longing for and fear of being attached to someone who might "transform" him; his tendency to devalue and leave therapists and spiritual teachers, rather than express anger toward them or work through the anxieties of establishing an intimate relationship. Some of these interpretations approached their mark. Nevertheless, in our sixth session, he apologetically announced that he had decided to change to another psychotherapist whose spiritual expertise seemed particularly useful to him.

Mirroring and idealizing transferences in the Eastern disciplines do not always lead to pathological acting out. As in effective psychoanalytic therapy, these dynamics may be therapeutic. The mirroring received by students and their idealization of the teacher may, indeed, fortify their sense of self. Not unlike the psychotherapist, the teacher affirms the student's desires for self-transformation and acts as a role model to be identified with as a source of strength and confidence in attaining this goal. Guiding the student through the destructuring process that leads to no-self, the master serves the selfobject function of validating, holding, and containing the student's experiences. In the Zen tradition, during week-long meditation retreats, the student each day visits the master in *dokusan*—a brief meeting in which the master assesses the student's progress and offers advice and encouragement, thereby revitalizing the continuity of the selfobject tie. By working more closely in an apprenticeship with a teacher, in what is called *shiho* study in Zen, students participate in a lineage of masters, perhaps even receiving "dharma transmission," which places them in a long and prestigious historical tradition that nourishes their self-esteem.

Students of Zen (e.g., Herrigel, 1971; Matthiessen, 1987) describe how the merging of pupil and teacher into becoming "one" later allows the student to separate while still carrying the teacher internally. Matthiessen compared it to a father-son relationship. As in psychotherapy, the selfobject bond eventually leads to the individuation of the student and the strengthening of the student's self structure via the internalization of the teacher's positive attributes. In addition to the self-affirming effects of idealization and mirroring functions, the student also benefits from the "twinship" transference (Kohut, 1984): the self feels strengthened by simply being alongside the teacher (and other students), who has similar needs, interests, and ideals. As compared to psychoanalysts, Zen teachers may not possess elaborate conceptual understandings of these selfobject transferences. However, many may be aware of and attempt to deal with such reactions. Some Eastern teachers (e.g., Kapleau, 1980b; Kauz, 1977) specifically mentioned the student's tendency to unrealistically idealize them. They advise their colleagues, who may be tempted to satisfy their own self-esteem and pride, to behave in a balanced way that does not exaggerate that idealizing nor punish the pendulum swings into devaluing the teacher. Such advice, some psychoanalysts might say, speaks to the need for an optimal equilibrium between frustrating and gratifying the selfobject transference reactions.

Other aspects of the therapeutic relationship between Zen student and teacher parallel those between patient and clinician. There must be an appropriate *interpersonal fit* between the two. Ideally, the subjective worlds of the teacher and student optimally overlap, thus maximizing the empathic bonding in how the training is subjectively experienced. Matthiessen (1987) noted that the powerful father-son feeling does not develop for all master-disciple dyads. The depth to which the student works with the master will depend partly on the student's *ability to tap the master's expertise*. Both therapists and Zen masters are like bells: people who tap them lightly get tiny sounds; those who strike hard receive loud, full rings. One's skill at engaging the master as a healthy selfobject may be included in this ability. The close bonding between the student and teacher also works best when, for the student, it is an *exclusive relationship*. Offering advice that sounds like psychotherapists talking to their patients, Kapleau (1980b) warned that students who try to work under two or more masters will ultimately fail. To each master, the student will appear lukewarm in commitment and will receive a lukewarm response. Coming from different training backgrounds and having different personalities, the masters may seem to be contradicting each other in how they deal with a student. Each may be correct in his own way, but the novice student will become confused, discouraged, and sapped of energy—resulting in both teachers being ignored or dropped. Last, the teacher-student dyad is a *reciprocal transformative relationship*. Ideally, as travelers on the same path to self-realization, they learn from each other, mirror each other (including both virtues and faults) and thereby enhance each other's identity development. Like Winnecottian psychotherapy at its best, the transformative exchange between student and teacher becomes a form of "playing" in the transitional space where one's own subjective meanings are mixed and matched with those offered by the other.

Becker (1960) took a more critical view of the relationship between Zen master and student. Challenging the works of both Fromm (1959) and Herrigel (1971), and supporting his argument with ideas from Stunkard (1951), he portrayed the master as a forbidding authority figure who stimulates in the student a state of infantile helplessness and the consequent dependence upon an outside source of security and satisfaction. The Zen koan symbolizes the impossible task of the child trying to figure out what the parent wants. The student's intense ambivalence and dependency toward the master is finally resolved by adopting the master's superego. Enlightenment, according to Becker, is the culmination of introjecting the teacher's value system. Ideally, it is a new superego that is more permissive than the old. Somewhat similar to the psychoanalytic patient, the Zen student does resolve the ambivalence to authority and attains a measure of independence from the personage of the master; but unlike the patient, the resolution involves only a partial individuation, since the Zen pupil is still symbolically tied to the master's superego.

The position of Fromm (1959) and Herrigel (1971) was that the master accentuates the appearance of authority in order, ultimately, to force the student to break it. Similar to psychoanalysis, students finally resolve their ambivalence and dependency by discovering that their self-transformation can lie in their own hands. The master serves only as a guide in this process—someone who has traveled down a similar, but not the same, road. Fromm therefore classifies Zen not as an "authoritarian" religion in which one relies passively on an outside power, but rather as a "humanitarian" religion in which the emphasis is on freedom and self-realization. To encourage the student to discover that freedom from monolithic dependency, the master may resort to extreme measures. In his desperate struggle to learn Zen archery, Herrigel spoke of how a great master first lets you get ship-wrecked before throwing you a lifeline. For Herrigel, the lifeline was the master's advice to let go of his fears and ambitions about archery, so the act could come spontaneously from within Herrigel himself. Finn (1992) described the Tibetan legend of how Milarepa urgently sought out his renowned teacher Marpa to help him drive away the demons who threatened him during meditation, only to be told that Milarepa already knew what he should do. As always in meditation, he should not fight the demons, but simply be aware of them; in fact, Marpa suggested, he should talk to and play with them. The demons turned out to be projections of Milarepa's own mind. When he willingly opened himself to them, they evaporated.

The student does, indeed, internalize the master. The basic

skills and knowledge that the student needs are acquired throughout the training. But at the peak moment of crisis and impending transformation, the master's absence is as powerful as his presence. In what self psychologists might call a "transmuting internalization," the student internally develops the intrapsychic functions that are needed when the now seemingly distant master empathically offers a lifeline. That lifeline, the master's last authoritative solution, is that one must find the solution within oneself. The whole process is one of playing with the paradoxical illusions of dependence and independence, separateness and connection.

Can a transformation, and even Zen enlightenment, occur without any Zen master? Can there be psychoanalytic insight and therapeutic change without any clinician? The legends of Buddha and Freud portray them as men who, despite having teachers who influenced them early in their development, individually pioneered new realms of intrapsychic transformation. The legends speak to the archetype that applies to all Zen students and psychotherapy patients: on some level they must do it "alone." Eastern teachers themselves have reported cases of Zen enlightenment without masters (see Ikemoto, 1971). Everyday life contains examples of psychoanalytic insights, even powerful ones, without a psychoanalyst.

The more basic prerequisite is that the transformative process always occurs *in a relationship*. It may be in relationship to nature, a ritual, a household object—anything in which "otherness" manifests itself, including a thought or perception being examined by the observing self. The dynamic polarity between self and other creates the transformative field in which the interpenetration and unity of self and not-self are realized. The desire for the other breaks the rigidity of the "I." Zen myth tells of the Chinese Buddhist philosopher Tao-sheng, whose enlightened mind was so profound that his contemporaries could not understand him. Expelled from the community as a heretic, he went into the desert to talk to rocks about how they, too, possessed Buddha nature. The legend holds that the rocks nodded in agreement. For many humans, however, it may be easier to discover the bond between self and not-self through a relationship with another human—there is more manifest overlap of subjective experience than with rocks! Other humans, particularly Zen masters and psychotherapists, also may facilitate the transformative process more efficiently than do rocks.

8

The Therapist as Warrior

The philosophical systems of Taoism and Zen had a major impact on many aspects of Eastern culture. One of the more difficult effects Westerners to understand is the influence of these systems on the Oriental's attitudes about fighting and warfare. For example, the United States, with its history of revolution and civil war, is no stranger to violence and combat; yet the limits of its understanding of warfare were clearly visible during its wartime encounters with the Japanese and Vietnamese. Deeply rooted in the principles of Taoist yielding and Buddhist selflessness, the Oriental soldier presented a force that often perplexed, and sometimes horrified, Western strategists.

It is the East's merging of warfare philosophy with religious spiritual philosophy that most puzzles Westerners. For Asians, throughout their history, the two have been inseparable. The earliest origins of Buddhist thought in India coincided with the development of martial theories and techniques (Reid & Croucher, 1983). Sun Tzu, a brilliant Chinese tactician whose book *The Art of War* (c. 350 B.C.) is still required reading in the military, was clearly influenced by Taoism, particularly the *I Ching*. Legend holds that Bodhidharma, the Buddhist patriarch who carried the teachings from India to China, taught martial art techniques to his students in order to strengthen their physical fitness, as well as enhance their understanding of Buddhist thought. His methods carried on throughout the reign of the Shaolin temples, where both Ch'an and Kung Fu formed the basis of training. In Japan, where the martial arts have blossomed over the past few centuries, the fighting spirit is cherished as a pure expression of Zen and Shinto.

Psychotherapy as Martial Art

Although, on the surface, the merging of warfare and spiritual philosophies appears perplexing and even contradictory, it is this blend that makes the martial arts accessible to Western theories about psychotherapy. The martial arts ultimately aim to cultivate a contemplative state of mind, rather than simply fighting techniques: therefore, martial philosophy harmonizes with the meditative disciplines and draws on the same transformative powers as does meditation. Some of the benefits that psychotherapy can derive from the study of meditation also can be found in the martial arts.

In addition, the martial arts specifically focus on the application of meditative awareness to concrete encounters with an opponent. By revealing the utility of the contemplative mind in a face-to-face encounter, the martial arts philosophy and techniques arrive directly at the psychotherapist's door. By exploring the practical, interpersonal uses of contemplative insights into circumstance, change, and transformation, martial arts offer advice for handling the encounter between clinician and patient.

There are innumerable facets to this spiritual or contemplative understanding of the interpersonal confrontation between oneself and the opponent: how to sense others' intentions, respond to their actions, handle the outcomes, as well as the overarching philosophy that explains why the encounter occurs and its ultimate meaning. These dimensions of the martial arts show how, similar to psychotherapy, they indeed comprise an art form that touches the universal sense of the aesthetic. Becker (1989) cited Jigoro Kano, the founder of judo, who stated that the martial arts consist of three elements: the culmination of plot *(tsukuri)*, the making of a decisive move *(kake)*, and the denouement *(kuzushi)*—an artistic pattern that is familiar to the clinician.

Of course, psychotherapists might claim that they do not consider themselves to be facing an "enemy" or "opponent" in their consulting rooms. So how could the martial arts be relevant? Surely, patients sometimes act, in a variety of conscious and unconscious ways, like adversaries in the path toward psychotherapeutic progress. This is implicit in the concept of resistance and defense. I also have heard colleagues discuss, in object relations language, the necessity of "battling it out" with the patient's toxic introjects. Some patients even fight off the clinician's attempt to empathize with their experience, and almost all patients, at some point in the transference, aggressively launch toward the therapist an assortment of affects. At the very least, psychotherapy is a game of strategy, move, and countermove—an exchange between contending intentions and subjective meanings.

On a deeper level, the connotations of "opponent" or "adversary" become irrelevant. All encounters between self and other involve some friction, opposition, or interchange of forces. This is the very essence of the experience of self and other. Overlying meanings of "opponent" are perhaps superfluous. Consistent with Zen and Taoist philosophy, the martial artist recognizes that the more essential principle is the confluence of adversary and ally, opposing and joining. It is the recognition of the interpenetration between self and other, including the interpenetration of the contentious and acquiescent dimensions of self and other. This realization is what makes the therapist a "warrior."

The Warrior Philosophy

In feudal Japan, the martial arts were strongly influenced by the *samurai* code of honor known as *Bushido*, "The Way of the Warrior"—a term that was popularized by Inazo Nitobe (1975). *Bushido* had its earliest roots in the concept of *wu-te* that Bodhidharma introduced to Buddhist monks in China sometime around A.D. 600. *Wu-te* emphasized discipline, restraint, humility, and respect for human life. For the feudal warrior, *Bushido* dictated a life of complete mastery over one's natural inclinations, unruffled serenity in the face of adversity, and the refusal to yield to sorrow or the exultations of victory. The *samurai* upheld unquestioning obedience to the feudal lord, even when it led to death—what Durkheim categorized as "altruistic suicide." However, some contemporary authors (e.g., Becker, 1989) believe that the *samurai* would not blindly follow their lords' demands if such actions deeply violated their conscience. Instead, they would commit *seppuku*, ritualistic suicide. In either case, dying for the lord or for the higher code of honor, *Bushido* was a philosophy of self-sacrifice.

The Way of the Warrior served powerful selfobject functions as a system of idealized principles. The code dictated that the warrior serve his family and village, and in turn, his identity was sustained by that communal self. Not only did the philosophy support his identity in life, but it also enabled him to participate in a transcendent realm where death, the sacrifice of the individual self, could sustain the vitality and continuity of the larger self that was *Bushido*.

Self-sacrifice, though rarely as extreme as demanded by *Bushido*, does play a role in psychotherapy. At times, the clinician may concede or renounce some aspect of self in order to serve a higher ego ideal. Following the principle of analytic neutrality, the clinician sacrifices the expression of his or her inner self. During the empathic immersion into the patient's experience, the therapist's own life remains at least partially sequestered. Setting aside their personal reactions, some clinicians follow without question the tenets of theory. Any pains suffered from the sacrifice of particular elements of the self are overridden by the sense that, on a more encompassing level, the self is being sustained by the selfobject functions of adhering to theoretical principles. Similar to *Bushido*, the survival of the theory, and the self's participation in that survival, outweigh the sacrifice.

Nearly all the great masters of the martial arts emphasized that their discipline was much more than a system for fighting and warfare. It was a way of life. It endorsed a wide range of (sometimes elusive) attributes, such as calmness, discipline, self-realization, self-acceptance, a flexible and open mind, harmony with all things, yielding and changing with life, devotion to family, friends, and community, and acceptance of death. During his karate training in Japan, Nicol (1982) and his fellow students, at the end of each practice, would fill the *dojo* with their chant, "To strive for the perfection of character; to defend the paths of truth; to foster the spirit of effort; to honor the principles of etiquette; to guard against impetuous courage!" (p. 11). In his contemporary and somewhat glamorized interpretation of the warrior philosophy, Trungpa (1988) equated the warrior's behavior with various dimensions of "bravery"—the bravery to overcome the fears of exploring oneself, developing oneself, opening up to others, and being compassionate. Renowned teachers such as Miyamoto Musashi (1982), the seventeenth century swordsman, and Zhuge Liang and Liu Ji (1989), who offered commentaries on Sun Tzu, also maintained that the warrior must be a cultured, well-rounded individual who is knowledgeable about the arts and various professions. Many eminent martial artists were, in fact, respected poets, writers, and painters. A diverse education, the masters claimed, would widen the warrior's field of vision.

We would be hard-pressed to state that there exists a clear, overarching philosophy that governs the actions of the clinician. The martial arts as a life philosophy may be more explicitly stated than that for psychotherapy. Nevertheless, many elements of the warrior's code have their parallels in the clinician's attitudes toward his or her work—attitudes that many clinicians, and patients as well, hold as values for living. Self-discipline; the mastery of one's inclinations; serenity in the face of adversity; refusal to submit to the excesses of one's emotions; an open and flexible mind; the bravery to explore oneself, search out the sources of fear, confront and change one's problems, and endure the vulnerability of an empathic immersion with others—all form a concise list of admirable characteristics for the psychoanalytic clinician and for people in general. Becker's (1989) more focused depiction of the *samurai* as "austere, calm, subdued, chaste" (p. 101) might be a fitting description of the idealized, classic version of analytic neutrality. For all clinicians, a wide-ranging set of interests and knowledge, including an appreciation of art and literature (as advocated by Musashi, Liang, and Ji) serves as a flexible, encompassing platform for understanding the patient.

The sense of duty and obligation to others pervades the martial-arts philosophy. It is a form of altruistic self-sacrifice that is highly idealized, perhaps at times naively. To understand fully the roots of the philosophy, we must not overlook the psychodynamic (and sometimes pathological) aspects of altruism that have been uncovered by psychoanalysis—for example, altruism as compulsive and masochistic (A. Freud, 1936), as an extension of an omnipotent "God complex" (Jones, 1913), as a manifestation of guilt (Erikson, 1969), as a rescue fantasy resulting from the transformation of aggression (Sterba, 1940), or as an identification with an idealized, altruistic figure in order to repair or defend against narcissistic injuries resulting from early object loss (McWilliams, 1984).

It would be a mistake either to extol the warrior philosophy as a pure form of psychological and spiritual well-being, or simply to condemn it as an expression of underlying pathology. Both would be an oversimplification of a more complex dynamic in which these seemingly opposing tendencies actually may generate and give meaning to each other. The warrior philosophy is an expression of the multifaceted constitution of the self in which the various planes of health and pathology, both psychological and spiritual, intersect and counterpoise each other.

The Pursuit of Self-Awareness

One of the pillars of psychoanalysis is the realization that clinicians must understand their own countertransference, including their specific reactions to particular patients, as well as the basic personality dynamics that led them to the profession in the first place. The challenge of understanding and grappling with oneself is an ongoing process that seems to have no limits.

The same principle holds true in martial arts philosophy. The masters emphasize that the ultimate battle is not with the adversary, but with oneself. The student's deepest struggles are not in learning techniques or developing physical prowess, but in confronting and mastering the insecurities, obsessions, fears, and misconceptions that threaten to block one's progress. A Chinese adage states that the secret of victory is to know both oneself and the enemy. Funakoshi (1981) described his students' confusion when he told them that to learn karate you must become weak, rather than strong. "He who is aware of his own weaknesses will remain master of himself in any situation; only a true weakling is capable of true courage" (p. 115).

When Herrigel (1971) undertook his study of archery in Japan, the eminent Master Awa introduced him to the "Great Doctrine." It stated that archery is a matter of life and death to the extent that it is a contest of the archer with himself. His goal is to hit himself, to find himself, in the act of archery. The archer becomes both the aimer and the aimed: "Do I hit the goal or does the goal hit me? All melt into one" (p. 70).

The Great Doctrine points to the polarity between self and not-self as the field in which this self-awareness crystallizes. In many of the martial arts, as in psychotherapy, the not-self is the presence of the other. The bipersonal context in which the self encounters the other is the reciprocal interaction of intentions and meanings between self and other. In this interaction the self struggles to clarify itself. For clinicians to advance an intervention toward the patient—as when martial artists advance a technique toward the opponent—they must gauge its meaning for the patient based on their understanding of its subjective meaning for themselves. To know where the arrow flies, one must know where it came from; it joins the aimer and the target. Martial artists can only respond effectively to the opponent when they realize how they tend subjectively to perceive the opponent's movement. To understand and respond to the patient, clinicians must understand their own intrapsychic realm of meaning that dictates how they find meaning in the patient's experience. By sorting through the bipersonal field—through the interplay of transference and countertransference, intersubjective conjunctions and dysjunctions—the self grapples with itself as it grapples with the other. Randon (1978) in fact stated that the opponent is the mirror of oneself; to fight the enemy is to fight oneself. He quoted Master Egami, who claimed that "the opponent becomes the master: he is like a part of oneself which one confronts" (p. 227).

The *dojo*, like the clinician's office, is the arena in which this struggle unfolds. For everyone involved, it is a microcosm of life with all its ambitions, anxieties, victories, and defeats. As a standardized setting with its own stable set of rules and procedures, this space draws out and highlights the unique characteristics of each person. In traditional martial art schools, the training is often severe and strict in order to push students to their limits, to accentuate their flaws and strengths so they are clearly visible. The same process may occur in psychotherapy, for both the patient and therapist, as well as in clinical supervision. Kauz (1977) suggested that within this space, victory and defeat become a way of life; they are not end-goals but just part of the overall process of self-realization.

There is a "fighting spirit" that sustains the individual through this process of self-analysis. Despite the obstacles, some patients (often referred to as "fighters") show enormous persistence in their psychotherapeutic work. This mysterious talent cuts across all levels of pathology, and complicated the psychoanalytic debates in the 1950s about "analyzability." Something like this spirit is present in the dedicated clinician and martial artist. Beginners in the martial arts usually report that they pursue their studies for the purpose of physical fitness or self-defense, whereas advanced practitioners state that they strive to perfect their mastery of the art. "What emerges is the sense of a lifelong quest for perfection, wherein each moment is intrinsically satisfying, but the experience is framed as part of an unlimited pursuit of growth and improved expression" (Levine, 1989, p. 311). Perhaps what fuels the fighting spirit is this self-sustaining idealization of an imaged, perfect self and of the striving toward that image. Clinicians and martial arts teachers who possess the patience and perseverance of this spirit serve as sources of idealization and identification in this pursuit. "Once we have disciplined ourselves in the true principles and have won the battle with ourselves, other people will naturally follow us" (Tohei, 1966, p. 19).

Aggression

The martial arts are highly effective, sophisticated methods for maiming and killing people. Aren't they intrinsically violent? Can we accurately claim that there is a psychotherapeutic value to a discipline that sits squarely in the domain of aggression?

Traditional psychoanalytic theory might claim that organized martial activities, even when deemed an art, are essentially a catharsis or sublimation of aggressive instincts. This observation must be taken seriously. Biographical analyses of martial artists often reveal evidence that confirms it. In the foreword to the autobiography of Gichin Funakoshi (1981), Genshin Hironishi humorously described this great master of Shotokan karate (an extremely deadly martial style that requires strict training) as a man who could not tolerate a stray sock lying on the floor, who could not even say the word "sock" while demanding that it be put away. Interpreted psychoanalytically, Funakoshi's compulsiveness may have been a defense against unconscious drives, especially aggression. In his own autobiography, Nicol (1982) described how he tried to exorcise his angry temperament through long, arduous sessions of repeatedly striking his fists into the *makiwara*, a straw mat fastened to a wooden post. From his review of the empirical research on the martial arts, Rothpearl (1980) concluded that a cathartic process is at work; by continually exposing students to aggressive situations in the *dojo* while requiring them to restrain themselves, they become desensitized to violence.

In Japan, where the martial arts have flourished, the role of aggression in these disciplines must be understood within a wider cultural context. According to Roland (1988), Japanese society entails an intense dependence and interdependence in which the we-self dominates over the I-self. Self-restraint—particularly the containment of ambivalence, anger, and aggression—has been elevated to an ego-ideal that helps ensure the smooth functioning of this interdependence. Open expression of anger toward hierarchically superior figures is strongly prohibited. The interdependent relationship between superior and subordinate is one in which the superior empathically senses and fulfills the subordinate's needs, whereas the subordinate idealizes and serves the superior. Junior people may feel deeply hurt and angry if the authority figure has not correctly sensed and responded to their needs; the authority may be enraged by disrespect and disloyalty. Roland notes that if these feelings cannot be controlled by simple containment or suppression, a number of symptoms may develop—somatization being a common one among the Japanese. In this context, it is interesting to note that several renowned martial arts masters, including Kano Jigoro in judo and Ueshiba Morihei in aikido, pursued the martial arts as a way to overcome illness and weak constitutions.

In some cases, martial studies may provide a context for a blatant acting out of aggression. Nicol (1982) admitted that, despite the philosophy of self-restraint and nonviolence, there persists in some karate schools a "satanic" underbelly of secrecy and militancy, where teachers beat unfaithful students and narcissistically grandiose students pick fights with unsuspecting victims. Whereas the traditional philosophy warns against such behavior, some contemporary training programs (often in the West) ignore this philosophy and dwell only on the fighting techniques. Such programs become easy prey to the acting out of psychopathology.

Enlisting one's art as an expression of hostility is not unknown to therapists in training. As a graduate student, confident that I had tucked some effective psychotherapeutic skills under my belt, I once decided to practice them on a fellow student who frequently talked about making money. Using basic techniques, I doggedly kept refocusing him on the fact that he was preoccupied with this topic. He vehemently denied it. His defenses bristled. His anxiety escalated. He needed money to bolster his identity, but could not acknowledge his fragile inner self that relied on money as a selfobject support. I had succeeded in poking my way into his narcissistic vulnerabilities.

My aggressive actions were the expression of my own narcissistic need to feel competitive, in control, and powerful. Disciplines that teach person-to-person techniques, including psychotherapy and the martial arts, can lead students to a phase in training that activates an interpersonal expression of the omnipotent self. They feel compelled to try out their skills, like toddlers who must investigate the limits of their developing powers. The therapist-in-training and martial student may feel tempted to test out against others their newly enhanced grandiose self. Nicol (1982) reports how karate students at the brown-belt level often develop an arrogant, cocky, and provocative attitude. Recognizing this situation, the *sensei* requires these students to spar with skilled black belts, who beat them soundly. They are taught humility. They must experience "the helplessness of a baby" (p. 108). There can be no pride or conceit. Training, Nicol suggests, pushes them up a hill to arrogance, only to knock them over. The *sensei* breaks down the students so he can then help build up their "spirit." Training throws them into the dynamics of omnipotence and shame. To pass through this dynamic is to attain spirit—the humility of recognizing one's limitations, the respect for an art that has an infinite depth beyond one's abilities to master it all, and the determination, nevertheless, to pursue that art.

In this respect, the graduate student learning psychotherapy resembles the karate brown belt. Graduate students often leave their training program feeling the same cocky sense of omnipotence. They think, "I know how to do psychotherapy." Unfortunately, there are no formal procedures for taming this grandiose self. Supervisors may try to chip away at it or shape it. Ideally, when novice therapists enter the real world of practice, their unsuccessful encounters force them into acknowledging their limitations. Gradually they develop the humility and spirit to do their work effectively.

The tools of the psychotherapist easily can be used for aggressive purposes. Even empathy, according to Kohut (1977), can be applied destructively. An empathic understanding of another's vulnerabilities can serve as a powerful weapon for attack. Hitler used his empathic powers to connect with the inner experiences of his people and to rile them into an omnipotent attempt to conquer the world. But acting out aggression as a means to express one's inner dynamics of narcissistic vulnerability and omnipotence runs contrary to the humility of the psychotherapeutic endeavor. There is a larger, encompassing philosophy or spirit that shapes the meaning and purpose of a technique, whether it is a punch or an empathic interpretation. Acted-out aggression plays no role in this warrior spirit.

Most advocates of the martial arts, including those who base their conclusions on empirical research, insist that aggression is not in keeping with the ultimate aims of the martial arts, that training instead will bring about a reduction of aggressiveness. It also produces other psychological benefits, such as an increase in self-esteem and self-confidence, empathy for others, and a sense of peacefulness and well-being (Becker, 1989; Fuller, 1988; Nosanchuk, 1981; Nosanchuk & MacNeil, 1989). There may be several factors that contribute to the alleviation of hostility in advanced students. Some aggressive dilettantes need violence to enliven their frail self structure. In a self-selection process, they may drop out of a training program that stresses nonviolence. For those who remain, the teacher, who models discipline and peace, sanctions hostile actions, and mirrors self-control, becomes an object of idealization and identification. In the advanced stages of study—as with psychotherapy—one develops an acute sensitivity to the emotions of the opponent, including anger. This empathy tends to inhibit one's own aggression.

Although some schools emphasize sparring with an opponent, this activity (which easily generates hostility in beginners) is usually considered a tangent to true practice in the traditional schools. Instead, there is an emphasis on the persistent repetition and perfection of *kata,* or "forms"—the standardized sequences of specific moves and postures that have been passed down through the centuries. This practice of forms is more than simply a cathartic or sublimatory outlet. It is a sustaining selfobject activity into which martial artists immerse themselves. As a highly contemplative exercise, it generates a self-affirming mastery of one's physical motions through space and of the complex array of thoughts and emotions that accompany those motions. The form becomes a somatic-sensory pattern, filled with subjective meaning, that embeds into self structure. As a formalized pattern of movement that dates back hundreds of years, it provides a self-sustaining context of continuity with the past and with the idealized masters of the past. Many types of aggression are by-products of a self that feels threatened by the loss of selfobject support. The practice of forms may lead to the alleviation of aggression—and to other psychological benefits—by furnishing a selfobject framework that fortifies self structure. This selfobject function extends to the entire martial arts milieu: the holding environment of the *dojo,* the relationship among students and teachers, the routines and philosophy of practice.

To appreciate fully the role of aggression in the martial arts and psychotherapy, we must avoid the oversimplified conclusion that aggression is something to be strictly avoided. Every master of these two disciplines would agree that destructive actions violate the fundamental spirit of the art. Aggression may be an intrinsic component of human nature, as traditional psychoanalysis claims. It may be the byproduct of a weak self structure that is threatened by selfobject failure, as claimed by self psychology. But the crucial distinction is between the destructive and constructive expressions of aggression. Kohut (1977) stated that nondestructive aggression is a component of the assertiveness of the grandiose-exhibitionist self; it plays a crucial energizing role in the tension arc between ambitions and ideals. Ego psychology would claim that aggression must be neutralized for the purpose of creating energy for the development of adaptive psychic functions. In both psychotherapy and the martial arts, where the encounter with the other invariably stirs hostilities, aggression can serve the goal of enhancing the demarcation of the self and its goals. It propels the self toward the attainment of its ideals. It magnifies the experience of self and is a source of meaning. Through hostility we experience ourselves and others more fully. As a manifestation of the creative, willing self, aggression can simultaneously connect the self to the other and aid in the separation and individuation of self. For Winnicott (1969, 1971), aggression was a source of vitality and motility. We need it to bump up against the other, to experience the boundaries between the self and other. It helps us recognize that there is something outside the self, the not-self, that can be engaged, encouraged, and struggled with. Winnicott also believed that the survival of the other in the face of our hatred and omnipotent need to destroy it reciprocally enlivens our appreciation of the realness of self and other.

Both psychotherapy and the martial arts stimulate these dimensions of aggression. Experiencing hostility enhances the texture of interpersonal contact. By possessing the knowledge and techniques to maim or destroy the other, we arrive at the realization of and respect for the aliveness of the other. By seeing that we too could be destroyed, we witness the reciprocity of this process (patients too possess the skills to attack the therapist at points of narcissistic vulnerability). At the most basic psychological level, the mutuality of mirroring or not mirroring pivots the self and other on the same fulcrum of being affirmed or negated. Ignoring the other destroys the other, but it also destructively hollows out the other's capacity to affirm one's self. Self and other continually weave in and out of mirroring, affirming, negating, and destroying each other. Self and other survive and regenerate each other. Creation and destruction, death and rebirth, hate and love, intertwine. This recognition of the mutuality and interpenetration of self and other is the full vision in psychotherapy, as it is in the martial arts. Aggression is but one facet of this vision. It is neither good nor bad, but rather one important element of the interpersonal process. It is contained by the larger spirit of empathy that opens one to the full range of affects, thoughts, and actions that arise between self and other, which join the self to the other.

For Tohei (1966), the most essential principle of aikido is not aggression, but "non-dissension." To understand this principle is to realize the universal in which there is no duality between self and other. Aggression against the other is derived from and becomes aggression against oneself. For this reason, martial students who fight mostly from their anger usually end up being easily defeated—they defeat themselves. The universal, Tohei claimed, is an absolute with which we have no cause to fight. Battles arise first when the idea of duality appears. They clothe the universal in the guise of good and evil, justice and inequity, victory and defeat.

Aggression often stems from fear—the fear that one's self will be undermined or destroyed. Perhaps the advanced stages of psychotherapy and martial arts training enable the practitioner to overcome aggression by being able to overcome the fear of the loss of self. Aggression dissolves into the wider, empathic grasp of the interpenetration of self and no-self, of self and other.

Basic Martial Concepts and Psychotherapy

As a philosophical and practical system with a history of hundreds, perhaps thousands, of years, the martial arts have developed a complex set of principles for encountering the other. The terms and their meanings often vary among the various schools. However, there are several concepts that are common to all. Perhaps it is their universality that makes these concepts particularly applicable to psychotherapy.

Mushin (Empty Mind)

Because the martial arts are a contemplative discipline, they strive to cultivate states of consciousness similar to those in meditation (see Chapter 6). In Japanese karate and Zen, *mushin* is the condition of "empty mind" or "no-mind." Similar to free association and evenly hovering attention in psychoanalytic listening, awareness is open and flowing. Attention is evenly distributed. It floats freely along the axes of the five senses and along the realms of thinking and feeling. No one sensation or mental activity sucks up the focus of mind. The mind flows easily from one awareness to another. This does not mean that the person (martial artist or clinician) perceives or acts without control or direction. Musashi (1982) noted that the juggler can juggle several objects without directly concentrating on any one of them, yet he or she still indirectly "sees" each object and fluently coordinates the entire activity of juggling.

Mushin requires letting go. In order for awareness to flow uninhibitedly, one must let go of any physical or psychological tension, including doubts, worries, anxieties, expectations, deliberations, or ambitions. All these affective and cognitive states cause the mind to freeze. Effort becomes an "effortless effort" where conscious control of perceptions and actions yields to the freer expression of unconscious influence. Hyams (1982) noted that when one lets go of caring whether one's effort is on target, it more likely will be on target. Desires and intentions to do something in particular block *mushin* and disrupt spontaneous, accurate effort. Too much concentration defeats itself; or, as Taoism states, "When you seek it you cannot find it." For the clinician, "trying" to make a good interpretation or an empathic response usually turns out stale and off-target. Because one lets go of effort, one also lets go of consciously focusing on the theory and technique of one's discipline. But one can only let go of one's discipline once it has been mastered. As in juggling, the letting go of effortless effort is a relaxing into one discipline that allows unconscious awareness to flow through that discipline.

For the martial artist and clinician, the emptiness and fluidity of mind in *mushin* enhances the ability to discern and reflect the states of mind within the other. The Chinese principle of *hsing I* (*hsing*, meaning "form;" *I*, meaning "intention," "idea," or "mind") refers to the ability to penetrate the form or outward appearance of the opponent and anticipate the other's inner thoughts and intentions (Reid & Croucher, 1983). In his martial philosophy of *Heiho,* Musashi (1982) similarly drew the distinction between *ken,* the superficial appearance of things, and *kan,* the seeing through or into the essence of things. He conceptualized *Heiho* as the resolution of the two: The warrior develops an intuitive sixth sense enabling him to anticipate the opponent's intentions by reading, usually unconsciously, subtle external behaviors. Clinicians, for instance, are familiar with such empathic phenomena as feeling a tear in their own eye before the client actually cries or even feels sadness. The momentary absence of *hsing I* for clinicians is reflected in such comments as, "I couldn't find my way into my patient's experience."

Mushin sensitizes the individual to rhythms between self and other that might not be discernible to ordinary states of consciousness. To sense rhythm is to sense the proportion, balance, and overarching order between self and other. Musashi (1982) stated that the warrior must learn the rhythms of each opponent and how they differ from those of other opponents, of how things progress and deteriorate, of failing and succeeding, of reaching and not achieving one's purpose. Sun Tzu (1983) noted that even within the turmoil and tumult of battle, i.e., within situations that appear chaotic to the cursory glance, there often lies a hidden, crucial pattern. If martial artists or clinicians can discern the intentions of the other before the other acts, as well as the rhythms of the other's behaviors and internal states of mind, then they can intervene quickly and effectively, often with minimum effort. The skilled warrior, Sun Tzu claimed, can see trends and take advantage of the opportunities they offer.

A curious and paradoxical effect of pure *mushin* is the intense power embedded in its complete vulnerability. Funakoshi (1981) related the story of the renowned karate master Matsumura, who defeated a younger, and perhaps better fighter without fighting at all. On the field of combat, Matsumura simply stood still and silent, in a completely casual and vulnerable posture. At that moment all his worries and anxieties, including his fear of dying, dropped away from the clear, unobstructed awareness of *mushin.* His apparent defenselessness confused and destabilized the challenger. His lack of anxiety about what was about to happen intensified that very feeling in the opponent. Working himself up into an acute state of tension and indecision, the challenger collapsed and forfeited the fight. He learned his greatest lesson when Matsumura later explained his insight that vanity and self-preoccupation are the only obstacles in life.

Something like this process occurs in psychotherapy. What often underlies such therapeutic qualities as analytic neutrality, empathy, and holding functions is a quiescent, flowing, and open state of awareness. This awareness exhibits strength and confidence in its apparently casual and vulnerable presentation. Its quiescence can draw out the anxieties in the patient, but its flexibility and strength also can support the patient's self-experience.

Continuing Mind *(Zanshin)*

Martial arts students are trained to enter the *dojo* with a sense of preparedness. Ideally, they maintain *mushin*—their open, flowing, and alert mind—throughout the practice. They should expect anything to happen while they are there. This contemplative attitude is not confined to the practice of forms or employed only as a tool for sparring with an opponent. Nicol (1982) described his fascination with the sense of spirit and concentration that the masters carried beyond their completion of *kata*. The perfect finish, the masters explained, is the spreading of the alert, open awareness beyond the boundaries of the form. In the perfect finish, the "mind like still water" continues flowing after the physical movements have ceased; you continue the same free-floating attentiveness to everything within and surrounding you. The internal essence of the *kata* extends beyond its superficial appearance. The masters called this *zanshin*—*zan*, meaning "to remain or continue," *shin*, meaning "heart" or "mind."

In the martial arts the "continuing mind" is a practical necessity. For the art to have any real application, *zanshin* must extend beyond the *dojo* itself. Students may train hard with full awareness during class, but then get mugged while carrying home their groceries, waiting to cross the street, or reading a book on the train. They are, colloquially speaking, "caught off guard."

A famous martial arts story tells about Matajuro, who went to the eminent Master Banzo to study sword. Expecting that he would start off by learning basic sword technique, Matajuro was greatly disappointed when Banzo gave him menial chores to perform around the house. For several days he worked with no hint from Banzo that weapon training would begin. One day, while Matajuro was sweeping, Banzo appeared with a large stick in his hands and struck his student. The next day, while Matajuro was drawing water, Banzo once again appeared from nowhere and whacked him as before. As the surprise assaults continued, Matajuro was able to dodge the stick and, eventually, sense Banzo's presence even before he appeared. His skill reached its peak on the evening he was kneeling over the fire to prepare a meal and Banzo quietly attacked from behind. While still peacefully attending to his supper, Matajuro used a pot cover and easily deflected the strike.

Clinicians may be tempted to experience their version of meditative awareness—whether they describe it as vicarious introspection, empathy, or evenly hovering attention—as being bounded temporally within the therapy hour, or spatially within the walls of the therapy room. As therapists approach and enter their offices, they may feel themselves spontaneously immersing into the contemplative state of mind. Associations about the upcoming patient may drift through awareness; a sense of alertness or preparedness sets in. The appearance of the patient triggers the distinct sensation that an intersubjective field has filled the room. The clinician is drawn into it. Settling into a meditative state, one is ready for anything to happen.

Often, the contemplative attitude confined within the form of the therapeutic hour is not sufficient. Like martial arts students who find themselves in a predicament outside the *dojo*, the clinician must learn the value of *zanshin*. In what often feels like a surprise maneuver, patients act out a variety of unconscious dynamics just before and after the session "officially" begins and ends. The clinician may be caught off-guard. Perhaps patients sense within the intersubjective field at the physical and temporal boundaries of the session the waxing and waning of the clinician's prepared awareness. Unconsciously, they may hope that their words or behavior are off the record, not to be interpreted. Even further outside the formal boundaries of therapy, clinicians may receive phone calls or find themselves in chance encounters with patients at the theater or grocery store. For both the therapist and patient, these situations feel very delicate, and very important.

Banzo's lesson for Matajuro was that there are no real boundaries for one's discipline. At the highest stages of study, one's discipline enters into one's everyday life. Reaching its peak effectiveness and applicability, the contemplative attitude of relaxed, open, and prepared awareness extends beyond the *dojo* and the therapy hour. Maintaining *zanshin*, the clinician can turn unexpected events outside the boundaries of therapy into highly therapeutic encounters. Like Matajuro's skill with the pot cover, clinicians may even use the chance meeting at the grocery store as a fortuitous therapeutic opportunity.

Methods for training a continuing mind, such as that employed by Banzo, conceivably could turn into an exercise in sadism. Matajuro's situation also could easily lead to paranoia, rather than to the peaceful, open awareness of *zanshin*. But the boundaries between anxious suspicion and relaxed attention, and between helpfulness and aggression, overlap at some dynamic point. On the Minnesota Multiphasic Personality Inventory, moderately high scores on the paranoia subscale indicate not paranoia, but rather, adaptive and mature interpersonal sensitivity. In some psychoanalytic supervision and training analyses, the clinician's attempts to analyze everything that happens—including why the trainee brought a cup of coffee to the session, or came a few minutes earlier than usual, or commented on the analyst's furniture—could become sadistic, interpretative overkill. But when employed effectively, like Master Banzo's training, such methods can help the trainee develop the sense of alert, flexible, and open attentiveness to all details that are necessary for analytic work. Often, what determines the effectiveness of such training methods is not the technique itself, but the underlying affect or intention with which the master, supervisor, or training analyst delivers the technique. If it genuinely is offered in the spirit of helpfulness and as an empathic attempt to understand the trainee, it will be accepted as such. If it is launched from a position of narcissistic omnipotence, oedipal competition, or anger, the consequences will be detrimental.

Centeredness

Martial artists often speak of the importance of being centered. To establish one's center is to create a focal reference or pivotal point for all actions. Without it, movement becomes uncoordinated and disjointed. Being centered creates a feeling of balance and harmony, in which efforts are neither overextended or held back. One is unified and poised between relaxation and readiness. There is a self-confidence or presence, called *sai* in Chinese, that is projected outward and easily recognized by others. Trungpa (1988) portrayed this sense of solidity and sureness as a position of firmly "riding in the saddle" (p. 75). Warriors are rooted and solid; nothing surprises or startles them; they hold their seat and posture regardless of what happens. This centering gives rise to their fearlessness.

The martial arts literature describes various outcomes of holding one's center during a confrontation with an opponent—effects that are reminiscent of various types of encounters in psychotherapy. In Tai Chi Chuan, being centered enables one to upset the opponent's balance while maintaining one's own; one acts like a rotating sphere that deflects attacks by being soft and yielding on the outside, but dynamic and strong on the inside (Jou, 1980). Similarly, the clinician's empathic and interpretative posture may appear delicate and pliant on the surface, but it is grounded in an internal resiliency and robustness that can deflect attempts to undermine it. For the student of aikido, being centered enables one to remain calm, peaceful, nonretaliatory, yet fully present in the face of the opponent's rising hostility—a psychological pose that can absorb and dissipate the opponent's anger (Tart, 1987). For the clinician, this calm but strong posture, a variation of the containing and holding functions described in the psychoanalytic literature, can metabolize and assuage a variety of intense affects. In their commentaries on Sun Tzu, Liang and Ji (1989) offer an explanation of centeredness that resembles the effects of analytic neutrality: To be centered is to maintain a balance, a posture of objectivity and impartiality, that is not disturbed by emotion. For Musashi (1982) this aspect of centeredness, like analytic neutrality, involved patience. One does not make the first move; one waits, centered and confident, until others make the first move, thereby revealing their intentions and weaknesses. He relates the story of two warriors who face each other in a standoff. The superior one waits, calm and confident. The inferior one, who cannot withstand the tension of waiting, anxiously makes the first strike, only to reveal his points of vulnerability.

Although there are no specific psychoanalytic terms that capture this experience of centeredness, it is a distinct feeling of confidence, balance, and solidity that clinicians experience regularly in their work. For example, clinicians are familiar with the scenario in which the patient devalues both therapy and the therapist. They recognize that the patient is indulging in distorted criticisms of the analytic work, that there is a narcissistic or conflictual basis to the patient's attack, that they really do know what they are doing despite the patient's innuendos to the contrary. Knowing all this, clinicians do not retaliate, intervene defensively, or feel pressured to explain themselves. They are not knocked off balance. Retaining their centeredness, they continue to empathically explore the meaning of the patient's reactions.

In their formulation of psychoanalytic phenomenology, Atwood and Stolorow (1984) described clinicians' ability to "decenter" from their subjective structures of experience, which may distort their empathic understanding of the patient's experience. Being aware of their countertransference reactions, clinicians can more accurately understand the sources of the patient's transference. Atwood and Stolorow used the word *decenter* to capture the idea that therapists are not unconsciously embroiled in countertransference; instead, they are able to disentangle themselves from the influence of their subjective structures and understand the intersubjective meaning of their reactions to the patient. They activate and step into the observing self that can become aware of any facet of subjective experience, including the potentially coloring and garbling effects of countertransference. But the term *centering* might have some advantages over the term *decentering*. It is, perhaps, more theoretically accurate to describe the rooting into the observing self as movement toward a nuclear, rather than peripheral, position. Also, the clinician's subjective experience of stepping into the observing self often is a feeling of centeredness, equilibrium, and groundedness in the face of the transference and countertransference that may threaten the stability of one's therapeutic posture.

In judo, when confronted by unusually difficult circumstances, the martial artist may employ a "sacrifice" technique. One deliberately forfeits one's balance and centeredness in order to surprise opponents, thereby disrupting their stability. It is an heroic effort, because the sacrifice is a last-ditch attempt to gain an advantage; if it fails, one is quickly thrown and loses the match. Analogous situations arise in psychotherapy, although they are rare. A colleague of mine described a patient with whom she had worked, unsuccessfully, for many years. The patient remained deeply entrenched in his characterological disorder. Finally, she decided to risk the assurance and solidity of her professional position by telling the client that, despite her best efforts, she did not believe that she could help him. At first startled and dismayed, in later sessions he gradually opened up to the analytic process and showed signs of benefiting from it.

For the martial artist, to be fully centered is to establish a grounding in the realm of the transcendent. In his study of archery, Herrigel (1971) learned that this centeredness meant a loss of the distinction between self and other, that by being both the aimer and the aimed the archer became the "unmoved center" (p. 6). Randon (1978) quoted Ueshiba Morihei, the founder of aikido, who suggested that being centered placed one in harmony with a domain beyond the individual self: "When an enemy tries to fight me, he faces the universe itself, he must break its harmony . . ." (p. 206).

Psychotherapists rarely speak about relying on a transcendent realm as a foundation for their work. Nevertheless, their centeredness often banks on the selfobject support provided by the larger professional community, the theories, and the eminent figures in their field upon which their confidence and sense of solidity rests. Confronted by the numerous pitfalls of transference and countertransference, the therapist turns to these mirroring and idealizing selfobject relationships to sustain their balance, composure, and stability. When patients engage the therapist, when they test the therapist's abilities, they must take on the larger theoretical, historical, and communal self in which the therapist's individual self participates.

Inscrutability

Traditional psychoanalytic theory places great emphasis on the importance of analytic neutrality, or playing the "blank screen." Even contemporary theorists, who may allow for a wider range of parameters in technique, still recognize the value of not disclosing aspects of oneself without a clear therapeutic intent in mind.

Martial arts masters—especially Sun Tzu (1971) and Musashi (1982)—also emphasized the merits of the warrior's inscrutability. Sun Tzu referred to the *Tao Te Ching*, which states that the great warriors of ancient times were subtle, mysteriously powerful, and unknowable. You should know the opponent, he suggested, but the opponent should not know you. Shape your enemies, but do not allow them to shape you. Musashi drew the distinction between *tatemae*, what you show to others, and *honne*, your real intentions that you should not reveal. The logic of analytic neutrality is to evoke the projection of transference onto the ambiguity of the blank screen created by the clinician. The patient's perceptions of the analyst are distorted by unconscious dynamics, but the more basic process is one of drawing to the surface previously hidden realms of meaning. Analogous strategies are evident in the martial artist's attempts to remain inscrutable. To shape one's opponents while remaining unshaped by them is to draw out their inner thoughts and purposes while concealing one's own. A variation of this tactic has been employed by Japanese businessmen who, arriving at a critical meeting, silently wait out the other businessmen until they speak first. Without revealing their own position, they compel the competitors to reveal theirs. Similarly, the clinician typically begins sessions in silence, allowing patients to disclose their state of mind; they avoid answering the patient's question, and instead encourage the patient to explore the meaning of the question.

Such techniques only work when patients allow an opening in their defenses and permit the therapist access to their internal experience. Entries cannot be forced. You have control over creating your own inscrutability, Sun Tzu (1971) stated, but the other's vulnerability depends on them. At best, inscrutability may facilitate such openings. Sun Tzu pointed out that if opponents do not know where you intend to advance, they must prepare their defenses in a great many places, thus weakening the strength of any single defensive position.

The same may be true of psychotherapy patients. Being unable to read through the clinician's neutral facade, they may expand their defenses across a wide range of issues, only to thin out their efforts and reveal points of sensitivity.

Jou (1980), a master of Tai Chi Chuan, suggested that the outer stillness of inscrutability is not simply static or inert. Beneath it lies dynamic motion, which Jou called "motion within stillness." With advanced training, the Tai Chi martial artist shifts obvious outward physical movements into almost invisible, finely tuned internal movements. Although appearing calm and motionless on the outside, the master, when confronted by an opponent, delivers a subtle but powerful force that overthrows the opponent. For the clinician, the outward movements are the array of interpretations and interventions that could be made (and usually *are* made by less experienced therapists) but in the case of the skilled clinician, are not. Instead, while remaining silent and calm on the surface, the clinician internalizes these potential interventions into an inner dynamic realm of free association, theoretical speculation, empathic attunement, and decision making. At the right moment, when the opportunity appears, this intrapsychic motion is transformed into a verbal intervention that, at its best, is subtle, but which carries considerable momentum and produces a powerful effect on the patient.

Sun Tzu (1971) called such subtle and highly effective techniques the method of "the sheathed sword." The skilled warrior, he claimed, wins with ease, without obvious effort. He wins without overtly fighting. Therefore, his victories may not bring him fame or credit for his endeavors. From the position of inscrutability, he takes advantage of opportunities that others do not see and intervenes at a level that is almost imperceptible to those who are expecting more dramatic measures. Similarly, in psychotherapy, there are interventions that are highly impactful on patients, but so subtle that the patients may not directly attribute the effects to the therapist.

A variety of characteristics contribute to the effectiveness of inscrutability—characteristics that also are relevant to the clinician. According to Sun Tzu (1971), one should be like water, without ascertainable shape. One conforms to the situation. Do not repeat tactics, especially when they succeed, but rather respond in a seemingly infinite variety of ways. For Trungpa (1988), the warrior's inscrutability comes from being confident and self-contained, from not struggling. Warriors do not need to be reassured. They have an inner conviction that does not require confirmation. They may appear noncommittal, but this quality is the result of not being interested in reassurance.

They do not need to be at the center of the scene, nor do they feel compelled to spell out the truth; they are satisfied with implying it.

Chi

One of the most important concepts in the martial arts is known as *chi* in Chinese, or *ki* in Japanese. Generally defined, it means energy. Jwing-Ming (1989) stated that it refers to any type of energy that demonstrates power and strength, and includes the energy itself, as well as the manner or state of the energy. He notes that many martial artists usually think of *chi* as the energy field that is internal to the human body, but *chi* also exists in nature, as in "heaven *chi*" and "earth *chi*." Each individual person, animal, and plant has its own *chi* field, and these fields of energy interact with each other in complex ways.

Most theories emphasize that *chi* is life itself. It is the energy that makes the various systems of the body alive, that underlies all bodily processes and functions. Following the dynamics of *yin* and *yang*, *chi* seeks to be balanced, and when a living thing loses that balance, it sickens and eventually dies if the equilibrium is not restored. This energy perspective of health and disease is the foundation for many of the Eastern systems for healing and well-being, such as acupuncture and acupressure, herbal treatments, meditation, and exercises such as Tai Chi Chuan. All these systems are designed to stimulate and balance *chi*. Whereas Western science often finds it difficult to accept these notions, Orientals point to the almost superhuman feats of strength, endurance, and control over bodily processes that masters attribute to their regulation of *chi*. Mackett (1989) described his observations of a *chi* practitioner who, much like Mesmer, cured patients of physical and psychological maladies via trance states that he induced, supposedly by projecting *chi* through his fingertips. Much of this sort of evidence is anecdotal.

The Orientals postulate that there are different types of *chi* that correspond to various facets of human experience, such as thinking, emotions, and spiritual awareness. In his description of aikido philosophy, Tohei (1966) hypothesized the existence of "plus" and "minus" *chi*, which correspond generally to positive and negative affective states. The various theories are extraordinarily subtle, complex, and, at times, confusing. The relationship between *chi* and emotion is especially perplexing. Is emotion a manifestation of *chi*? Is *chi* a separate energy that affects emotion? Does emotion affect *chi*? All these propositions seem to be true. For example, Jwing-Ming (1989) seemed sometimes to be saying that negative emotions are a form of *chi*, and sometimes that negative emotions block *chi*. To complicate matters even further, he stated that *chi* cannot be understood apart from two other basic concepts—*jieng*, the essence or primal substance from which a thing is made and that provides the true nature of the thing; and *shen*, the spirit, mind, or soul that is the center of being which calms the mind and firms the will.

Because psychoanalysis focuses specifically on understanding cognition and affect, it seems to be a more precise theory about these psychological phenomena than are the theories based on ideas about *chi*. Nevertheless, it is tempting to compare the Oriental's notions of *chi* to the drive/instinctual model of intrapsychic functioning that has dominated traditional psychoanalysis. Perhaps *chi* is another name for *libido* or *eros*, as conceptualized in classical theory or in other revisionist perspectives (e.g., Brown, 1970). The analogy that chi is like electricity generated within the human psyche (Tohei, 1966) surely parallels ideas in the psychoanalytic economic model. Dating back to Freud's (1895) *Project for a Scientific Psychology*, psychoanalysts, like Eastern thinkers, have struggled to explain how the structures and functions of the intrapsychic world are derived from internal "energies." The resulting theoretical complexities, subtleties, tautologies, and metapsychological confusions have been no less troublesome than the Oriental speculations about *chi*. For example, on the heels of the debates about how drives and intrapsychic structures interact, Fairbairn (1952) pointed out that there is no true distinction between energy and structure. They are inseparable; energy IS structure. Such conclusions lead us to the realization that concepts about "libido" and "drive" are as elusive as those about *chi*, even though many theorists and practitioners still rely heavily on them.

One apparent difference between psychoanalysis and theories about *chi* is the assumption held by many Eastern thinkers that *chi* can be controlled by the mind: it can lead, store, preserve, balance, concentrate, and transfer *chi*. In psychoanalytic theory, there is little room for the mind, particularly the conscious mind, to manipulate drives and affect. Theory often skirts the tricky ontology of the self as a willing agent. One notable exception might be Rank's (1945) emphasis on will and the implicit idea in other psychoanalytic theorizing that there exists a willing self (see Chapter 3).

The premise that the mind can control *chi* reflects the more general assumption that the mind can control the body. Here psychoanalysis will more readily agree. According to Nicol (1982), martial arts training cultivates the awareness that the body is a manifestation of the mind and the ability to use the body to express the mind. The mind and body are integrated. There is a "body-mind" (Klein, 1984) that can be strongly influenced from the mind's side of this synthesis. In a modern age when most scientific theories reduce all human phenomena to biology, psychoanalysis, like Oriental philosophy, instead emphasizes the mind's profound influence on the body. Physical health and pathology often are manifestations or concretizations of intrapsychic dynamics. The body is a "theater" for the expression of mind (McDougall, 1989).

Defining *chi* as energy would seem to place the concept outside the bounds of contemporary psychoanalytic theories, such as self psychology and some object relations approaches, that abandon the traditional psychodynamic ideas about intrapsychic energy. However, theories about *chi* also emphasize that it is essentially relational in nature. *Chi* is a force of interconnectedness and unification among all things. Tohei (1966) stated that plus *chi* constitutes the interconnections between people; it is the source of love and nurturance. Such ideas bear some similarity to object relations theories that state that drives are always relational in nature; they constitute the affects that connect self to object and self-representations to object representations (Greenberg & Mitchell, 1983). We might even speculate about *chi* as being the affective or ontological vitality of the "intersubjective field" (Atwood & Stolorow, 1984) that exists between the clinician and the patient; it is the dynamic binding of the clinician's subjective realm of meaning with that of the patient. Within the therapist or patient, the common subjective experience of feeling momentarily energized when the therapist and patient "connect" may be the conscious manifestation of this *chi*. It is interesting to note that Grotstein (1990a, 1990b) attempted to interpret the psychoanalytic understanding of meaning in one's self and object world, and the affect that sustains that meaning, in terms of the unified field theory in modern physics.

Martial arts philosophy states that *chi* connects the individual not only to other people, but to the world as a whole. Tohei (1966) claimed that the primary purpose of his art, aikido, is to join the individual to the universal *chi*. According to Tohei, *chi* is the real substance of the universe from which come all movement and stillness, all joining and breaking apart, and all mutual actions that give rise to the universe. Aikido regulates the flow of *chi* within oneself, between self and other, and between self and the universal. The result of connecting to the universal are feelings of calm, peacefulness, and love.

Psychoanalytic clinicians rarely describe their therapeutic objective as an attempt to join the individual to a universal force. Nevertheless, psychoanalysis does acknowledge the connectedness of the individual to realms that transcend the individual psyche. Self psychology points to the individual's immersion into a profound and complex selfobject world that consists of a wide spectrum of interpersonal, social, and cultural processes—a selfobject network that bolsters and soothes the self. Breaking with the traditional idea that the intrapsychic world is a distinctly separate and individual entity, Sullivan (1964) similarly stated that the person is an organism embedded into a complex configuration of relationships with the environment. In all such theories, it seems to be *affect* that is the primary source of this connectedness. In Grotstein's (1990a) view, affect may be connected to a unified field "that embraces far more than the emotional" (p. 257). Perhaps *chi* is the Oriental's vision of this universal field of interconnectedness.

The Dynamics of Soft and Hard Techniques

The martial arts draw a distinction between styles that are "soft" and those that are "hard." The soft styles, such as judo, aikido, and tai chi chuan, involve movements that are more yielding, pliable, and adaptive. Incoming forces are not opposed directly, but are accepted, joined with, and redirected using minimal strength. Motions are curved or circular. Emphasis is placed on staying close to opponents and sensitively resonating with their movements. Working with balance is essential. By contrast, hard styles, such as karate, involve motions that are more straightforward, forceful, and focused. Fighting from a distance, one confronts incoming forces directly by blocking and countering. Defenses are challenged. Motions are linear and strong. Whereas soft styles are described as "esoteric," relying more on internal sensitivity and receptiveness, hard styles are "exoteric," relying on the disciplined strength and agility of the external portions of the body (Reid & Croucher, 1983). The distinction between the two styles often is expressed in terms of the polarity between *yin* and *yang*.

McWilliams (1991) proposed an analogous distinction between soft and hard styles in psychoanalytic therapy. In the history of psychoanalysis, she claimed, the debates about therapeutic technique often implied a contrast between styles that are "maternal" and those that are "paternal." Maternal styles entail interventions that are gentle, accepting, closeness-inviting. More explicitly compassionate and resonant, maternal therapists yield to and immerse themselves in the patient's experience for the purpose of holding and soothing, as in self psychology. Flexibility of technique is emphasized. By contrast, paternal styles are stimulating, confrontive, and forceful. Emphasizing differentiation and separateness between therapist and patient, the clinician challenges defenses and more directly probes for unconscious issues. Rules about technique are disciplined and strict. McWilliams suggests that the distinction between the two styles is based on archetypic themes, and does not imply that males are always paternal and females always maternal. When used appropriately, both styles are also empathic in the sense that they match the needs and intentions of the patient. Both promote psychological growth. Irrespective of the content of the intervention that is made, its maternal or paternal quality is determined by the clinician's underlying attitude or affective tone.

As the Taoist philosophy of *yin* and *yang* suggests, polarities are never distinct and separate entities. They give rise to and sustain each other. They are embedded within each other. Advanced martial artists recognize that soft and hard techniques are mutually enriching. A truly skilled practitioner mixes and interpenetrates both. At the peak level of effectiveness, the two are seen as inseparable. This insight also holds true for the clinician. McWilliams (1991) stated that skilled therapists combine maternal and paternal styles. The patient's type of psychopathology, the type of dynamic issue being explored, and the stage of therapy are all factors that may determine which style is appropriate. Alternating between the two highlights the therapeutic impact of each. Technically advanced interventions also might fuse aspects of both maternal and paternal styles—as in gentle, compassionate interpretations that are subtly stimulating and confrontational.

The sections that follow explore various technical aspects of the soft and hard styles and how the two are related. They also explore the harmonious dualities arising out of the *yin/yang* polarity of soft and hard—such as the harmony of yielding and advancing, stillness and action, formlessness and form. The final section on technique examines some psychotherapeutic implications of "unorthodox" martial strategies.

Yielding

One of the fundamental principles of Taoism, as clearly stated in Lao Tzu's *Tao Te Ching*, is that the soft and yielding overcomes the rigid and strong. This principle is captured in the Chinese notion of *wu wei*, achieving action through nonaction, and the Japanese concept of *ju*, winning by giving way. The soft martial art styles emphasize this approach and draw on a variety of analogies to highlight it, such as the metaphor that one must feel like flowing water or soft clay, or Klein's (1984) idea that one must react like a spring that compresses and absorbs all the physical and emotional energy delivered by the opponent. Effective yielding requires that one be centered; otherwise, giving way becomes an uncoordinated and unbalanced action.

The effects of yielding in the martial arts have their psychological equivalents in clinical work. Yielding to and absorbing the other's aggressive reactions (or other affective responses) may alleviate the intensity of those reactions—which, in psychotherapy, may correspond to a catharsis that plays itself out, the soothing effects of empathy, or the metabolizing functions of a holding environment. By yielding to and evading attacks (which means not running away or striking back) one may also cause opponents to exaggerate their movements and lose their balance. They attempt to advance against a target, but find no target there. Like patients attempting to tackle the clinician's analytic neutrality, they end up tripping over themselves or getting in their own way; expecting to find a solid target, they overextend their efforts. In the case of psychotherapy patients, they stumble onto their own unconscious dynamics and overextend their efforts in the form of transference.

Effective yielding is not entirely soft. Centeredness requires an internal vitality and strength at the core of yielding: *yang* within *yin*. Martial artists use the analogy of a steel bar wrapped in cotton, or a peach that is soft on the outside and hard on the inside. In karate, one meets a blow to the body by remaining relaxed and pliant on the outside, in order to absorb the initial force; then, as the blow penetrates, one meets and repels the remaining force with a strong inner "spirit" (Nicol, 1982). Similarly, the clinician's empathic posture absorbs the patient's subjective experience and affective reactions; but a strong inner core repels any strong affect from disrupting the clinician's centeredness and from inflicting psychological damage on the clinician. This inner solidity assures patients that they will not corrupt, hurt, destroy, or engulf the therapist.

Joining and Leading

In judo and aikido, yielding involves more than simply giving way to an incoming movement. It entails joining, leading, and redirecting the movement. One moves off the line of the approaching force, harmonizes oneself with it, and, by adding a small amount of energy to that force, leads it even further in the direction it was headed or smoothly redirects it onto another path, usually the path of least resistance. By accepting and leading the movement, one takes control of it. This yielding or *ju* allows the incoming momentum to spend itself or throw itself off balance.

Tart (1987) described how he applies these principles of aikido to everyday conversation. When others challenge or attack something he has said, he moves off the line of the attack and says something that expresses his agreement with some element of what they have stated. After having established this alliance with them, he then gently leads the argument to the conclusion that he intends to communicate to them, even though that conclusion may be quite different from that held by the challengers. As they arrive with him to the conclusion, the opponents more easily accept where they have been led. The less gentle variant of this strategy is to join and lead the challengers, and then upset their balance and "throw" them from their position by introducing an idea that obviously contradicts what they had posed.

These strategies can be applied to situations that are emotional, as well as intellectual or cognitive, and to a variety of affects other than anger and hostility. Psychotherapists often join and harmonize themselves with the experience of their patients, whatever that experience might be—thus establishing a therapeutic alliance—and then proceed to lead the patient's awareness to deeper, unconscious dimensions of the issues at hand. The process of gradual, empathic immersion into the patient's subjective world often entails a subtle redirecting of the patient, rather than simply following the patient's experience. The process of interpreting, which often is most effective after joining the patient, may entail throwing the person from his or her intrapsychic equilibrium into a new insight into unconscious dynamics. The new insight may contradict aspects of what the patient previously experienced on a conscious level. The sometimes controversial technique of "joining the resistance" follows a similar pattern. By accepting and joining the patient's defenses or resistances, by adding additional energy to the direction of those defenses, the clinician can gradually lead the patient into a more productive path or throw the patient from the status quo of his or her resistance. Silverberg (in press) suggested that such work with resistance may be one of the most powerful aspects of psychotherapy.

Martial artists point out that the highest level of skill in joining-and-leading enables one to influence the opponent on an extremely subtle level. Hyams (1982) described how you can lead opponents' energy (*chi*) without their mind feeling disturbed; if you steer their *chi*, the rest of them follows along. Even before opponents initiate a movement, you sense their intention, their *chi,* and lead it without having to deal with the physical movement. Redirect the mind and the body follows. It is a process of leading the opponent's attention. Similarly, skilled clinicians can sense, join, and guide the patient's intentions even before the patient's ideas, words, or affects have fully surfaced to a conscious level.

Joining-and-leading is a distinctly empathic process. In the martial arts, blending with the attack helps one empathize with the attacker's position and point of view. Leonard (1989) stated that the ultimate goal is not to control or master opponents, but to serve them. One becomes so sensitive to their intentions and needs—physical or psychological—that one knows precisely where they want to go and what they want to do. Blending with them, one helps opponents do what they intend. The thrower is not separate from the thrown; together they enter a unified dance that rejoins them to "the harmony of nature" (Leonard, 1989, p. 180). "We blend into a single motion, a small ripple in an endless sea of existence" (p. 177). In psychotherapy, the empathic-introspective process contains similar elements of serving, blending, and harmonizing.

Adhering

Yielding and joining require that one follow the other's movements closely. In the martial arts, this is known as "adhering." Musashi (1982) called it the "body of lacquer and glue" (p. 46). You stick closely to the opponent's actions, not allowing any gaps. However, the distance should be optimal, allowing you room to move freely and to avoid becoming entangled with the opponent. The Japanese refer to this as *maai*—the "ideal space" in which you are close to the opponent, but the opponent cannot use that closeness to control you (James & Jones, 1982). One grasps the opponent, but is not grasped by the opponent. The basic point, according to Liang and Ji (1989) in their comments on Sun Tzu, is to forget oneself and follow the other, like the cat that quietly, intently watches the mouse. Do not make the first move, which may be awkward and misdirected. Instead, simply follow and observe, which involves movements that are more light and agile. In a perfect equilibrium between self and other, bend when opponents advance, expand when they contract, and remain still when they are motionless. Match speed with speed and depth of movement with equal depth.

By following the other's actions without initiating your own, you are able to measure the rhythm, strengths, and vulnerabilities of the opponent's movements. As Sun Tzu (1971) suggested, a general must know the terrain before the battle begins. Good warriors first assess their opponent and sensitize themselves to trends and changes. By doing so, they can take advantage of opportunities that may arise, as well as deal with the unexpected.

In psychotherapy, clinicians use empathic mirroring to adhere to the patient's experience. Giving up their own memories and desires, they attempt to attach themselves to the patient's subjective explorations. But empathy is never a perfectly continuous or evenly layered process. The empathic-introspective energy of the intersubjective field ebbs and flows. There are disruptions and gaps in adhering to the patient's experience, sometimes because of momentary, sporadic lapses of attention, or the more persistent interference of unmastered countertransference. Ideally, therapists' empathic observing of patients is a light and agile mindfulness. They match the patient's speed and depth of intrapsychic change; they patiently wait when the patient's progress has stalled. Maintaining an optimal distance, they avoid becoming entangled in the patient's unconscious distortions and allow themselves enough free space to move into an interpretation or some other therapeutic intervention. Without making the first move (an aspect of analytic neutrality), they assess the status and fluctuations in the patient's experience. By initially adhering to and following these trends and changes, they can detect openings in the patient's stance. These openings may be lapses in defenses that allow for an interpretation, or openings that permit the clinician's empathic pose to enter into deeper intrapsychic issues.

Advancing/Attacking

Proponents of the hard styles in the martial arts state that there comes a time in an encounter when one must attack. Even in the soft styles, the techniques of yielding, joining, adhering, and leading at some point turn into the initiation of a movement against the opponent. One must at times advance, rather than simply wait.

"Attack" may be too strong a word to be relevant to the interventions of the clinician in psychotherapy. However, the therapist does at times advance toward the patient in a manner that is more assertive than the techniques of yielding and adhering. Defense interpretations are advances against the structures that block therapeutic progress. Interpretations in general are advances against repressive barriers, and are designed as incursions into deeper layers of subjective experience.

Even self psychologists, who sometimes are criticized for the apparently passive quality of their empathic posture, can be assertive in their penetration into unconscious experience. Kohut (1984) related the case of a patient who arrogantly tossed himself onto the analytic couch and proceeded to describe how he had been stopped for speeding on the way to his session. The police officer had been inclined to let him off, but the patient acted so belligerent that the officer was provoked into giving him a ticket. In an unrepentant tone of voice, the patient recalled similar incidents over the years when his driving "like a bat out of hell" had involved him in several accidents. Kohut silently listened to his outpouring for several minutes. When the patient's verbosity finally subsided, Kohut paused, then stated that he was about to give the most important interpretation he had so far offered in this analysis. The patient was utterly surprised at such an announcement, the likes of which he had never before heard from Kohut. After several seconds of silence, Kohut said very firmly and very seriously, "You are a complete idiot." There was another moment of silence, after which the patient broke into laughter and visibly relaxed. They spent the remainder of the session openly discussing for the first time the patient's self-destructive tendencies and emotional tantrums.

Advances toward the other do not necessarily have to be quick, sudden, or forceful to be effective. Musashi (1982) claimed that in sword duels, speed is not important. A master works with ease without any loss of timing. Experienced practitioners conducting their art form do not look busy, whereas inexperienced people often feel that they are lagging behind even though they are working briskly. Without initiating a clearly definable advance, Musashi stated, the skilled swordsman renders motions that are gradual, flowing, and continuous, eventually culminating in a cut. As in psychotherapy, where clinicians may gradually build their comments toward a final, decisive interpretation, all the movements are part of the closing move. In the most efficient execution of this advance, nothing is wasted. All the therapist's comments, and all the words and ideas in these comments, are concise, powerful, and to the point. As Sun Tzu (1971) stated, never make a useless move, and take no step without a clear purpose.

Judo masters state that the best expression of energy is to achieve the best possible result from the least possible force; another translation for *ju* is "delicacy" (Randon, 1978). Liang and Ji (1989), in their commentaries on Sun Tzu, similarly emphasized the value of minimalism in battle: Do not overextend your position when advancing—as in premature interpretations in psychotherapy, which may intensify defenses and drive important issues underground. By anticipating events ahead of time, one can make small moves that later yield large effects: "Do the great when it is still small" (p. 17). By making casual, interpretative "hints," the clinician can plant a seed in the patient's thoughts that later blossoms into productive therapeutic work.

An advance will never be effective unless there is an opening. Sun Tzu (1971) stated, "One may know how to conquer without being able to do it" (p. 19). By adhering to the other's movements, one senses the moment when an opening occurs—when, in the case of psychotherapy, the patient is ready to hear an interpretation. With contemplative awareness, clinicians ride the momentum of the tide of events until an opportunity appears; they feel out the intersubjective field for revealing fluctuations in the resonance of empathic introspection. Musashi (1982) called such openings *suki*—the space between two objects or interval in time that allows something to enter. In the encounter between self and other, it appears as a momentary stopping of the mind's activities. A gap appears in the other's stream of consciousness. For the psychotherapy patient, it may be a brief pause in verbalizations, a sudden break in defensive posture, or a moment when a new realm of subjective experience unlocks to the clinician's empathic attunement. That moment is the opportunity to advance and enter.

As the martial artist or psychotherapist approaches that instant, he or she may experience a concentration or tightening of the mind known as *kime* in Japanese karate. The practitioner excludes extraneous thoughts and localizes all attention on the immediate moment. It requires the ability to focus and direct all power and energy to a single point, while retaining inner calm and balance. Randon (1978) compared *kime* to a laser beam that penetrates to deep regions by passing safely and easily through outside layers. Karate masters can strike a stack of bricks and shatter one specific brick several layers down, while leaving those on top intact. When making a timely interpretation in psychotherapy, clinicians may experience this focusing of their attention and affect on the intervention. In some situations they may use this concentration of effort to effectively penetrate past any distractions or residual defenses within the patient.

One school of thought concerning martial technique emphasizes the cultivation of the singular, definitive attack. Musashi (1982) called it *utsu*—the convergence of all one's effort and concentration into one decisive and flawless blow. It commits you to a course of action from which there is no return. Some sword masters perfected the art of moving almost instantaneously from a casual standing posture, with their sword sheathed, to a forceful, focused, and deadly cut. There was no room for error. Concerning karate, Funakoshi (1981) stated that when you strike a blow, "you must have no doubt whatsoever that one blow decides everything" (p. 105). Stated even more dramatically, Herrigel's (1971) archery master Awa proclaimed, "One life, one shot." Letting go of the arrow into a perfect hit is only the outward manifestation of the inner events of the archer. Good shots filled with spiritual richness, he claimed, travel deeper and further.

Some schools of thought in psychoanalysis emphasize the technique of the singular, definitive interpretation. The clinician waits and quietly listens with evenly hovering attention until a pattern of the patient's unconscious slowly crystallizes. At least three pieces of evidence supporting the validity of an interpretation must be sifted from the patient's associations before the interpretation can be presented. Ideally, the evidence integrates an aspect of the patient's past relationships, present relationships, and transference to the clinician—what some therapists refer to as an intersection of the there/then, there/now, and here/now. But clinicians do not derive the evidence only from the patient's experience; they must also sort through their own associations and countertransference to gather and integrate the material. If they can present the evidence in a single, concise, and definitive interpretation that comes from the richness of their own intrapsychic world, as well as from that of the patient, it will travel far and deep. This school of thought acknowledges and accepts the fact that only one such interpretation might be offered during the course of a session, or even several sessions. Otherwise, the clinician remains silent.

Randon (1978) outlined Master Anzawa's categorization of the qualities of good and poor shots in archery. The list easily could be a menu for good and poor interpretations in psychotherapy. There are shots that are controlled or careless; overcautious or hasty and thoughtless; possessing clear vision or lacking in prescience; uniform or disorderly; profound or superficial; anticipated or unexpected; selfless or self-centered; ripe or premature; trained or undisciplined; launched by correct positioning or by incorrect movement.

The ancient martial arts masters also offered a variety of other ideas about advancing and attacking that may inform the clinician's interpretative maneuvers in psychotherapy, particularly the interpretation of defenses. Musashi (1982) suggested that one may advance against the corners of the other's position, thereby weakening the center; or move against one strong point, and when it weakens, move against another strong point, and then another—a process of zigzagging that creates openings in the other's overall posture. He also advised the use of "mountain and sea change" (p. 75). If you use a move and it fails, it is unlikely to succeed on the second try. Never use a tactic three times. Be unpredictable. If the opponents expect mountain, give them sea; if they expect sea, give them mountain. Create confusion or momentary distractions by feigning an advance, then move into the openings that appear as a result of that moment of unbalance. Sun Tzu (1971) suggested that if the opponent is defended simultaneously in several places, some positions will be much stronger than others. Avoid the heavily defended sites and advance on those that are weaker. He advised one to become more focused and earnest the further one penetrates into the other's territory. Other such techniques (some of which may strike the clinician as unorthodox) will be discussed later.

The martial arts offer insightful observations not just about the techniques and attitudes that lead up to an advance on the opponent, but also about what occurs afterward. These insights parallel those concerning psychotherapy. Herrigel (1971) indicated that after the perfect shot in archery, the heart continues to beat evenly and quietly; concentration is undisturbed. Although the shot was perfect, the archer feels that the day has just begun; "He feels in the mood for all right doing and all right not-doing" (p. 61). Archers must not grieve over bad shots, nor rejoice over good ones. If they do celebrate, it is as if someone else had made the shot, or as if the shot originated from some realm "beyond" oneself. They are free from the buffetings of disappointment and pride (a dilemma often experienced by beginning psychotherapists). In their commentaries on Sun Tzu, Liang and Ji (1989) stated that, "When you have won, be as if you had not" (p. 20). Do not relax even after your advance has been successful; remain aware and prepared. "Accept a surrender as you would take on an opponent" (p. 129). Wait and see if the person's surrender is genuine or not. Successful interpretations in psychotherapy unlock the unconscious, and therefore may produce unexpected results, including unforeseen transference reactions. Interpretations that appear to be successful—for example, those with which the patient immediately agrees—may not be correct at all.

The Harmony of Yielding and Advancing

In the perfect blend of hard and soft styles in the martial arts, as well as in the art of psychotherapy, yielding and advancing complement one another. When they are most effective, hard and soft techniques are inseparable. The Tai Chi Chuan exercise known as "push-hands" clearly demonstrates this insight and serves as a beautiful analogy for the psychotherapeutic process. In push-hands, two partners stand in close proximity and engage each other in complex patterns of fluidly interlocking motions where each person senses and responds to the other's yielding and advancing. The goal is to locate the other's center and use that point to displace the person from their balance. An analogous dance of sensing and responding to the other's cognitive-affective fluctuations occurs between therapist and patient in psychotherapy. For the therapist, locating the patient's center means penetrating to central, unconscious issues. The therapist uses that center as a pivotal point for displacing the patient from the static equilibrium of pathological formations and onto new paths for healthy psychological development. For the patient, retreats are the defensive avoidance of the clinician's attempts to find this center, whereas advances are the transferential reactions and other affective responses that are impelled toward the clinician.

Jou's (1980) analysis of push-hands effectively summarized these harmonizing dynamics of yielding and advancing that have been alluded to throughout this section on hard and soft techniques. His ideas readily translate into the principles employed by therapists. In *tsou*, or "leading by walking away" (p. 242), one gives no resistance to an incoming force. One must use *ting* (awareness, careful listening) in order to sense, adhere to, and follow that force; one cannot know how or where to yield unless one can discern the force's direction and magnitude. In *nien*, one advances when the opponent retreats by continuing to sense, adhere to, and follow the other's movement. Like *tsou*, *nien* also relies on *ting* to detect the course, speed, and strength of the motion.

Tsou and *nien* must be reciprocal, balancing actions that are joined seamlessly together by sensing and adhering. Jou uses the analogy of a swinging door between two people. If one yields too much, contact with the other person will be broken (e.g., the clinician's break in empathic contact when hastily retreating from transference reactions). As a result, one's advantageous position and opportunities for locating the other's center are lost. When yielding too late, one clashes with the incoming movement. In *nien*, if one advances too quickly, resistance will be encountered (e.g., the resistance encountered by premature interpretations); if one advances too late, contact with the other and the opportunity for locating the center is lost. The effectiveness of both *tsou* and *nien* rely on timing.

By balancing *tsou* and *nien*, one can yield, but also hold one's ground by maintaining contact. One may use this balance to create *hua*—the holding and neutralizing of the other's force, which, in psy-chotherapy, corresponds to the empathic holding and soothing of the patient's affective reactions. *Hua* is the efficient harmonizing of *tsou* and *nien*.

By balancing *tsou* and *nien*, one also can subtly follow the other's movements (including retreats) and detect openings for *fa*—the attack/advance on the other's center that allows one to displace other people from their position. Knowing the exact moment when the opening appears enables one to use minimum force, but still be extremely effective. By harmonizing *tsou* and *nien*, one senses when, where, and how to advance. Early advances meet resistance and waste effort. Late advances allow others time and energy to adjust their stance and counter one's movement.

Other martial arts masters have offered insights concerning the balance of yielding and advancing. Musashi (1982) noted that when one is deflecting or dodging the opponent's advances, one must keep in mind ways for turning those yielding motions into one's own ad-vance toward the opponent. Liang and Ji (1989) stated that learning how to yield completely will teach one how to advance. Recommend-ing the technique of "varying the substantial and insubstantial," they also suggested that when the opponent attacks at a certain point, one should make that point insubstantial, but at the same time become substantial at another point and use that point to advance; it is a method of "folding up" in which withdrawing and advancing coin-cide. When you poke the head of a snake, it responds with its tail, and vice versa. Finally, Cheng Yi (see Liang & Ji, 1989, p. 18) stated that "if you do not press any contention that you should not press, and go back to find out the real truth, you will change insecurity into security . . ." Rather than continuing to advance interventions that don't seem to be working, clinicians are well advised to yield, reex-amine their strategies, and discover more therapeutic alternatives.

The Harmony Between Stillness and Action

The martial artist, like the psychotherapist, strives to maintain a state of balance between stillness and action. Tohei (1966) claimed that people who participate only in the quiet disciplines, such as medita-tion, easily fall into the habit of idealizing calmness and tend to stag-nate in that sedate inactivity. On the other hand, those who prize the active disciplines respect only activity and easily become frenzied in their bustling about. Some therapists also tend to stagnate (perhaps narcissistically) in their contemplative free associations without initiating enough therapeutic interventions, whereas others get swept up in a whirlwind of questions, comments, and interpretations.

Ideally, one balances stillness with action. In a martial or therapeutic encounter, one may pause for a variety of reasons: to find one's rhythm, assess the other's intentions, alter one's strategies, or disrupt the other's cadence by not following a predictable pattern. Like the pause between notes in music, stillness is an integral component of the composition (Hyams, 1982).

In Tai Chi Chuan—and Taoist philosophy in general—the transition from stillness to action, from *wu chi* to *tai chi*, lies at the heart of all processes of change and transformation. How does the martial artist move from the posture of contemplative stillness into an active advance on the opponent? How does the clinician shift from the silent awareness of evenly hovering attention into a verbal intervention? The ancient martial artists intensely studied this polarity between motionlessness and motion to discover the secrets of the perfect balance and transition between the two.

While studying archery under the great master Awa, Herrigel (1971) struggled with this essential lesson. With the arrow carefully positioned and the bow fully drawn, when was the best moment to let the arrow go? In the perfect shot, Awa explained, the arrow flies on its own; stillness spontaneously transforms into action. Herrigel waited for this moment to come, but his own efforts defeated him. His expectations and anticipations sabotaged his technique and concentration. Straining his strength, with the bow pulled to its limit, Herrigel found himself growing impatient, tense, shaky. Doubts about himself and the teachings infiltrated his thoughts. Anxiety disrupted his focus on the present moment. The shot failed.

Psychotherapists, waiting to make the "perfect" interpretation, may encounter the same dilemma. Their expectations, desires, and ambitions for that perfect moment disrupt their attention. They wonder if they will miss their chance. They drown in the cognitive strain of planning the impeccably phrased intervention. Their anxiety builds. Empathic contact is lost. The interpretation may become entangled and confused with their own personal doubts and insecurities. Finally, they feel pressured to speak—but the effort is too late, too hasty, off target.

An ancient Zen saying states, "You may find your own character at the moment of shooting." Anticipating and waiting for the perfect shot throws one into the depths of one's own intrapsychic world. Herrigel (1971) described how a flurry of memories, feelings, and desires surface because one has touched previously unreached realms. The perfect shot arises simultaneously from the aim to the target and to one's inner self. Letting go of the shot, according to Master Awa, is a matter of life and death. One's whole being should enter it: "One shot, one life" (p. 34).

The perfect shot waits at this point of highest tension. But one cannot consciously plan or force it. Master Awa explained to Herrigel that he should not think about what he had to do. There could be no intention. The shot goes smoothly when it takes the archer by surprise, when it occurs spontaneously. You immerse into yourself, and allow anxieties and doubts to surface if they must; but you stay at that point of highest tension until the shot falls from you. When the tension is fulfilled—when, for the therapist, the affect of transference and countertransference blossom together—the shot will fall by itself. Attaining a paradoxical harmony of calm and tension, one reaches an egoless state of no-self in which the spontaneous, fluid mind is not attached anywhere in particular but is present everywhere. The tension is purposeless, without ambition or desire. Hits are outward manifestations of these inner events, of internal purposelessness and selflessness at their highest. Good shots filled with this spiritual richness, Awa stated, travel far and deep.

Following the principles of *yin* and *yang*, stillness and action are embedded in each other. In the martial arts and psychotherapy, one seeks motion within stillness and stillness within motion. A quiet outward appearance encloses an inner core of dynamic awareness. Quick, forceful advances are most effective when they arise from and are sustained by inner calmness. Tohei (1966) used the analogies of the spinning top, which reaches its most stable point when at peak speed, and the calm center at the eye of the hurricane. Ideally, stillness and action give rise to and sustain each other.

The Harmony of Form and Formlessness

All disciplines require the mastering of techniques. The techniques constitute the outward form or appearance of the discipline. Although learning techniques is necessary, it is not in itself sufficient for penetrating to the true spirit of the art. Musashi (1982), for example, claimed that the martial schools that simply emphasize technique without developing the underlying philosophy and attitude of *Heiho* are weak and ineffectual. Funakoshi (1981) made similar comments about karate practitioners who emphasize the logistics of technique: they have lost the heart and soul of the art. Mastering the form is a stepping stone to other dimensions that are more hidden, more form-less, and ultimately more powerful.

The beginning stages of training in any discipline emphasize the repetition of basic skills. In the martial arts, the ritualized rehearsal of *kata* gradually build power, speed, and fluidity in the application of technique. From repeatedly striking the *makiwara* with his fist, over and over again, Nicol (1982) learned that it was an exercise that grad-ually molded concentration, rhythm, strength, and the awareness of distance and timing. Through disciplined training, one learns to sub-stitute techniques for other, instinctive responses that may be inap-propriate, ineffective, or harmful to the art. Because there are too many techniques to learn all at once, Funakoshi (1981) noted, the stu-dent must fully understand each one before moving on to another. The tireless repetition of basic skills eventually enables the student to see the complex relationship among those skills. They are all inter-related; there are underlying, universal principles. Sun Tzu (1971) stated that even when there are only a few basic techniques, the com-bination and interaction of those techniques are infinite. Although there are only five musical notes and five primary colors, he noted, the range of music and color compositions is without end and reaches to principles that transcend the basic elements. While teaching these basic principles, teachers at first may simplify instructions by creating rules, but as students progress they discover the exceptions and qual-ifications of the rules. The form of the discipline starts to crumble as they move toward deeper, less tangible insights.

These ideas readily apply to psychotherapy training, as in the example of learning the basic therapeutic technique of reflection. Be-cause it seems relatively simple, students use it over and over again in their beginning cases. Gradually, they learn to appreciate the rhythm, timing, and power of the technique. When introduced willy-nilly, or just to have something to say, reflections serve little purpose. Stu-dents learn to reflect affect—including painful affect, thereby over-coming their natural, colloquial inclination to reassure people and steer away from unpleasant emotions. They learn that reflections, when used effectively, are closely related to interpretations. They re-alize that sometimes a powerful reflection is to say nothing at all. The ultimate insight is that this technique is but a manifestation of the more fundamental psychotherapeutic process of uncovering the un-conscious.

Funakoshi (1981) related a story that supports the idea that the student must fully master a specific set of techniques or one theoretical approach before attempting to learn others. A dramatic-ballad singer studied under a strict teacher who insisted that he rehearse—day after day, month after month—the same passage from the Tai-koki, without being permitted to go any further. Finally, over-whelmed by frustration and despair, the young man ran off to find another profession. One night, stopping at an inn, he stumbled upon a recitation contest. Having nothing to lose, he entered the contest and, of course, sang the passage from the Taikoki that he knew so well. When he had finished, the sponsor of the contest praised his performance. Despite the student's embarrassed objections, the sponsor refused to believe he had just heard a beginner perform. He insisted on knowing the name of his instructor, who, the sponsor proclaimed, must be a great master. The student eventually became known as the great master Koshiji.

By practicing a technique repeatedly, it becomes thoroughly internalized. It can be applied fluidly, spontaneously, creatively, without the burden of self-consciousness. Movements become simple and elegant. At that point, the martial arts masters claim, the technique flows through the clear, open awareness of *mushin*. In fact, *mushin* is attained through the practicing of *kata* and the ritualization of technique. Musashi (1982) called this *munen musho*—the ability to apply technique spontaneously, without conscious thought, effort, or intention. The perfect shot in archery, Herrigel (1971) explained, does not even feel like the repetition of a technique. It feels as if one "were creating it under the inspiration of the moment," as if it "comes from the center" (p. 62).

In the Chinese martial arts, the concept of *hsing I* captures the interaction between technical form and its inner intention or meaning (Reid & Croucher, 1983). At the highest level of study, one no longer shows outward form *(hsing)*, as in the beginning phases; or feels the intention or meaning of the form *(I)* without showing the form, as in the intermediate phases. At the highest level, one acts without *hsing* or *I*; there is no form and no preoccupation with the meaning or intent of the form. One returns to the point of origin. One is free and flexible to respond to all possibilities.

At that level, the technique is no longer a technique. It has become part of one's personality, an extension of it. The skilled martial artist and the skilled clinician perform their work not as the application of a set of skills, but as an expression of themselves. There is no need to consciously articulate one's mastery, because the art is strongly felt, strongly experienced. In his comparison of the martial arts to psychoanalysis, Parsons (1984) stated that the "examination of what the analyst is doing reveals it as a way of being for the analyst, an embodiment of who he is" (p. 457). Once clinicians have passed the initial phases of mastering techniques and theories, they move into the advanced phases of molding the techniques and theories according to their own personality structure; they learn how to use themselves, their own intrapsychic dynamics and subjective meanings, as the agents of psychotherapeutic change. A single interpretation with a single patient is the culmination of years of clinical practice interfused with the cultivation of one's personality: "One shot, one life."

Technical knowledge, therefore, is not enough. One has to transcend technique so that the art becomes what the masters called an "artless art" that arises out of the unconscious. "The bow and arrow," Herrigel (1971) stated, "are only a pretext for something that could just as well happen without them, only a way to the goal, not the goal itself . . ." (p. 8). When techniques and theories are surpassed—when they are perfectly assimilated—practitioners resemble the novices they once were when they knew nothing. They regain the same state of innocence in which they were unaware of and unhampered by rules, procedures, and theories; they have reached the "way without a way." Nardi (1984) referred to the Japanese martial concept of *rinkiohen*, the fluid, chameleonlike adaptability to all circumstances that goes beyond the haphazard application of techniques, and instead relies on the spontaneous expression and unique synthesis of various skills, according to one's own being. The original forms move into formlessness. "I have no principles," a *samurai* saying proclaimed, "I make *rinkiohen* my principles."

Suzuki (1970) referred to this advanced level of knowledge as the "beginner's mind" in which knowledge is forgotten. In the expert's mind there are limited possibilities; in the beginner's mind anything is possible. A famous Zen story tells of a professor who visited a Zen master. It was obvious by his conversation that he intended to impress the master with his knowledge of Zen philosophy. The master poured his visitor a cup of tea, and kept pouring even after the cup started to overflow. When the startled professor pointed out the apparent error, the master replied, "How can I show you Zen unless you first empty your cup?" Emptying one's cup means transcending the forms of theory and technique to enter the realm of formlessness that gives birth to theory and technique. One's self, one's own mind, is the vehicle into that replete realm. "Out of the fullness of this pres-

ence of mind, disturbed by no ulterior motive, the artist who is released from all attachment must practice his art . . ." (Herrigel, 1971,
p. 42).

If the martial arts and the art of psychotherapy become an expression of self, then the art becomes one's life. The philosophy—the
heart or spirit that underlies the techniques—is not restricted to the
discipline; it becomes one's life philosophy. A *samurai* maxim stated,
"A man who has attained mastery of an art reveals it in his every
action."

Unorthodox Strategies

Traditionally, psychotherapists are portrayed as straightforward and
honest in their methods. There are no attempts to manipulate the patient, no tricks, no hidden agendas. But contrary to the conventional
view, the forthright approach does not always work. Clinicians have
come to realize that the direct, aboveboard techniques that work so
well with neurotic problems sometimes fall short in the treatment of
severe personality disorders, narcissistic pathology, and psychosis.
Even those psychoanalysts who are reluctant to stray from the principles of analytic neutrality and the rule of abstinence recognize this dilemma. Ever since Eissler's (1953) speculations about the need to
introduce "parameters" into treatment, analytically minded clinicians
have experimented with techniques that are more covertly strategic in
design—techniques that sometimes resemble the so-called "paradoxical" therapies. Every therapist has heard and read about such methods. An analyst joins in and even outdoes his patient's delusions
about traveling to other planets. An extremely histrionic patient pops
out of her convulsions when her psychologist enthusiastically pulls
out a camera to take a snapshot of her drama. During the treatment of
a man who is terribly afraid that his anger will destroy his doctor, the
therapist insists that he bring his rage into the session "so we can feel
closer."

Martial artists have attempted to perfect such covert, indirect
strategies. This was especially true of the great Chinese tactician Sun
Tzu. The art of maneuvering, he claimed, was to make the indirect
route the most direct: "turn the devious into the direct and misfor-
tune into gain" (1983, p. 30). Similar to what clinicians learned about
unorthodox therapeutic techniques, Sun Tzu's insight was that what
appears to be a circuitous or even counterproductive path for affect-
ing the other's position actually may be the most impactful tactic.
Trickery and "deception" played a major role in his philosophy:

All warfare is based on deception. Hence, when able to attack, we must seem unable; when using our forces, we must seem inactive; when we are near, we must make the enemy believe we are far away; when far away, we must make him believe we are near. (1983, p. 11)

"Deception" is a strong word that would make many psychotherapists uncomfortable. However, clinicians often do not immediately disclose to their patients their therapeutic strategies or diagnostic assessments. They may hold on to an interpretation for weeks, months, or years before offering it. The time must be right. In particular, the classic psychoanalytic posture of analytic neutrality carries with it an element of "deception" that is reminiscent of Sun Tzu. Until the interpretation is made, the patient, while revealing her- or himself, cannot see past the analyst's silent, blank screen. The analyst has a strategy that is unknown to the patient until the advance is made. One of Sun Tzu's most basic principles is that we try to discover the opponent's dispositions while remaining invisible ourselves. This enables us to keep our forces concentrated, while forcing opponents to divide their forces to protect all fronts, thereby revealing their vulnerabilities.

Sun Tzu's classic work *The Art of War* is filled with examples of deceptive strategies that are worthy of the psychotherapist's consideration. Throwing out an odd or unaccountable behavior will make the opponent stop and think, which often creates an opportunity for you to advance. Set up a false formation that diverts and divides the other's energies; "induce others to construct a formation while you yourself are formless" (1983, p. 94). When opponents are strong, use humility and courtesy to make them overconfident, then wait for an opening in their position. Feign weakness to find an opening when opponents slacken their posture or make a revealing move. In a similar vein, Musashi (1982) recommended the technique of "intoxication," in which one pretends to be relaxed and easy-going, giving the opponent the feeling that one is inferior. The attitude is transferred to the opponent, who also relaxes and lets down his or her defenses. By contrast, he also suggested the strategy of "moving the shadow." When unsure of your opponent's intentions, pretend that you are about to attack forcefully, which will cause the opponent to reveal his or her plans. In judo, many of these techniques fall under the category of *kusushi*, or "breaking balance." For opponents who thwart your efforts by being passive or prepared, you can upset the balance of their position by exaggerating or feigning weakness. It is an attempt to destructure the other's status quo while creating opportunities for restructuring (Gleser & Brown, 1988). Some of these strategies, though appearing deceptive on the surface, can be employed empathically. The clinician implicitly expresses the hope of opening up pathways to a deeper understanding of the unconscious.

Such techniques of deception are never used carelessly, excessively, or without regimen. Sun Tzu stated that to feign disorder, one must be disciplined; to feign cowardice, one must be brave; to appear weak one must be strong. He also suggested that the most effective overall approach to create change and opportunity is to combine and alternate obvious strategy with unexpected, unorthodox strategy.

Sun Tzu's book is filled with other suggestions about tactics that might be useful to clinicians. How and when these suggestions can be useful will depend, of course, on their suitability to particular patients and on the therapist's skill in applying Sun Tzu's ideas.

Participating in Transcendent Realms

That mastering martial techniques can be a self-transformative process should not detract us from recognizing the important social functions of the martial arts—functions similar to those in the world of psychotherapy. The martial arts comprise communal networks consisting of complex systems of beliefs, values, and customs, all of which potentially serve the selfobject function of supporting the sense of self. Within the individual *dojo*, a social context is provided for the reenactment and amelioration of family dynamics. Kauz (1977) suggested that the master serves as the demanding but idealized father figure who compassionately nurtures the growth of the students. As a multifaceted combination of teacher, parent, and professional guide, he models social, moral, and spiritual values, and not simply martial techniques. Senior students play the role of benevolent sisters and brothers. Following the tradition of Japanese society and culture, the social order is clear. The unambiguous hierarchy of status and interpersonal responsibilities may be reparative for those people who come from families in which roles were confused or reversed.

The instructors and masters also benefit from the communal selfobject functions of working with students. Although being idealized may bolster their sense of self, Tohei (1966) warned that conceit can block their personal progress in the art, as well as their abilities as teachers. He suggested that the more important benefit is the mirroring that takes place between instructors and students as fellow travelers along a universal path. They reflect each other's development, their respective virtues and weaknesses. As a communal act, the martial arts lead both student and teacher to an idealized, transcendent realm of meaning and truth that sustains the sense of self. In his philosophy of Shotokan karate, Funakoshi (1981) asserted that teachers should not think of students simply as students, because their abilities may someday surpass the master's own. The true spirit of the martial arts is the recognition that it is a way of life in which everyone, student and teacher alike, participates in a realm larger than the individual self. "By extending help to others and by accepting it from them, a man acquires the ability to elevate the act into a faith wherein he perfects both body and soul, and so comes finally to recognize the true meaning of karate-do" (p. 110). We may think of experienced clinicians, therapists-in-training, and patients as similar travelers along a universal path.

Rather than simply boosting the teacher's narcissism, the student's idealization can join student and teacher in this path to a connectedness with the transcendent. When students become dissatisfied with their skills, as compared to those of their teachers, and feel they will never attain the same level of expertise, they feel encouraged and sustained by the fact that the teachers often feel the same way about their own teachers—a process that also occurs among psychotherapists. This lineage of idealization creates a continuum of learning and inspiration that drives one's progress toward a transcendent goal. This continuum is supported by the legendary stories of the great ancient masters (or the master psychotherapists) who demonstrated seemingly superhuman feats of skill and knowledge. Whether the stories are true or not may be irrelevant; they serve important instructive and selfobject functions.

For both the psychotherapist and the martial artist, an important aspect of practice is the sense of belonging to a structured, disciplined society, larger than the individual self, that has a long, distinguished history. The feeling that one participates in this lineage serves the selfobject function of bolstering the cohesion and continuity of the individual self.

As Hyams (1982) and Trungpa (1988) suggested, lineage also connects one to the realm of primordial wisdom. In the martial arts, the ritualistic practice of forms and kata that have been passed down through the centuries enables one to touch the warrior ancestry of all humanity. For therapists, exploring the meaning of a dream, similarly, may join them to the visions of the human mind beheld by Freud, Jung, and the ancient sages of the unconscious that preceded them. These realms of wisdom into which one immerses oneself are profound, vast, unlimited. Because the martial artist and psychotherapist attempt to perfect their skills and knowledge in a sphere that is limitless and ungraspable in its fullness, their struggles connect them to the transcendent. Those who are looking for quick instructions and easy answers soon drop out of the discipline. Those who endure are attracted to the infinite and steadfastness of purpose in pursuing that which can never be fully mastered. Paradoxically, they connect to the ungraspable realm of the infinite that both transcends the self and sustains it.

9

Tai Chi Images: The Tao of Psychotherapy

Psychotherapy is a subtle, intricate process. As the art and science of psychotherapy advances, we search for new, more comprehensive frameworks to organize our understanding of its complexities. Some of these frameworks evolve into highly abstract conceptual systems. Rooted squarely in the contemporary technological and scientific *zeitgeist*, some models draw on advances in neurology, physics, engineering, or computer science.

Here, I propose a model that is more intuitive and imagistic than objectively conceptual and abstract. It draws more on ancient thought than on contemporary science. At first glance, it may appear to be an example of "Orientocentrism" (Rubin, 1992a), falling prey to the mistaken tendency to glorify Eastern thinking and subjugate Western principles to those ideas. Instead, I intend it as a format for containing and harmonizing Eastern and Western insights. Together, both the cup and the tea it holds make the act of drinking possible.

The Tai Chi System

Almost 4000 years ago, the great Emperor Fu Hsi, founder of the first Chinese dynasty and a devout scholar of Taoist philosophy, created the system known as the *Tai Chi*, which can be translated as the "Supreme Ultimate." Although appearing far from modest in selecting this term, Fu Hsi intended it to indicate how the Tai Chi captures the essence of all processes of change—natural, social, and psychological. For those who are familiar with Chinese meditation techniques, acupuncture, the martial arts, or the exercise system know as Tai Chi Chuan, the word *chi* refers to the energy within the physical or spiritual self that mediates change and transformation. The earliest known definition of *chi* is "ridgepole," the horizontal beam in a house upon which the two sides of the roof rest. The two sides of the roof symbolically represent the *yin* and the *yang*, which, according to Taoist philosophy, constitute the two fundamentally opposing yet balancing principles of nature. It is the equilibrium and creative tension between these two forces that gives shape and direction to all processes of change. *Yang,* symbolically represented by a solid line (_____), is associated with positive, masculine, strong, firm, light, heaven, rising, and father. *Yin,* symbolically represented by a broken line (___ ___) is associated with negative, feminine, weak, receptive, yielding, darkness, earth, falling, and mother.

The Tai Chi system created by Fu Hsi is an imagistic model for depicting the variety of interactions between *yin* and *yang.* The diagram illustrated in Figure 9.1 (also known as the *Pa Gua*) contains several basic components. First, there is the visual symbol of the Tai Chi, now widely recognized even in our Western culture, of the black and white "fish" swimming gracefully around each other. Along the various positions of this figure are eight "trigrams"—*Chien, Sun, Kan, Ken, Kun, Chen, Li, and Tui*—that represent all the possible triadic combinations of the *yin* and *yang* lines. Each trigram is associated with a specific image from nature and a variety of attributes accompanying that image. These aspects of the Tai Chi system have specific meanings and applications in a variety of Taoist practices, including diet, meditation, medicine, and Tai Chi Chuan.

The Tai Chi offers the opportunity to apply an intact system from Eastern philosophy to Western psychotherapy, rather than simply borrowing isolated concepts, as is typically the case in scholarly studies of East/West integration. In addition to the spiritual themes embodied by the Tai Chi, this system also can offer concrete, practical information about social and psychological processes. It is this latter approach that I emphasize in this chapter. However, I would like to make it clear that I do not present the Tai Chi as the supreme, ultimate method of merging Eastern and Western ideas, but rather as one example of how an integration can occur. It is important to note that Fu Hsi's model is but one part of the much larger philosophical and spiritual system that is Taoism.

The eight trigrams are the building blocks of the 64 hexagrams that constitute the *I Ching,* or Book of Changes—one of the three major texts of Taoism (the other two are Lao Tzu's *Tao Te Ching* and the *Book of Chuang Tzu*). These 64 hexagrams, each consisting of six lines of *yin* and/or *yang,* are constructed from all the possible dyadic combinations (8×8) of the trigrams. For each hexagram, the *I Ching* describes an associated image, the advantages and disadvantages of the social, psychological, and spiritual situations associated with that image, and judgments about how to act in those situations. The *I Ching* has occupied the attention of some of the most eminent scholars in

FIGURE 9.1

The Tai Chi Figure and the Eight Trigrams

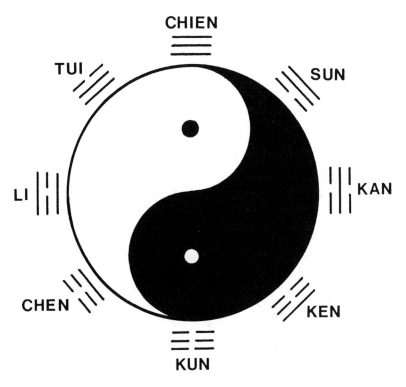

	Image	Attributes
SUN	wind	gentle, penetrating, gradual, simple
KAN	water	depth, danger, profundity, anxiety, mystery
KEN	mountain	stillness, waiting, stubbornness, calm, resting
KUN	earth	yielding, nourishing, receptive, adaptive
CHEN	thunder	excitement, shock, inciting movement, activity
LI	fire	clarity, illumination, intelligence, attachment
TUI	lake	satisfaction, openness, pleasure, joy, fullness
CHIEN	heaven	creative, strong, firm, enduring

Chinese history, and is considered one of the most important books of world literature. The mathematical scheme underlying the *I Ching* also inspired Leibnitz, the eighteenth century philosopher and mathematician, to develop the binary system, which now constitutes the basis of all computer languages. This fact alone—that the mathematical design underlying contemporary computer science is the same as that proposed by ancient Taoist masters—suggests that there is an archetypal form that unites Eastern and Western thought. It the form of *yin* and *yang*, of balancing opposites, of duality and polarity.

According to Taoist philosophy, the imagery of the Tai Chi and *I Ching* capture the essence of change and transition. The ancient scholars believed these symbols could be used to understand the complexity and subtlety of *all* processes of change, be they natural, social, or psychological. For this reason, these ideas often attracted the attention of Western psychology. Most noteworthy was Jung's application of the *yin/yang* polarity to the study of intrapsychic dynamics—in particular, the concept of *anima* and *animus*, the male and female components of the personality that fluidly balance each other in the fully actualized individual. During the course of psychotherapy—particularly during an impasse—Jungian therapists sometimes consulted the *I Ching* as a book of divination that revealed insights into the therapeutic situation via the process of "synchronicity" (Jung, 1951/1971). Synchronicity is the process by which phenomena in the world parallel or reflect each other through a hidden, acausal connection.

Here, I propose the imagery of the Tai Chi and its eight trigrams as a framework for understanding the psychotherapeutic process—in essence, as an imagistic model of psychotherapy. I am not suggesting that it be used as a tool of divination based on synchronistic events. Rather, my assumption is that psychotherapy, as a distinct process of interpersonal and intrapsychic change, falls within the realm of the Tao, the archetype of all processes of change, which is expressed in the imagery of the Tai Chi. The imagery of the Tai Chi figure and its eight trigrams can encompass the various microcosmic and macrocosmic aspects of change that occur within minutes or years in the course of psychotherapy. It embodies the process of attaining insight, the transitions in emotional states, and the metamorphosis of the self. It applies to the experiences of both the patient and clinician, and to the various transformations of the relationship between patient and clinician.

Like the cup that holds tea, the Tai Chi system can serve as a container for holding and organizing one's ideas about psychotherapy. It is a flexible framework into which we can place, explore, and reshape our theories. As such, I do not intend it as a substitute for current Western notions about psychotherapy. Rather, I see it (like the ancient Taoists, I believe) as a vehicle for reinterpreting our theories by filtering them through a paradoxical mixture of subjective intuition and universal forms. Because my orientation is primarily psychoanalytic and phenomenological, my application of the Tai Chi system acquires this flavor. But the system can be applied to *any* psychotherapeutic theory, and in each case it takes on a new meaning. Going beyond the teacup metaphor, the Tai Chi can allow its own framework to adapt to the ideas that the framework organizes: The container can alter its shape according to the characteristics of that which it contains.

I place special emphasis on the *imagistic* qualities of the Tai Chi. The Tai Chi figure is a distinctly and uniquely visual representation of the process of change. The trigrams, too, with their associated attributes and symbols, express ideas through visual imagery, as well as through a variety of other imagistic modalities—kinesthetic, auditory, tactile, even olfactory and gustatory. For instance, to understand the trigram *Li* (fire) and how it applies to psychotherapy is to understand how fire looks, moves, smells, and feels. This style of thinking in images is quite different from the verbal modes that usually dominate our Western cognitive styles. Language and verbalizations tend to represent experience in an abstract, logical, objective, and linear code. However, imagery, as a sensory-perceptual format, has two distinct advantages: It more effectively captures the emotions of an experience, and it more efficiently encodes the multiple, complex meanings of the experience. For these reasons, imagery plays a crucial role in the organization and transformation of the self (Suler, in press-a). As an affective, holistic vehicle for understanding the processes of change, one image is worth a thousand words—and is therefore a worthy method of exploring the multiple (perhaps infinite) determinants of the psychotherapeutic process. It also is important to note that the Chinese language itself is highly ideographic, consisting of "picture-grams" rather than alphabetic strings, which brings it closer to more fully encoding the complexity of variables and simultaneity of patterns that occur in nature (Watts, 1975b).

Some people may claim that explaining psychotherapy via the Tai Chi would be a highly ambiguous endeavor, leading to very subjective results. Interpretations of the Tai Chi figure and its trigrams would seem to be as much a product of the interpreter's psychology as anything else. I wholeheartedly agree, adding that the subjective, ambiguous elements of the Tai Chi are precisely its strength. Psychotherapy is ambiguous, as is life. Indeed, negotiating the subtle intricacies of the psychotherapy process requires the capacity to cope with ambiguity. It is an art of ambiguity—and a crucial tool of this art is the ability to delve into the subjective experience of both the patient and of oneself as the clinician. As revealed by contemporary psycho-analytic phenomenology (Atwood & Stolorow, 1984), the psychotherapy process can only be understood as an intersubjective field where the cognitive-affective schemata of the clinician shape and direct his or her exploration of the patient's inner world. Therapists do not simply "discover" the person's underlying dynamics, but rather help "articulate" those dynamics through their own personality structure. Psychological hermeneutics (Messer, Sass, & Woolfolk, 1988) similarly describes how subjectivity cannot be avoided in social science research. Meaning can only be revealed within a subjective context. Believing that one can rely on a completely objective theory is a self-deception. Ancient Taoists understood this, and so created an epistemological vehicle that incorporated this wisdom. The advantage of the Tai Chi is its ability to embrace the art of ambiguity and subjectivity, rather than whitewash it with claims of supposedly pure, objective theorizing.

To employ the Tai Chi, one enters it as the type of transitional space described in object relations theory, particularly in the work of Winnicott (1953, 1971). Like the child's blanket or teddy bear, the Tai Chi is, in part, objectively given by the external environment and partly created through the person's subjective meaning infused into it. The Tai Chi serves as an intermediate zone somewhere between the objective and subjective, where reality and imagination intermix, where one playfully shapes the externally given elements according to one's own ideas and wishes, and is in turn shaped by those elements. It is the zone where creativity flourishes. Pointing to the fact that the Tai Chi acts as a transitional space is my reply to criticisms that the images of the trigram system must be culture-bound, that the manner in which these images were interpreted by people thousands of years ago in a drastically different culture bears no resemblance to how we would interpret them today. On the subjective side of the transitional space, the Tai Chi allows for, even encourages, these cultural differences. On the objective side, it offers images from nature that have universal, archetypal meaning. The very characteristics of the elemental images present an objective, universal truth. No matter where we go on this planet, water flows downhill and fire produces light. The meaning we attribute to these facts may vary among cultures and individuals, but the image defines a range within which these meanings must take form. Although images may be particularly effective as transitional phenomena, any creative and powerful concept in any discipline is creative and powerful to the extent to which it provides a transitional space that allows for a variety of applications and interpretations.

The ideas offered by the Tai Chi images may not follow conventional logic and reason. They often embrace contradictions and paradox. The language of imagery, like that of dreams, lies close to the unconscious, where everyday, logical discriminations have little weight. At the deepest intrapsychic levels, paradox governs the self and its therapeutic transformation.

The Secrets of the Swimming Fish

As a first step in applying the Tai Chi to psychotherapy, let's examine the visual form of the Tai Chi symbol. It was often used by the Taoists as an object of meditation. For us it can serve as a context to free associate, to uncover and explore our concepts about psychotherapy.

The Tai Chi figure is, most fundamentally, a circle. In fact, the precursor of the Tai Chi is the Wu Chi, the empty circle—the stillness preceding the very first moment of action. As an archetypal, even mystical image, the circle symbolizes unity and completeness. Across all the numerous theories about psychotherapy, the most consistent, universal theme is the striving for wholeness within the self—whether we express that in terms of self-actualization, the integration of conscious and unconscious, of self and object representations, of id, ego, and superego, or the harmonizing of cognition, affect, and behavior. This circle, which surrounds the swimming fish (but only implicitly, because its form arises from the outer surfaces of the fish), signifies the overarching, yet mysteriously intangible self that unifies all elements of the intrapsychic world: the "superordinate" self that forms the final bedrock through which psychoanalysis cannot pass.

The creation of the circle also draws the distinction between inside and outside, between what is the self and what is not. Surely, a goal of the psychotherapeutic process is to clarify who you are and are not, to delineate and bolster self-boundaries. Because the figure is a circle (and not, say, a square or triangle), it suggests that these boundaries are fluid and changing, rather than rigidly static.

The act of actually drawing the Tai Chi symbol can further reveal its symbolism (see Figure 9.2). To progress from the static Wu Chi to the more dynamic Tai Chi, one must create two smaller circles, one on top of the other, within the larger circle. The joining of the opposing halves of these circles creates the reversed "S" between the dark and light fields. This theme of "two within one" is essential to the Tai Chi, as it is to personality development and psychotherapeutic process. The complex constellation of personality dynamics bounded within self-unity arises from one's history of dyadic relationships. Psychology has long recognized that the self evolves

FIGURE 9.2

Creating the Tai Chi Figure

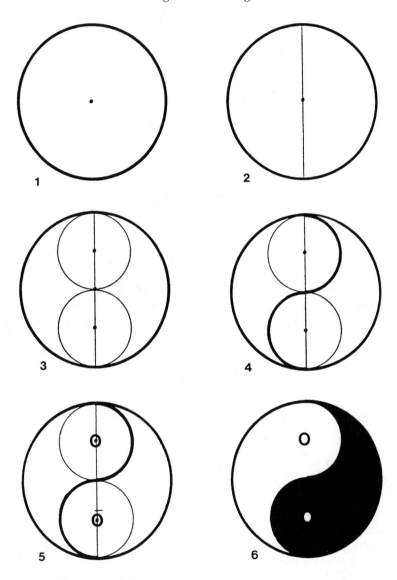

through a series of interpersonal contacts with significant others. The dyadic relationship becomes internalized, represented within the self. So, too, psychotherapy establishes an interpersonal context between two people—an intersubjective whole—that sets into motion the unification of self and ultimately becomes embodied within that unity. But the representations of parental imagoes or of self and other within the intrapsychic system ideally should not be isolated, self-contained units; unassimilated, repressed introjects provoke pathology. Instead, the two circles within the larger circle of the Tai Chi figure are hidden and joined seamlessly. Like the integrated system of self and object representations for which psychotherapy strives, the inner circles function silently, smoothly, efficiently.

The two circles within one also convey the spiritual theme, suggested by Suzuki (1970), that the self is both two and one, which includes the paradoxical dualities between self and other, self and no-self. The self is distinct from the other, and it is one with the other. The self is distinct from no-self, and it is one with no-self.

The circularity of the Tai Chi, which is enhanced by the swirling movements of the dark and white fields suggests that the psychotherapy process is cyclical, rotational. Here the Eastern vision seems to contradict the traditional Western concept of progress (both ontogenic and phylogenic) as being linear and directed toward a specific end-state. Surely, we wish to retain our belief that psychotherapy aims for a goal—namely, the goal of alleviating symptoms and actualizing the self. But the Tai Chi rejects the notion that this movement is a march straight forward, and points instead to the rhythms of circularity within the process of change and development. Newly uncovered issues in the course of therapy must be cycled back and understood in the context of previously explored themes, and vice versa. In his integration of psychoanalysis and behavior therapy, Wachtel (1977) suggested that the therapeutic process is a spiral. Alleviating the anxiety associated with a problematic issue frees the patient to become aware of another, related, but deeper issue, which leads again to anxiety, which, when worked through, leads to yet another issue, and so on. Freud's statement that psychoanalysis turns an extraordinary misery into an everyday suffering hints at a denial of the linear finality of attaining a cure. That successful patients often regress at the end of therapy also suggests that symptoms do not vanish, but rather, play a new role within the intrapsychic system.

All theories about psychotherapy implicitly or explicitly emphasize the "going back" motion that is, paradoxically, required for the progression forward. It is implied in the ubiquitous prefix re-, in such words as reverting, restoring, replacing, regressing, reviving. Psychoanalysis most clearly endorses the need to move through the past in order to progress forward. The evolution of the self through insight was clearly and succinctly summarized by T. S. Eliot: "We shall not cease from exploration, and the end of all our exploring will be to arrive where we started, and know the place for the first time." The word *religion* is derived from the Latin *re-ligare*, "to bind back"—back to the original source or ground of the self. So, too, Lao Tzu, the founder of Taoism, described the actions of the Tao simply as "returning."

Drawing the Tai Chi requires a series of locating centers and halving. As illustrated in Figure 9.2, one first locates a center and draws the initial, empty circle (Wu Chi); then halves the circle with a diameter and halves the radii of that diameter to locate the center of two new circles. Next, one halves and joins opposite sides of those circles and returns to the center of each to draw the "dots" at the center of the dark and light fields.

Psychotherapy also is a process of locating centers and halving. Halving is the act of dichotomizing, discriminating between pros and cons, identifying opposing feelings, revealing the polarities in personality structure. But the psychotherapeutic process also involves locating centers. Recalling the definition of Chi—the ridgepole upon which the two sides of a roof rest—we can think of psychotherapy as the process of realizing the unitary dimension or centering point that underlies a polarity in feeling or behavior. A patient may uncover hate as well as love for her father, but only her understanding of the power of attachment as the ridgepole between these two feelings will enable her to settle into a center where this conflict can be resolved. In therapy, the masochist might discover his hidden sadistic tendencies, but it is the realization concerning issues of control and power—the fundamental fulcrum—that will enable him to experience the center of this polarity, and move beyond it.

According to Buddhist philosophy, as soon as one draws a distinction between this and that—as soon the first dichotomy appears—other distinctions and differentiations follow, resulting in a plethora of discriminations. This also holds true for the psychotherapeutic process, where the act of distinguishing between this and that side of a conflict, or of any polarity in personality structure, invariably leads to further differentiations among the complexities of one's thoughts, feelings, and behaviors. This, essentially, is the process of "working through"—exploring the interconnections among intrapsychic dynamics. But the complementary therapeutic process is finding a center, a stable reference point, that unifies and gives an integrated meaning to the complexities of intrapsychic dynamics.

The dovetailing of the black and white fields within the Tai Chi expresses the mutual creation and inseparability of opposites, of *yin* and *yang*. Psychotherapy sets into motion this dynamic interaction of polarities; it frees the personality structure from the static tensions of intrapsychic conflicts and strives for the fluid harmony, symmetry, and balance of polarities. When distorted, warded off, or frozen in place by repression and defense mechanisms, the diametric poles of the intrapsychic world lose their ability to give form to one another. Opposites, Freud said, lie close to each other in the unconscious, and the course of psychotherapy steers toward the realization and actualizing of their mutual arising and inseparability. Love and hate, joy and grief, ambition and lassitude, hope and despair—all forms of ambivalence have meaning and definition because of the contrast of opposites. The infinite variety of polarities that are discovered in psychotherapy awakens one to the rich dynamics, depth, and subtlety of psychological life. The overall course of psychotherapy itself is a balance of diametric processes. It entails the adaptive regression of integrating fantasy, illogic and emotion with practicality, reason, and rationality; a mixing of primary and secondary process, of destructuring and restructuring the self. All together, these form the essence of creativity (Suler, 1980).

The imagery of the Tai Chi figure reflects specific insights into how opposites interact. The swimming fish seem to dance around, chase, or push each other, in what can be read as a state of playful tension. This is a fitting image, too, for the transferential/countertransferential interaction between patient and therapist. At that point where the *yang* culminates to its fullest magnitude (at the top of the figure), the first traces of *yin* appear. The reverse is also true at the bottom of the figure. In psychotherapy, the intense peaking of an emotion or behavior may mark the subtle transition to an opposing emotion or behavior. Joking that rises to a burst of laughter may turn to tears; a borderline patient builds to a full-blown devaluing of the therapist before the first signs of idealization surface. The Tai Chi figure also shows that the heart of the *yin* territory contains a dot of *yang*, and the heart of the *yang* a dot of *yin*. In psychotherapy, embedded within an emotion, thought, or behavior is its opposite. A patient refuses to talk, but always comes to session on time. With words of enthusiastic appreciation, a patient brings the therapist a gift for her office, but the fact that it is obviously the wrong color betrays a hidden animosity. As noted by Eigen (1986), during the most intense psychotic episodes there remains a hidden, sane part of the schizo-phrenic that observes the decompensation—and within normal peo-ple there lies a deeply buried "psychotic" core.

There is yet another duality expressed by the Tai Chi figure that is not immediately obvious, perhaps because it is so fundamental. The figure was drawn on a blank page; it arises from a contentless background, from emptiness. A creative tension exists between form and formlessness. In psychotherapy, periods of entering blankness and void (when one feels stuck and there is nothing to say) mark a transition into a zone of pure potential. It is not a static emptiness, but one replete with vibrant possibility: Something previously hidden and unrealized always surfaces. As stated by Eastern philosophy, the definition and features of the self are rooted in selflessness, in no-self. It acts as the essential, pivotal point for psychological growth. The psychotherapy process activates the dynamic interplay between self and no-self, figure and ground, which nourishes intrapsychic life.

The Tai Chi emerges from the Wu Chi, the empty circle, but also contains the Wu Chi within it. The dots at the center of the *yin* and *yang* fields suggest yet other empty circles, Tai Chi that have yet to form. They are islands of pregnant stillness waiting to be actualized, unexplored territories embedded within the present intrapsychic realm: Tai Chi within Tai Chi, worlds within worlds. During the psy-chotherapeutic process, as one delves deeper into the unconscious, new universes continually open up. Self-exploration is a process with no definitive end.

The Trigram Images and Attributes

The images and attributes of the trigrams can be applied to psy-chotherapy as a means of attaining new perspectives and insights concerning the process of psychological change. The insights may pertain to transformational processes within the patient, the clinician (including the clinician's interventions), or their relationship. The tri-grams may be particularly relevant when their imagery appears in the associations of the therapist or patient—in dreams, memories, or metaphoric expressions—not unlike the archetypal images described by Jung. In some cases, it might even be useful to present and focus on a Tai Chi image as a specific therapeutic task—in a sense, using the context of an image and its attributes as a transformational space (Bollas, 1986) for facilitating change. For example, personal growth workshops (Kahn, Kroeber, & Kingsbury, 1974) have encouraged participants to adopt a specific Tai Chi image that feels personally applicable, to explore their associations and fantasies about that image, to construct rituals and ceremonies involving it, and even to under-take "field trips" where one meditatively encounters the natural element depicted in that image (i.e., if one selects *Ken*, the mountain, one goes to a mountain).

To use the images to understand the psychotherapeutic process, clinicians may rely on their own intuitive knowledge to explore their meaning and application. The image of "thunder," for example, stirs up a variety of intuitive associations and affects. The attributes that traditionally have been assigned to the images can serve as guidelines for this associative process. These attributes have been interpreted in a variety of ways by scholars of the *I Ching* and the Tai Chi system. Some of these interpretations are classic, such as the ancient *Shuo Kua* in the Wilhelm/Baynes (1950/1967) translation of the *I Ching*. For an additional source of information on how to interpret and apply the trigram images, one may also double each trigram, thereby turning it into a hexagram, and locate it within the *I Ching*. For example, the trigram *Chien* placed over the trigram *Chien* (heaven over heaven) becomes the hexagram *Chien*, which consists of six solid *(yang)* lines. For each hexagram, the *I Ching* offers a description of its image, as well as interpretations of the situations associated with that image, its inherent dangers and opportunities, and "judgments" as to what course of action is most wise. Note, however, that doubling a trigram endows it with extra layers of meaning that may, in some cases, go beyond the meaning of the more basic trigram. Also note that all 64 hexagrams of the *I Ching* could be applied as a conceptual framework for understanding the psychotherapy process, although the level of depth and complexity would far exceed that in this discussion. In addition to the two classic English translations of the *I Ching*—the Legge (1964) version and the popular Wilhelm/Baynes (1950/1967) volume—a variety of more contemporary translations have been published (e.g., Wing, 1982).

Let us now discuss some possible interpretations and applications of the eight trigrams, starting with *Sun* and progressing clockwise around the Tai Chi figure. Positioned around this figure, the three trigram lines are read from the inside out—in other words, the bottom of each trigram is positioned next to the Tai Chi circle, whereas the top is on the outside. In this discussion of the trigrams, all quotations from the *I Ching* are taken from the Wilhelm/Baynes (1950/1967) translation.

SUN (Wind)

Sun is known as "The Gentle." Its attributes are: gentle, penetrating, gradual, simple, honest. The quality of penetrating, but doing so gently and gradually, is indicated in the trigram structure by one *yin* line beneath two *yang* lines.

Sometimes the most effective interventions in psychotherapy are those that are subtle and gradual, like a gently penetrating wind. This approach is particularly important in the beginning phases of therapy, when resistance may be strong. The *I Ching* suggests that even the seemingly rigid and immovable slowly yield to such a force, as long as the force perseveres (which gives it power) and is guided by a clearly defined goal that moves it always in the same direction. So, too, in psychotherapy, patients with rigid defenses or severe characterological disturbances slowly respond to the therapist's enduring attempts to penetrate to a deeper level of understanding the patient's symptoms, as long as that effort is evenly delivered, tempered by patience, and thoughtful in purpose. Like the wind that "disperses the gathered clouds, leaving the sky clear and serene," the therapist gradually can sweep away the obstructions and confusions arising from denial, acting out, and other defensive attempts to thwart the therapeutic process.

Kohut's (1977) persevering attempts to understand and cure patients with narcissistic disturbances were a testament to the spirit of *Sun*. Previously considered unanalyzable, such patients could talk endlessly about trivial matters or present a defensive facade of grandiosity that could not be interpreted by traditional methods. The technique of mirroring—simply reflecting back the gist of the patient's communication—proved to be the gently penetrating wind that gradually uncovered and remedied the inner conditions of self-depletion and emptiness that afflicted these patients. But effective mirroring never occurs willy-nilly. Like the gently penetrating wind, it has a clearly defined goal, always working in the same direction ultimately to uncover and restore the deficits in self structure.

According to the *I Ching*, the gradual, inconspicuous results of gentle penetration may not be striking to the eye—but they are often more enduring and complete than rapid, surprise attacks. This is "success through what is small." Such advice from the Taoist masters would seem to favor the gradual, sometimes almost imperceptible changes resulting from long-term therapy over the comparatively rapid effects of short-term treatments that endorse forceful, swift interpretations. However, the *I Ching* also warns that there are disadvantages to gentle penetration. When pushed too far or repeated excessively, it may result in exhaustion, humiliation, or crippling doubts.

From the very first day, Sal created a troublesome double bind in our therapy sessions. Unable (and sometimes simply refusing) to talk about himself, he skillfully ignored and avoided my attempts to explore his thoughts and feelings, even those concerning the most mundane of daily events. At the same time, he was unable to tolerate silence, which escalated his anxiety to the point of blocking and cognitive disorganization. Any attempts to interpret these dynamics only made them worse. Suffering from a rather severe schizoid disorder, he was unable to articulate to me or to himself his inner thoughts and feelings. As he entered at the beginning of one session, before even sitting down, he remarked, "Don't ask, because I don't know," and fell into his typical, awkward silence.

The treatment approach I adopted for Sal followed the path of *Sun*. I encouraged him to talk about events and issues external to himself and his symptoms. Essentially, we engaged in chit-chat about the weather, current events, and TV. But, like the gently penetrating wind, I used these discussions to gradually, consistently steer us toward a goal: to find openings and move toward his own ideas, feelings, and fantasies. After several years of this work, his internal world became more and more accessible. His ability to articulate his own experience slowly improved. However, as warned by the *I Ching*, I learned that my strategy could become overly persistent. On several occasions, when I lingered too long in trying to help him express his feelings about a particular topic, he reacted with frustration, anger, and humiliation, because he felt unable to reply. He experienced me as dogging him with the same questions, even though he insisted he did not know how to answer them. The challenge for me became the task of learning to distinguish between an effective penetrating wind and one that was overly intrusive and taxing.

Although the characteristics traditionally attributed to the trigram *Sun* are gentle, penetrating, gradual, and simple, the *Shuo Kua* also suggests another interpretation that is quite different—in fact, almost contrary to the traditional one. Winds advance and retreat; they are changeable, indecisive. Surely, such characteristics describe how some patients approach therapy, particularly in the beginning phases. Yet they also may outline ideas for an effective therapeutic strategy. Being able to advance and retreat flexibly will enable the therapist to test the intensity of the patient's defenses and effectively pace the therapy. Being able to change directions will enable one to approach issues from various angles, making it easier to find a way "in." Even the quality of being "indecisive" can work therapeutically. Some patients will more easily accept interpretations that are suggested tentatively, hypothetically, than those that are launched as hard facts. The "Detective Colombo" style of intrapsychic investigation appears less threatening, and encourages the patient to let down his or her defenses.

KAN (Water)

Kan is known as "The Abysmal." Its attributes are: depth, danger, profundity, anxiety, mystery. The trigram consists of a *yang* line between two *yin* lines.

This trigram is associated with the image of water as it moves downward, as in a ravine or canyon. The ravine bears a twofold symbolism. It signifies danger and anxiety, as well as the sense of profundity and mystery associated with movement into great depths. The structure of the trigram (one *yang* line between two *yin* lines) reflects both these conditions. The *yang* line is read as being both dangerously hemmed in by the *yin* lines, and mysteriously hidden by them. The ways in which the mind encounters danger, and the mysteries associated with them, are the subject of *Kan*.

The psychotherapy process is, metaphorically, a descent into the depths of the unconscious. During the course of therapy, the patient will encounter danger—intrapsychic danger. The *I Ching* warns against two possible reactions. One may be tempted to escape immediately, which is analogous to the "flight into health" so typical of the early phases of psychotherapy, when patients get a first glimpse of their unconscious dynamics. The second tendency is to grow used to the danger and conform to it in a nonproductive, harmful way. Pathological adaptations to anxiety, such as somatizations or addictions, sometimes arise in therapy as the patient approaches previously warded-off affects and fantasies. Comparing this danger to a ravine or abyss, the *I Ching* suggests that one should imitate the actions of water. Water "merely fills up all the places through which it flows; it does not shrink away from any dangerous spot nor from any plunge, and nothing can make it lose its own essential nature." It infiltrates and fills every depression, remains in the situation until a way out shows itself, and then moves on. The movement is always downward. This captures the essence of the psychotherapeutic process very poetically. While proceeding along the line of least resistance, one must thoroughly explore the meaning of every danger that is encountered, and then continue downward. As long as one takes the time to explore carefully a particular issue, no matter how danger-ous or anxiety-provoking, a way out—a path to deeper, yet related, issues—will always show itself. Dwelling unnecessarily on that issue can be detrimental to the therapeutic progress. Although the move-ment of *Kan* uncovers danger and anxiety, it is also the path of insight into deeper, more profound mysteries.

The *I Ching* emphasizes the need to be thorough and depend-able, to do what one must. The movement of water is predictable; its essential nature does not change. "In danger, all that counts is really carrying out all that has to be done in thoroughness—and going for-ward." This is the attitude that the clinician can convey about the therapeutic process. The direction of therapy is always clear: to un-derstand the patient. Despite the dangers encountered, it must move forward, and when it does, it will succeed. Such an attitude supports and inspires confidence in patients, particularly at those points when they feel overwhelmed by intrapsychic danger. Even when the thera-pist is not sure what is causing the crisis, the attitude that their joint efforts to understand will nevertheless continue—reliably and thor-oughly—is therapeutic in itself. As stated by the *I Ching*, "If one is sincere when confronted with difficulties, the heart can penetrate the meaning of the situation."

The *I Ching* also suggests that great accomplishments should not be expected in situations of great danger. It is sufficient to reach small gains, or simply to get through the danger. To attain this, it offers a bit of practical advice: "To enlighten someone, we begin with what is lucid and proceed simply from that point."

KEN (Mountain)

Ken is known as "Keeping Still." Its attributes are: immobility, wait-ing, stubbornness, calm, resting. The qualities of inner stillness and resting, with an outward appearance of stubbornness and resistance, is indicated in the trigram structure by two *yin* lines beneath one *yang* line.

At times in psychotherapy, nothing seems to be happening. The patient appears stuck, blocked, stubborn in the face of the therapeutic process. Some clinicians believe that the essential therapeutic task is always the analysis and chipping away of the mountain of resistance. Traditional psychoanalytic theory views the patient as locked into conflict between id and ego, with the unconscious portions of this conflict barricaded from influence by layer upon layer of defenses. Facing the therapist and the possibility of change, mountainous forces within the patient paradoxically resist progress.

Yet moments of inaction may indicate more than a blockade arising from a tight knot of intrapsychic defenses. Contemporary psychoanalytic theory (e.g., Kohut, 1984; Weiss & Sampson, 1986) suggests
that what appears to be resistance actually may be the patient's deliberate pausing, unconsciously, before moving to a deeper level of exploration. In this stage of waiting, the patient may be testing the
clinician to determine whether the therapeutic relationship is safe
enough to continue. For example, Sal's silence was more than simply
an attempt to avoid the anxiety and shame of revealing his inner feelings and fantasies. It was also a test to determine whether I could tolerate him, whether I had the patience to stick it out. When it was clear
that I did, that I could be trusted not to abandon him, he was able to
move forward.

Hesitation implies an intrinsic need to move forward. When a
pendulum reaches the height of its arc, it pauses a moment before its
movement continues back. As stated by the *I Ching*, rest is a state of
polarity that always posits movement as its complement. The image
of the mountain signifies that movement has reached its normal conclusion; its stillness represents the end and beginning of change. "It
is a mysterious place where things begin and end, where death and
birth pass into each other." The *Shuo Kua* compares it to a seed that
acts as the link between the beginning and end of plants. It also
points out how the structure of the trigram *Ken* (one *yang* line above
two *yin* lines) looks like a gate or doorway. Hence, it describes *Ken* as
the "gatekeeper" or "guardian" who watches, protects, and, given
the right circumstance, permits entrance.

In psychotherapy, when patients appear resistant or complain
about being stuck or about how therapy is having no effect, unconsciously they may be sitting on the brink of an important change. A
colleague reported such a complaint from a patient who, in the next
session, described a dream in which she was speeding down a hall-
way in the psychologist's chair. Such phenomena are related to the
experiences of derealization and depersonalization in patients who
unconsciously sense imminent and rapid intrapsychic change. Outer
inaction and stillness may constitute a "breather" before further work
can be engaged, or a stage of assimilation in which prior therapeutic
gains are being consolidated.

Other interpretations of *Ken* readily lend themselves as advice to
the therapist. According to the *I Ching*, the stillness of the mountain
image represents a "resting in what is right"—a meditative focusing
of one's thoughts on the immediate situation. It is an inner calm that
allows one to see a situation more clearly and objectively (this may

apply to the patient, too). The *I Ching* warns against acting impulsively and letting one's thoughts wander from the issues at hand. Regardless of what difficulties or uncertainties face the clinician, if this inner stillness can be maintained, "a course will become bright and clear." This, in fact, might be perfect advice when confronting resistance and impasses.

Finally, it is interesting to note the application of *Ken* in Tai Chi Chuan, the Taoist style of martial arts. To shove or knock over the opponent, one uses the side of the body, particularly the shoulder and upper arm, to displace the adversary. Like a massive, still mountain, one essentially occupies the space where the opponent used to be, forcing him or her out. A therapist described to me a patient who insisted on talking only about how he organized various nuts and bolts he had purchased at a local hardware store. All attempts on the part of the therapist to interpret this resistance or redirect the session to more productive issues failed. Finally, she decided to join the patient. She asked numerous, detailed questions about the nuts and bolts, and offered a gamut of ideas about alternate ways of organizing them. Within a few sessions, the client dropped this discussion and began exploring important intrapsychic issues.

A similar situation was described by Lindner (1954) in his case of "the jet-propelled couch." When confronted by the rigid delusions of a brilliant engineer who claimed he visited alien civilizations, Lindner wholeheartedly joined the delusion. He not only encouraged the storytelling, but grew more and more vicariously thrilled by these adventures into outer space. Lindner admits that he became more delusional than the patient, until one day the patient—sheepishly afraid to disappoint Lindner—disclosed that he no longer believed the delusion. The cure, Lindner concluded, was a matter of displacing the patient out of his delusion. Two objects cannot occupy the same space at the same time. This, essentially, is the application of *Ken* in Tai Chi Chuan.

KUN (Earth)

Kun is known as "The Receptive." Its attributes are: yielding, nourishing, receptive, adapting, devoted. The receptive and yielding quality is revealed in the trigram structure by three *yin* lines.

At the fullness of *yin* and darkness, positioned at the bottom of the Tai Chi figure, *Kun* can represent the unconscious in its purest archetypic form. Rather than being simply a reservoir of repressed affects and memories, as conceptualized by Freud, *Kun* more represents the Jungian vision of an unconscious that is nourishing and adaptive. According to the *I Ching*, these beneficial attributes of *Kun* can only be actualized through a dynamic interaction and balancing with its opposite trigram, *Chien* (heaven), which is associated with the attributes of strength, firmness, and endurance, and represents the force known as "The Creative" that gives shape and form to all things. Standing alone or in opposition to *Chien*, the yielding influence of *Kun* can be harmful. Ideally, it is the receptive space in which the creative force of *Chien* takes its action—a kind of prepsychological space that precedes and enables the building of intrapsychic structures. According to the *I Ching*, it "releases active forces." Not unlike the creative interaction of unconscious and conscious in adaptive regressions such as artistic work, *Kun* must be activated and led by *Chien* in order for the psychological world to become actualized. The creative and receptive complete each other. Whereas the Creative gives form to things, the Receptive allows them to unfold and thrive. Contemporary psychoanalytic theory, particularly object relations and self psychology, often speaks of self structures that develop from the prepsychological precursors of structure. However, these theories seem to lack a conceptual dynamic to explain such processes. The Tai Chi vision of the *Kun/Chien* polarity might offer such an understanding.

Dipping into the unconscious, precursory realm of *Kun* during the course of psychotherapy may stir anxiety and a sense of danger. Fear and resistance will be common reactions to the possibility of entering a place where psychic structures are destructured in order to be restructured, where space, according to the *I Ching*, mysteriously "opens out" to allow new possibilities to form. Here, a receptive yielding to hidden forces must supersede deliberate, conscious strivings. As described by James (1902) in his classic study of religious experiences, a moment of devoted "letting go" is crucial to the transformation of the self.

True to the image of the earth that yields and nourishes, the facilitating activity of *Kun* manifests itself in a variety of ways during the psychotherapeutic process. For the patient, it appears as the willingness—and ability—to yield to unconscious influences, as well as to the therapeutic process in general. Allowing oneself to enter the transformational space (Bollas, 1986) is, essentially, *Kun*. It is the willingness and ability to yield to the influence of the therapist and the process of change. The *I Ching* warns against relying too much on one's own strength, and advocates the need to be led by a helper or guide. As such, paranoid and narcissistic patients who resist the therapist's influence (as well as those who become excessively dependent or merged) may be conceptualized as suffering from a pathology of *Kun*.

For the therapist, *Kun* manifests itself as the ability simply to listen to the patient. To ignore the power of simple listening, as novices and clinicians overly eager to "help" sometimes do, is to overlook the power of *Kun*. This robust therapeutic effect appears in other deceptively simple interventions, such as reflection or showing concern. To account for the transformational impact of such activities, psychoanalytic theory has derived the concepts of empathy, holding environments, "containing" the patient, and "metabolizing" affect. In all cases, the common denominator is the activity of *Kun*—of yielding to the patients' communications and affects, providing a space for them to unfold, and nourishing them, regardless of what they may be. "The earth in its devotion carries all things, good and evil, without exception." "It attains what is right for all without artifice or special intentions." To allow *Kun* to thrive, the therapist must forgo trying too hard and forcing his or her intentions. "If he tries to lead, he goes astray; but if he follows, he finds guidance." Although *Kun* is receptive and yielding, it nevertheless is devoted and persevering in its ability to carry all things, "like a foundation that endures forever." Empathy and holding environments, at their therapeutic best, possess these same characteristics. The *I Ching* calls this "furthering through perseverance."

It's interesting to note that the traditional technique of analytic neutrality, including the so-called "blank screen," also possesses many of the characteristics of *Kun*. It, too, involves a yielding and adapting, an opening of space to allow all things to manifest themselves and unfold, an abstinence on the part of the therapist, whose inclination is to do something specific, and devoted perseverance. At the deep process level of *Kun*, traditional and contemporary psychoanalytic technique may bear more similarities than is apparent on the surface.

CHEN (Thunder)

This trigram is known as "The Arousing." Its attributes are: excitement, shock, inciting movement, activity, growth, expansion. An upward, arousing movement is indicated in the trigram structure by the strong *yang* line beneath two *yin*.

According to the *I Ching*, sudden forces "moving upward from below," like lightning and its accompanying thunder, can cause fear, terror, and trembling. At the peak of such moments of shock, presence of mind is easily lost; one is robbed of reflection and clarity of vision. Opportunities for constructive action may be overlooked, and one may be tempted to let fate take its course. In psychotherapy, these sudden forces may be the unpredicted eruptions of repressed affects, memories, or fantasies that lead to panic, confusion, and acting out.

However, the *I Ching* notes, the shock is only momentary, and in the best of circumstances can induce productive movement. *Chen* entails beginning or arising. It spurs a person into beneficial action, as long as that person moves carefully, thoughtfully, with caution. The *I Ching* suggests that "fear brings good fortune," and that "an enlightened person, when badly frightened, seeks to improve himself." Once the ordeal passes, there is a sense of relief, perhaps even laughter and joy, as well as a reverence for the manifestation of these shocking forces. The therapy patient's sudden experience of the unconscious often arouses awe and respect for the intrapsychic life and for the psychotherapeutic process. In response to that fearful reverence, "he sets his life in order and searches his heart." The *Shuo Kua* describes these effects of the Arousing as "decisive" and "spreading out." To gain from the shocking experience, the *I Ching* suggests that one remain still until composure and clarity of mind is restored. One must attain some degree of distance and "move to higher ground." In psychotherapy, this is accomplished by stimulating the patient's observing ego and providing a holding environment in which the clinician's composure sustains the patient's ability to endure and assimilate the experience.

Dan had always expressed doubts about the relevance of discussing his childhood for overcoming his anxiety attacks and pervasive shyness. In his second year of therapy, he reluctantly attempted to recall his earliest memories of his father, who had died from a brain tumor two years prior to Dan's seeking treatment. At the time of the father's death, Dan's alcoholic mother informed him that his father, on several occasions, had been arrested for exhibitionism. In this session, recalling only a vague feeling of having been "suppressed" by his father, Dan fell into silence, unable to articulate or even think of anything. I suggested that perhaps he might be able to see an image pertaining to his relationship with his father. His face turned white and his hands tightened on the armrests of his chair. He jumped up, began pacing the room, and described vivid sensations of choking, defecating, and intense anxiety. He stated that an image had flashed through his mind, though he could not see it clearly. By the end of the session, after much pacing and long periods of silence, he stated his dawning realization that his father had "done something sexual" to him when he was a small child.

The thunder of *Chen* had erupted into this session. Although at first terrified, and literally trembling, Dan was awed by the power of his unconscious. It aroused him into movement. In later sessions, he cautiously (and at times with considerable resistance) approached the question of what, exactly, his father had done to him and how it had affected his life.

LI (Fire)

Li is known as "Clinging." Its attributes are: intelligence, clarity, brightness, illumination, attachment, dependency. The trigram structure—one *yin* line between two *yang* lines—can be interpreted as fiery in that the brightness of the two *yang* lines clings to the inner *yin*. Like fire, and in contrast to water *(Kan)*, the movement of *Li* rises upward and outward.

The image of fire can signify clarity of mind, intelligent awareness, and reason, as well as the energy, enthusiasm, and inspiration that can accompany clarity of mind. Whether or not fire is beneficial depends on how it burns—which is determined by the source to which it clings. "Clarity of mind has the same relation to life that fire has to wood. Fire clings to wood, but also consumes it. Clarity of mind is rooted in life, but can also consume it. Everything depends on how the clarity functions." The *I Ching* warns that at times of high energy, there is a tendency for reason and intelligence to consume itself. One throws oneself away in the enthusiasm. In psychotherapy, overly ambitious enthusiasm, including the intellectual enthusiasm arising from the "high" of self-discovery, can quickly lead to dead ends and disappointments. As the *I Ching* states, "matters end badly when a man spends himself too rapidly and consumes himself like a meteor."

Clarity of mind, like fire, will quickly exhaust itself unless it clings to a stable source that sustains it. Otherwise, it cannot be tamed and directed productively. "A luminous thing giving out light must have within itself something that perseveres; otherwise it will in time burn itself out." In psychotherapy, intellectualizations quickly fail if they are cut off from one's core emotional dynamics. For patients to achieve an enduring clarity of mind that illuminates their experience of the world and themselves, a stable, secure sense of self first must be established. Intelligent awareness and clarity in thought and perception depend on this underlying, cohesive self, an idea expounded in object relations theory and self psychology. According to the *I Ching*, attaining this inner "seriousness" and "composure" preserves the brightness of mind needed to come to terms with the innumerable impressions that pour in from the outside world. For the psychotherapy patient, it is the clarity to see their transferences and parataxic distortions for what they really are.

Attaining this clarity of mind is also a matter of allowing oneself to cling to the social and spiritual realms. "By cultivating in himself an attitude of compliance and voluntary dependence, man acquires clarity without sharpness and finds his place in the world." Apparently, the *I Ching* recognizes that ideas based solely on one's own perceptions and inner constructs may warp or follow misleading tangents without the correcting influence of others. In fact, this advice suggests the importance of depending on selfobject relationships. Concerning the spiritual realm, the *I Ching* states, "In order that his psychic nature may be transfigured and attain influence on earth, it must cling to the forces of spiritual life." This clinging is the realization of the interpenetration between self and no-self, the rooting of the self in the no-self that sustains and enriches it.

The image of *Li*, therefore, captures three sources on which reason and clear thinking depend: the intrapsychic, the social, and the spiritual.

Of course, these qualities apply to the therapist as well as the patient. The clinician could have no therapeutic impact, if not for the attributes and processes embodied by *Li*. "Through his clarity of nature, he causes the light to spread farther and farther and to penetrate the nature of man ever so deeply."

TUI (Lake)

The image of the lake is known as "The Joyous." The attributes of this trigram are: fullness, satisfaction, excess, openness, pleasure, and expansiveness. The trigram structure—one *yin* line resting atop two *yang* lines—depicts how true joy rests on firmness and strength within, manifesting itself outwardly as yielding and gentleness.

Similar to *Li*, *Tui* expresses the benefits of being sustained by a nourishing source. Whereas *Li* emphasizes the cognitive benefits (clarity of mind, reason), *Tui* highlights the affective gains (joy, pleasure, satisfaction). The lake is a refreshing, vitalizing force for all things surrounding it. So, too, in psychotherapy, the development of a stable, cohesive self structure nourishes the psychological life of the patient. The experience of openness, satisfaction, and joy, according to the *I Ching*, rests on internal solidity and strength. "Quiet, wordless, self-contained joy" thrives despite external circumstances and "remains free of egotistic likes and dislikes." *Tui* is "the quiet security of a heart fortified within itself." Without this sustaining center, the *I Ching* warns, one is empty and easily tempted by "indulgences and lowly pleasures"—a situation that is reminiscent of Kohut's (1977) description of addictions, perversions, and other compulsions as attempts to fill narcissistic deficits in the self. "They attract external pleasures by the emptiness of their nature. Thus they lose themselves more and more . . ." If joy is not based on inner steadfastness, it degenerates into the false optimism and "uncontrolled mirth" of a false self.

The hexagram *Tui* (the lake resting on a lake) further suggests that one is sustained by being related to others. Two lakes connected refresh each other and do not dry up easily. For this reason, the *I Ching* advises the cultivation of relationships with others and the need for interpersonal encouragement and accord. By testing your ideals and exploring your deep feelings with others, you overcome rigid, habitual styles of thinking, and your personality becomes more flexible, refreshed, and multifaceted. "In this way learning becomes many-sided and takes on a cheerful lightness, whereas there is always something ponderous and one-sided about the learning of the self-taught." Similar to the previous trigram, *Li* (fire), the advice associated with *Tui* reflects the psychotherapeutic principle of fortifying the flexibility, harmony, and cohesiveness of self structure through the development of selfobject relationships—first a self-nourishing relationship that the patient develops with the therapist, then, ultimately, with other people outside therapy.

The trigram *Tui* is associated with the mouth, with being open, receptive to and communicative with others—in Freudian terms, healthy oral needs. At some point in therapy, virtually all patients recognize the need to connect to others, to allow themselves to develop a self-nourishing dependency, to be in accord with the social environment in general. Joy and satisfaction will follow. The *Shuo Kua* visually interprets the trigram structure (a *yin* line atop two *yang* lines) as breaking open at the top, like the bursting open of a ripe fruit that has dropped to the ground. The basic lesson: One must open up. For some patients, it's the simple but profound realization that you have to talk with others, about feelings, fantasies, ambitions in order to survive. For some patients, the act of coming to therapy is itself the manifestation of *Tui*.

CHIEN (Heaven)

Chien is known as "The Creative." Its attributes are strong, firm, determined, successful and enduring. These characteristics are represented in the trigram structure by three *yang* lines.

Chien represents the primal, creative energy or power that lends substance and form to all things. It constitutes inspiration, initiative, and will. It makes actual what is potential. The *I Ching* describes it as the "urge to life," that which "furthers and is right for each being." Whereas *Kun* (earth) is the formless but fertile ground that sustains all states of being, the course of *Chien* alters and shapes all things until each attains its true, specific nature. The dynamic interplay between the two constitutes the reciprocity between the formless potentiality of the no-self and form-structuring activity of the self. "The way of the creative works through change and transformation, so that each thing receives its true nature and destiny and comes to permanent accord with the Great Harmony; this is what furthers and perseveres." Whereas *Kun* possesses spatial qualities (the fertile space through which form arises), *Chien* is more temporal in nature. The "furthering" quality of this creative force involves continuous movement and development that endures through time. Along this temporal path, each thing receives the nature appropriate to it, which the *I Ching* refers to as "destiny." On the psychological level, it instills confidence in oneself, a sense of integrity and justice, of being true to oneself, of having direction and purpose, a feeling of beauty, clarity, and harmony with the world.

Chien covers a broad base of ideas found in psychoanalysis, personality theory, and philosophy in general. As the inspiration-filled "urge to life," it resembles to the traditional psychoanalytic concept of Eros, Rank's (1945) discussions of will, and Nietzsche's mystical vision of the "will to power." Humanistic theories of psychotherapy speak of the need to tap the forces of self-actualization that dictate what each person is destined, ideally, to be. Recent psychoanalytic theories (e.g., Kohut, 1977, 1984; Weiss & Sampson, 1986) similarly imply the importance of unlocking the internal, intrinsic drive toward the resolution of conflict and the development of self structure. It is a drive that, despite the deadlocks of pathological symptoms and unfortunate external circumstances, endures through time, lying in wait for the opportune moment and the opportune therapeutic relationship to continue its movement. The image of heaven may represent, in Kohut's terms, the fundamental ambitions and ideals—the internal nuclear programs—that provide the tension arc of organizing, structuralizing energy for developmental movement. *Chien* is the essence of the willing self. As such, it follows the path of the separation and individuation of the self. As stated by the *I Ching*, the specific, unique nature actualized in each person by *Chien* "fixes a boundary that separates each individual being from every other." Many clinicians realize that the psychotherapeutic process is not so much doing something to make the patient change, but rather unleashing the forces of *Chien* to allow development to occur spontaneously.

Much of the therapy I conducted with Sal, the patient mentioned earlier, was tedious. Only gradually did he acquire the ability to talk about himself. I subjectively experienced our sessions the way he must have experienced his everyday life—directionless, apathetic, numb. Once he described himself as "living my own death." He often drifted through the week in a quasi-dissociated state and was unable to recall in therapy anything he had done. Having received little mirroring or any kind of reaction, positive or negative, from his parents (even when he told them he was gay), he could barely hold on to any sense of hope or enthusiasm for life. Although he suffered from what might be described as a pathology of *Chien*, there were moments when this vital urge for life did surface spontaneously. On those rather rare occasions when he broke through to the unconscious— when he remembered a childhood experience that helped explain his present situation, or finally recalled a dream—a surge of energy and enthusiasm followed. He understood something about himself! Things made sense! On those occasions, his old interests in music were spontaneously revived. He started writing songs—optimistic songs, rather than his usual, depressing ballads about unrequited love. He began reading books on how to publish music. He searched for a new job that would enable him to save money for a music publishing business. Although he succeeded in some of these endeavors (he did get a new job), the power of his aspirations and creative will at times faded. The "furthering" quality of *Chien* was still unstable.

Similar to its discussions of *Li* (fire), the *I Ching* does offer a warning about the enthusiasm and energy bounded within *Chien*: "The main thing is not to expand one's powers prematurely in an attempt to obtain by force something for which the time is not yet ripe." But the *I Ching* does not clearly specify what such an unripe time involves; it seems to imply inopportune situational factors. We should also keep in mind that the course of *Chien*, following the path of the *yin* and *yang*, must wax and wane. Creative growth and structuralization cannot endure forever without naturally subsiding (at some point instinctively returning to *Kun*) or encountering new obstacles, internal or external. Psychoanalytic theory, on the other hand, has done much to clarify the internal factors that obstruct the kinds of changes associated with *Chien*, including the oedipal guilt and anxieties associated with success and failure, as well as the pre-oedipal fears of abandonment, engulfment, and object annihilation associated with separation and individuation.

Trigram Structures and Relationships

In addition to the images associated with the eight trigrams, we may also use interpretations of the trigram structures as tools for understanding the psychotherapy process. In the previous section, for each trigram, I briefly described these structures and how they related to the trigram images and attributes. But there is significantly more depth and subtly in how to visually interpret the patterns of the three *yin* and *yang* lines. These interpretations enrich and expand the application of the trigram images. The structural patterns can help explain a variety of psychotherapeutic phenomena, including how the patient communicates and behaves, and how the clinician intervenes. Because the trigrams are multilayered (layered in threes), they can capture the depth and multifaceted qualities of the interactions between patient and clinician. They are particularly effective at representing simultaneously the juxtaposition of conscious and unconscious processes.

For example, the trigram *Ken*, the mountain, consists of a solid *yang* line above two broken *yin* lines. Some patients may present themselves as outwardly stubborn and resistant, but inwardly they are in fact yielding and receptive. One of my patients consistently fought me off, refusing to acknowledge that therapy helped—but he always came on time, started to grow his hair like mine, and, when he acquired a higher-paying job, mumbled under his breath that he wanted to pay more than the reduced fee. The trigram *Chen,* the image of thunder, consists of a strong *yang* line beneath two *yin,* which suggests patients who appear calm on the surface, but sit tentatively, on the brink of an upward-rising intrusion from the unconscious. In some cases, the trigram structure may add a totally new level of interpretation that goes beyond the more straightforward interpretation of the image and attributes. Although *Tui* usually is associated with joy and openness, the *Shuo Kua* notes that its structure (a *yin* line above two *yang* lines) represents someone who outwardly appears yielding, kind, and receptive, but is inwardly stubborn—the Tai Chi depiction of the passive-aggressive personality.

One can only imagine the even higher levels of complexity and subtlty involved in applying the 64 hexagrams of the *I Ching* to the psychotherapy process. Each hexagram consists of six lines, which entails the interaction of the upper and lower trigrams with each other, as well as with the two overlapping "nuclear" (internal) trigrams constituted by lines 2-3-4 and 3-4-5. It comes as no surprise that Confucius, nearing the end of his life, stated that he wished he could survive another 50 years and devote the time to studying the *I Ching*.

Fu Hsi's circular arrangement of the eight trigrams around the Tai Chi figure presents the trigrams in polarities. Opposite trigrams lie opposite each other. In the case of the images, this is most clear in the fact that heaven *(Chien)* lies opposite earth *(Kun)*, and fire *(Li)* from water *(Kan)*. In terms of the trigram structures, the positions of the *yin* and *yang* lines are mirror images of each other, when comparing opposite trigrams: Wherever there is a *yang* line in one trigram, there is a *yin* line in the opposite trigram (note, again, that the bottoms of the trigrams lie near the Tai Chi circle, so that the trigrams are read from inside to out).

Although the trigrams are presented in opposite pairs, they are not conceptualized as opposing each other, but rather as complementary. As polarities they enhance, balance, and give rise to each other. For this reason we may apply these polarities to exchanges between the patient and therapist. For example, manifestations of *Chien* in the patient—including inspired, self-enhancing strivings, as implied in the image of "The Creative," or outbursts of strong affects (i.e., rage) as implied in the forcefulness of three *yang* lines—may receive the complementary response of *Kun* from the therapist. Here the receptive, yielding intervention of *Kun* would include mirroring the ambitions and ideals, or the empathic "holding" and "containing" of the unmodulated affects. A patient presenting as *Ken*, who appears on the surface as a mountain of resistance but is internally pausing before making a therapeutic advance, may receive a therapeutic intervention resembling *Tui*. The clinician offers an overt acknowledgment and acceptance of the resistance (the yielding *yin* at the top), but also a more subtle, hidden encouragement or even push to advance (the two *yang* lines below).

Communicative exchanges involving embedded hollowness and embedded firmness are encompassed by the *Li/Kan* polarity, where either a *yin* line is positioned between two *yang (Li)*, or a *yang* between two *yin (Kan)*. One year into therapy, Mary stated that she had learned a great deal about herself, but that she now wanted to terminate. Our work, she claimed, felt as if it were stalling out and that we had accomplished all that we could. She said that it was difficult telling me this, that she was afraid I'd be disappointed or hurt by her leaving, and she worried that I might try to convince her to stay. She presented as *Li*, feeling illuminated about herself and clear about her decision. On the outside, (the outer *yang* lines) she appeared solid. But embedded within, her presentation was actually hollow, false (the inner *yin* line). I sensed that an erotic transference had been brewing, that she wanted to escape confronting it by terminating, but I also sensed that I could not interpret this directly without further fueling her "flight into health." So I adopted the complementary tactic of *Kan*, an intervention where the firm, even "hot" interpretation (*yang* line) was embedded safely between two yielding comments (outer *yin* lines). I told her that I understood how difficult it was to express her feelings, that there might be all sorts of feelings that are difficult to express toward me—feeling afraid, worried, attracted to me, competitive with me—who knows what. The outer comments about being afraid, worried, and competitive were the outer *yin* lines that yielded. They were easy for Mary to hear because either she had already said it herself or it was not immediately relevant to the transference. It was the inner comment about being attracted to me (the inner *yang* line) that constituted the heart of the interpretation. She could consciously choose to disregard it while it nevertheless made an unconscious impact. In this context, *Kan* enabled me to make an interpretation without exactly making it.

In addition to working with the trigram polarities in the Fu Hsi arrangement, we also can interpret the relationships of the trigrams according to their sequence. In the Fu Hsi arrangement, starting at the 1:00 position and moving clockwise around the Tai Chi figure, the sequence is: *Sun, Kan, Ken, Kun, Chen, Li, Tui, and Chien*. An alternate sequence, proposed by Chou Wen-Wang in approximately 1100 B.C. and known as the King Wen arrangement, is: *Li, Kun, Tui, Chien, Kan, Ken, Chen, Sun*. This sequence represents the way the hexagrams are ordered in the *I Ching* and is thought to reflect cycles in nature, whereas the Fu Hsi arrangement is thought to reflect polarities, as discussed earlier. The extension of Fu Hsi trigram arrangement into the 64 hexagrams follows an identifiable mathematical progression (the one that inspired Leibnitz to create the binary system). However, no one has been able to discover a mathematical code for the King Wen arrangement, which has led scholars to believe that the arrangement is only accessible through intuition.

Although the King Wen arrangement is usually considered the better representation of cycles in nature, the Fu Hsi sequence also possesses a poetic rhythmic pattern, one that applies particularly well to psychotherapy. The process begins with a gentle, gradual, but enduring immersion into the deeper, unconscious structures of the self (*Sun, Kan*). Anxiety and resistances may be encountered along the way (*Kan, Ken*), so the process may need to rest or pause, perhaps to allow the patient to consolidate gains and test the waters before proceeding (*Ken*). Facilitated by the therapist's empathy and a holding environment, the patient reaches a point where the unconscious receptively opens up and yields its secrets *(Kun)*, sometimes with shocking results that can spur the patient to movement *(Chen)*. The ultimate benefits are the creation of a stable, cohesive self that serves as the basis for clarity of mind *(Li)*, feelings of joy, satisfaction, and openness to others *(Tui)*, and the creative urge to progress even further in the actualization of the self, its ambitions and ideals *(Chien)*. This creative urge always seeks more; in Nietzsche's words, "Life wants more life." As such, it sets the cycle in motion again.

Circling clockwise around the Tai Chi figure (the two intertwined fish) intuitively corroborates this pattern. The movement from top to bottom (the gradual immersion into the darkness of *yin*) corresponds with the descent into the unconscious, insight, and the destructuring of the habitual components of the self. The movement from bottom to top (the gradual ascent into the light of *yang*) corresponds with conscious assimilation and mastery, and the restructuring of the self. This periodicity may pertain to the entire course of therapy, to smaller cycles within individual sessions, or something in between.

The Tao of Psychological Transformations

If one were to look for a summary of how the Tai Chi relates to psychotherapy, one might find it in the three definitions of Tao suggested by Chu Chai in his introduction to the *I Ching* (Legge, 1964). The Tao is change and transformation; it is invariability; it is ease and simplicity—three characteristics captured visually by the Tai Chi figure.

In psychotherapy, the complexity of intrapsychic dynamics and of the various changes and transformations that occur can be overwhelming. The self moves through endlessly complex, subtle fluctuations. Although the same issues may arise over and over, you never step in exactly the same river twice.

Yet beneath it all lies an unchanging force, an invariable principle that is both unique to each person and common to all. It is Tao as the internal force of gestation, the ordering process that is rooted in chaos and moves toward the unity of intrinsic potentials. It lifts the patient through change and transformation to the actualization of the latent, nuclear self.

Although one struggles through a complex maze of ceaseless transformations, the final therapeutic attainment is ease and simplicity. In the cohesive, adaptive self, the complex array of structures and processes are joined seamlessly, effortlessly, unself-consciously, just as a pianist performs without concentrating any deliberate effort or awareness on his or her fingers. This ease and simplicity enables the liberation of the invariable ordering process that is the self's nuclear plan. Ideally, the psychotherapy process follows this path—the path of *wu wei,* where one can let things happen according to their own design.

10

Vision Quest

The Vision Quest Concept

In primitive cultures, a method for gaining psychological or spiritual insight was the *vision quest*. People would undertake the quest as a rite of passage into adulthood, to discover an essential aspect of their identity, or to find the meaning of or solution to a crisis that confronted the clan. For the spiritual leader of the group (the shaman or medicine man) the quest was a periodic ritual of receiving guidance, wisdom, and inspiration from the forces or beings that dwelt in the unseen realms behind everyday reality. The seeker would wander into the wilderness alone, searching for a sign or vision, perhaps in a dream, that would reveal some truth. Deprived of food, water, and shelter, often for several days, the person self-induced a heightened need state and altered consciousness. Hallucinogens or self-torture were sometimes included in the practice. The combination of an altered state of consciousness with the intense desire and expectation for discovery often triggered an experience, or a series of experiences, that led to insight. Afterward, the shaman or medicine man might help the person interpret the vision.

Various techniques and rituals for attaining insight into higher truths were practiced among ancient cultures (Campbell, 1972, 1976). Variations on the vision quest ritual, as described, played a particularly important role among many of the tribes of the Plains and Plateau Indians (Albers & Parker, 1971; Benedict, 1922). To discover the special powers that made a person unique among his tribe, or when confronted by disease, war, and death, the Indian would seek a guiding vision from a guardian spirit. In his widely read book *Black Elk Speaks*, Neihardt (1959/1972) recounted the story of Black Elk, a Sioux warrior and medicine man whose visions foretold the downfall of the Indian nation at the hands of the white settlers. In a less well-known but equally poignant work, Brown (1974) describes his own vision quests to gain an understanding of the psychological and social implications of the clash between the Indian and white cultures, and of the ultimate fate of the Indian people.

Historical evidence seems to suggest that the Indian tribes were descended from Asia, and that their culture, including their religion and spirituality, has its roots in the Orient. Some well-known writers on Buddhism—for example, Peter Matthiessen (1987)—are convinced of this shared lineage between Native American spirituality and Zen. The vision quest theme of wandering in search of truth overlaps with the mythical and actual emphasis on journeying and pilgrimage in the Orient. Tibetan Buddhism contains many stories of the journeys and visions of Milarepa, the most important religious figure in Tibet (Lhallungpa, 1982). Peter Matthiessen's (1978) account of wandering through the Asian mountains in search of the snow leopard, a story that was as much archetypal in spirit as it was autobiographical, gained widespread recognition. The very origin of Zen lies in the fact that Bodhidharma, one of the patriarchs of Buddhism, journeyed across the Himalayas from India to China, where his teachings became Ch'an, the historical predecessor of Japanese Zen.

Marian Mountain (1983) described the importance of leaving one's "old hometown," that place of familiar perceptions and attitudes, the conventional and usually egotistic hold on reality that offers safety, comfort, and predictability. Instead, she stated, Zen calls for wandering because it is the Buddhist way of expressing one's ordinary life and ordinary mind. Not to cling, to avoid a clutching monkey-mind, is the very essence of Zen. Quoting D. T. Suzuki (p. 8), she noted how the Sanskrit word *apratistha* means "not to have any home where one may settle down"—or, perhaps more accurately and paradoxically, "to settle down where there is no settling down." She also quotes Suzuki's translation of a verse from a Japanese book on swordsmanship:

> Wherever and whenever the mind is found
> attached to anything
> Make haste to detach yourself from it.
> When you tarry for any length of time
> It will turn again into your old hometown.

Not having any home may seem like a terribly disorienting, toxic experience. The longing that starts one on the Zen path, Matthiessen (1987) suggested, is a kind of homesickness. However, perhaps paradoxically, homelessness may also highlight feelings of rootedness and fulfillment. In fact, it is one of the definitions of *nirvana*. The great Zen patriarch Rinzai described apratistha as a characteristic of the Enlightened Man of No Title:

> He is the one who is in the house and yet does not stay away
> from the road; he is the one who is on the road and yet does not
> stay away from the house. Is he an ordinary man or a great
> sage? No one can tell. Even the devil does not know where to lo-
> cate him. Even the Buddha fails to manage him as he may de-
> sire. When we try to point him out, he is no more there; he is on
> the other side of the mountain. (quoted in Mountain, 1983, p. 8)

This Buddhist concept of wandering as the source of insight and enlightenment may be one of the origins of the Native American's vision quest practice. Indeed, it is a universal, cross-cultural phenomenon, remnants of which exist in various forms in our contemporary culture. Themes about wandering and searching often have been the focus of popular literature, such as the "on the road" ventures of Jack Kerouac (1955) and William Least Heat Moon (1982), or the mystical wanderings of Carlos Castaneda (1972). Even the common walk or drive by oneself "to have time to think" bears elements of the vision quest. The idea of setting off by oneself on a journey of discovery—of being the wanderer, the searcher—is an archetypal theme that has surfaced in the lives of ordinary people, as well as mythical heroes and great spiritual leaders, such as Odysseus, Siddhartha, and Christ. Similar to the vision searchers of earlier cultures, the person sometimes aims his or her quest toward universal insights of a social or spiritual nature. For other people, the quest may be a more personal pursuit for self-understanding. However, universal and personal insights are often intertwined. As revealed in the Jungian vision of the collective unconscious and discussed also by Campbell (1972), the conflicts and strivings within the life of the individual often are rooted in archetypal, transpersonal themes. For Jung (1961) himself, the vision quest was an ongoing exploration into these archetypal roots, a lifelong process of interpreting his dreams and visual fantasies—of seeking signs through meditation, during travels to remote cultures, and even in his journey through a near-death experience.

I became interested in the vision quest while teaching an undergraduate course on psychotherapy. Because the course emphasized insight-oriented approaches, I was looking for a confidential, yet potentially effective, exercise for the students that could enhance their understanding of therapeutic processes and their own intrapsychic dynamics. One day the idea struck me that a modified, less intense version of the vision quest—a kind of self-directed psychotherapy— might be the answer. The project provided us the opportunity to study some of the transformational features of the quest and its underlying intrapsychic processes. The vision quest emphasis on insight and the implicit assumption about "unconscious" realms of experience indicated the value of applying a psychoanalytic interpretation to this ancient practice. In addition, the theme of wandering, of breaking attachments to one's old hometown, indicated the power of Buddhist interpretations. The vision quest seemed to be perfectly blended for exploration via a synergistic combination of Eastern and psychoanalytic insights.

I gave the participants instructions that highlighted the essential features of the vision quest: (1) solitariness—they had to do it alone, and although they might meet people along the way, extended conversations should be avoided; (2) a wandering away from their usual environment without any predetermined destination in mind, allowing intuition or instinct to carry them along the way; (3) a wandering of thoughts and emotions to accompany the physical circumambulation; (4) self-reflecting and self-questioning—posing to oneself, as a reference point for the wandering, either a specific question about some issue in one's life, or a more open-ended question of an existential or spiritual nature, such as "Who am I?" (5) an attitude of searching, looking, expecting a solution or insight into the question proposed, perhaps in the form of a purely internal realization, either gradual or sudden, or perhaps in the form of a sign or vision from the world around them.

The quest lasted four hours, just a fraction of the time primitive peoples devoted to the endeavor, but a more realistic goal for the students. They kept logs of what transpired, which, in addition to my discussions with them, allowed me to share and help them interpret their experiences. In their logs I offered comments and questions designed to enhance their intellectual and personal understandings of the experience; some of my feedback resembled interventions I make in my psychotherapy work. I introduced the project to the students as a voluntary exercise, and I encouraged them to consult with me before, during, or after the quest if they had questions or needed assistance.

The year that we first attempted the exercise, the students (and, secretly, I) were skeptical about whether it would be effective. To our surprise, when they returned from their journeys almost everyone agreed that it had had a significant impact on them—a result that encouraged me to report the findings of what became an ongoing project (Suler & Genovese, 1988; Suler, 1990a). Over the next four years I continued to collect data, including the personal accounts of students, colleagues, psychotherapy clients, and my own personal experiences (a total of more than 100 vision quests).

This modified version of the vision quest obviously differs from the ancient practice of the Native Americans, especially regarding the cultural/historical context and the intensity of the altered consciousness induced. However, many of the essential ingredients (those that echo Eastern themes) remain: the act of wandering, the relation of self to world during the wandering, and the insights that occur along the way.

Wandering: Free Association and Destructuring

People often sense a psychological hurdle over which they must jump before they can even begin the quest. Wandering away from one's routine lifestyle stirs a variety of subconscious feelings that may undermine one's determination to engage the quest. Searchers experience undertones of nervous anticipation and excitement about what might happen. They sense a vague anxiety rising from the feeling that they are on a journey with an unknown destination, that they are leaving behind and separating from the familiarity and safety of their everyday activities. The threat of uncovering the unconscious, and of leaving one's old hometown, peeks out from behind the facade of conventional consciousness. Some experience guilt and doubt because our achievement-oriented culture does not endorse such meanderings. For those who conceptualize the quest as a task to be mastered, there is performance anxiety. The quest stands before the person as an archetypal reminder of the shaman's journey, and of choice and free will—ideas to which our culture pays much lip service, but which, on deeper, unconscious levels, as Fromm (1965) suggested, trigger existential anxiety.

One of my colleagues was working with a psychotherapy patient who had a longstanding interest in myth, shamanism, and Eastern philosophy. They discussed the possibility of her undertaking a vision quest as a means of enhancing her progress in therapy. On the morning she intended to begin the quest, she experienced such intense anxiety that she could not leave the house. Agitated and distraught, she decided to conduct the exercise while remaining at home. Afterward, what stood out in her memory was reading an apocalyptic newspaper article about worldwide devastation due to climatic changes. With her therapist, she described her fear of failing miserably at the exercise. On a deeper level it was a fear that her cherished ideal of being a wandering shaman—the fantasy that bolstered her identity—might be a false, unrealistic grandiosity, that her sense of self might be devastated, leaving only depression and emptiness behind.

Of the large majority of participants who succeeded at launching themselves into the quest, some carried with them a specific question or issue in mind. Typically, they were issues not unlike those presented at the beginning of psychotherapy: difficulties in interpersonal relationships, especially with parents and love relationships; anxiety, depression, low self-esteem; conflicts about dependence and independence, success and failure; facing decisions about the future, especially choices about careers and marriage; fears about object loss, death, and the meaning of life. The core themes, consistent with the developmental task of college students, centered on separation/individuation, self-identity, and intimacy. Other participants undertook the vision quest with no specific question in hand. They equipped themselves only with an illusive expectation that they would learn something about themselves, or about "reality."

With or without a specific question, the participants rarely pursued the quest in any organized fashion. Those who did attempt a rational, systematic attack on their question met with frustration and minimal success. The essence of the quest is both a psychological and physical wandering, a loosely structured free association or stream of consciousness and perception, not unlike that in psychoanalysis and insight meditation. The students described the quest as "daydreaming," "a relaxing of the mind," and, in words that echo those of a Zen master, a "letting go of your thoughts and feelings." The experience of derealization, of "being in a dream" (also similar to meditation) was common. The searcher's attention drifts between observations of the external world and internal thoughts, feelings, and fantasies. Previously forgotten memories and dreams begin to surface and are punctuated with periods of heightened affect—depression, sorrow, anxiety, or elation. People often describe the feeling of trying to reach lost or hidden parts within themselves, of being more aware of inner conflicts and contradictions, as if the Freudian idea of ambivalence or the Jungian vision of the complexes and *yin/yang* bipolarity of personality structure becomes clearer to them. One searcher, troubled and confused by the recent death of a close friend, sensed the archetypal polarity of reason and emotion:

> I feel like I am telling a story right now. Like I am writing this to someone but I don't know who. I think it is the cool, rational side of me talking to the emotional, irrational side of me. The rational side is saying that Margaret died for whatever reason—so let it go. The irrational side doesn't feel it's enough.

During the quest—unmoored from the familiar physical and psychological surroundings of one's old hometown, released from the routine tasks of everyday living—the entrenched boundaries of the self begin to loosen and unravel. Logical thought, reality testing, pragmatic intentionality, and other aspects of secondary process are temporarily suspended. Once the rigidities of personality structure relax, one is able to retrieve the freed, previously unseen pieces of self and object representations that bob to the surface of consciousness. The barriers against primary process and warded-off aspects of the self open up. Often, this loosening of defenses causes an activation of visual imagery, which is an important system for representing self-experience. One searcher (whose defensive barriers and personality structure may have been borderline to begin with) experienced vivid images from a past dream:

> A face appears far off in the distance and grows closer and closer to mine. It is almost touching mine when I wake up out of breath. It scares me because it is the face of the devil . . . I must be feeling guilty about something. I try to push it out of my mind.

The wandering of the vision quest is a wandering of the focus of consciousness along the infinite axes of the intrapsychic world, and it leads the person to a fuller rooting in the self that is the source of that consciousness. As in insight meditation and psychotherapy, searchers often describe the experience of "stepping back" to look at themselves. This stepping back into the origin of consciousness is a grounding in the noological space of the "detached" self where existential meaning and purpose can be determined. It is the movement into the observing self that is centered and without boundaries, that can observe any thought, emotion, or process that constitutes the object self, but cannot be observed itself. This rooting into the observing self occurs through the deautomatization and negation of the self-as-structure, a process symbolically enacted in the rituals of self-torture (cutting off fingers, tearing away pieces of flesh) that sometimes occurred during the vision quests of the Native Americans. The wandering of the vision searcher reverses and destructures habitual patterns of thinking and feeling, frees the stream of consciousness, and grounds the person in the observing self that is aware of that stream and in the willing self that may take action on it. One wanders along the road but remains in the house. One settles down in a place where there is no settling down.

Wandering during the vision quest is not chaotic or random. It is filled with meaning and intentionality. It is a living, projective test in which the participants, consciously or unconsciously, drift to surroundings that reflect their intrapsychic life. They selectively structure their perceptions and actions in accordance with the external environment. At times, the paralleling of the internal and external worlds takes the form of archetypal symbolism. One searcher walked back and forth across a bridge while questioning the decision to marry her boyfriend; another sat below a weeping willow tree while recalling her childhood experiences with a neglectful, emotionally distant mother. One participant, who had once jokingly referred to himself as a "latent schizophrenic," spent his quest sitting on the dividing median of a busy highway. Searchers often feel drawn to a particular place, at times carried along almost involuntarily by an impulse without fully realizing why—as if being directed by an unconscious part of themselves. The visionaries of the Plains and Plateau Indians sought places that possessed spiritual and magical powers; the contemporary searcher seeks places that are powerful with personal meaning and emotion. For those concerned with the past—preoccupied by regrets, unresolved conflicts, and longings for something lost—the pull was toward old, familiar settings; recollections of early object relationships were common. Searchers exploring new realms of themselves ventured into unfamiliar and sometimes risky territories.

The external world through which the person wanders, whether it symbolizes the past, present, or future, provides the potential for uncovering new dimensions of self and object representations. To discover special powers and attributes, the unique aspect of one's identity, the Indian searched for a vision from a guardian spirit. So, too, contemporary searchers look to the surrounding environment for revelations about tapping the undeveloped or unrealized aspects of their identity—and about the obstacles that block that discovery.

One shy, introverted woman, who lamented the subjugation of her artistic self to the part of her that insisted on a practical, successful career, decided to break away from the trail in the woods near her home. She followed a stream into an unfamiliar area, driven by the feeling that she was looking for something, that she needed to know where the stream stopped. When she discovered that it ended in an old, murky pool of brown water, she suddenly remembered a dream—a dream about being hunted as she explored a stream. At that moment, while reflecting on the dream, she heard gunshots in the distance. Her dream was recurring in reality! Terrified, she thought the hunters might accidentally shoot her, so she ran frantically through the woods until she stumbled upon a familiar road. Feeling stupid and angry with herself, she wondered whether she should have taken a chance by wandering from the trail in the first place.

Such surprising parallels between the internal and external worlds, between fantasy and reality, are reminiscent of Jung's (1951/1971) concept of synchronicity—the acausal, meaningful connection of simultaneously occurring psychic and physical events. While reading the logs written by the vision searchers, I often was reminded of the Eastern notion of the unity and interpenetrating connectedness of self and world, of the blending representations of self-in-the-world and world-in-the-self. But not all apparently synchronous events are strictly acausal. The paralleling of the external and internal worlds often is a complex causal interweaving of these two realms. The searchers' states of mind led them, often unconsciously, to certain locales, and those environments reciprocally altered their stream of consciousness, often directing them to new, productive avenues of thought and feeling. The meaning of these interconnected, apparently synchronous events may be clear to the reader of the logs, but not always to the participants themselves. When searchers suddenly realize the impact of an external event on triggering an insight—when the insight manifests itself in this event—they have received their "sign."

Signs and Visions

The instructions for the vision quest encouraged the participants to be watchful for a cue or message from the environment. Something would happen or appear before them, precipitating a new understanding or insight into the question they had proposed to themselves. It was an expectation for a "sign," similar to the Indian's expectation for a vision. Many participants did report such events. The signs delivering the most impact were those that appeared suddenly, by surprise, catching the person off-guard—which suggested the influence of unconscious processes. The sign happened "out there," but at the same time gripped one's intrapsychic world by revealing an important idea, memory, or emotion. An old man who passed by became the image of the father "who must have loved me underneath all that drinking." A bird's song proved that there was hope for a failing relationship. Seeing water flow around a dam was realized as the potential to overcome obstacles. A tree stump suggested that one was "stumped" in life. The sign also could take the form of a situation that coalesced around the individual, as in the case of the person who found himself stuck driving between two school buses on their afternoon rounds, which provoked associations about his feeling trapped at college and by the course his career was taking.

The woman who felt troubled and confused by her friend's death undertook a series of three vision quests, several weeks apart, to help clarify her feelings. After each journey we met to discuss her experiences. During her second quest, while wandering through a cemetery, a sign suddenly came to her in the form of a bouquet of flowers sitting by a gravestone—a juxtaposition of life and death, the mutual arising and inseparability of opposites—that caused her to relive her friend's funeral and uncovered the clashing emotions of the mourning process: her feelings of abandonment, sorrow, anger, and guilt. To her the flowers represented her friend, and at first she perceived them as beautiful, but then suddenly she was gripped by confusion and frustration:

> It's beginning to drive me crazy that I'm alone. I don't know why I just don't leave this cemetery. I feel trapped by my own self—like there is some sort of answer in here—and then I don't think that way at all. I feel confused and negative about everything—which isn't like me. I'm beginning to hate this place. I hate these flowers and I hate the emptiness of this place. I feel like screaming but there is no one even here to hear me.

That night, she dreamed of being on a vision quest along a beach, when a strong wind blew her into the ocean. The undertow threatened to drag her down, but, suddenly, a stranger appeared and pulled her from the water. During our talk she interpreted the dream as being "saved from drowning in my unconscious thoughts." The dream vision revealed the intrapsychic impact of the quests, as well as her desire to be rescued—which was, in part, a transferential reference to me, and also an important theme throughout her life. The dream expressed her identification with her friend. It conveyed her unconsciousness' acknowledgment of death and the loss of self (even the "oceanic experience") as the inevitable counterpoint of existence. She spent her last quest walking around and around a traffic circle near her home, thinking about her life ahead, but reaching no definite conclusions—a sign that there were more issues yet to resolve.

For some searchers, the meaning of the sign was instantly clear; it may have triggered a fresh insight or simply heightened their awareness of something that they already vaguely knew about themselves. Other searchers were struck by the feeling that the event was indeed important, though they were not immediately certain how to interpret it. As they thought about the sign during the remainder of the quest, the layers of its meaning began to unfold, sometimes facilitated by the appearance of new signs. Associations tended to accumulate and interact dynamically over time. Some searchers only realized their sign and its significance in retrospect, after the quest had ended, which revealed the influence of unconscious incubation and the new perspective attained through the passage of time. The appearance of the sign and the person's working through its meaning corresponds to the inspirational and elaborational phases of regression in service of the ego (Kris, 1952), a process that some theorists have used to explain the experiencing and assimilating of mystical encounters (the oscillations between self and no-self). In the inspirational phase, the ego suspends its restrictions against the unconscious, allowing the primary process mechanisms of condensation, displacement, and symbolism to reveal insights into new realms of experience; whereas in the elaborational phase, the barriers are reestablished and ego functions resumed in order to decipher, refine, and integrate the raw insight.

Similar to the role of the shaman in earlier cultures, I helped the searchers interpret the meaning of their visions. In many cases, I needed only to suggest what the sign might have been in order to trigger their insights. During her quest, one searcher ruminated about her relationship with a hostile, apparently schizophrenic mother, her search for independence, and her overly ambitious need to overcome problems by herself; yet she also felt withdrawn, lonely, isolated from others, "like I'm from the wrong culture." I suggested that her sign, the symbol or self-representation of how she had adapted to her family, was the turret atop a house which had captured her attention during the vision quest at the same synchronistic moment that she heard the lyrics of a song (by Sting) playing on a distant stereo, "If I built this fortress around your heart." When I suggested this interpretation, her eyes flew wide open. "It's perfect!" she said. "It's me!"

It is important to note that the searchers were not always aware of the environment, or susceptible to the appearance of signs. "I was solely into myself—I didn't know if it was day or night, cold or hot." "Nothing around me even fazed me." Similar to the insight meditator, rather than maintaining an evenly enduring sensitivity and receptiveness to the external world, the vision quest participant experiences an oscillation between intrapsychic preoccupation and outer-directed cognizance, a rhythm of withdrawal and contact. Perhaps it is this rhythm that sets the psychodynamic stage for the appearance of signs.

Indian wisdom stated that the sign appears when the person merges and is one with the surrounding world. Similar to mystical states of consciousness, the loosening of ego boundaries permits a freeing of self structure, allowing an intermingling and dynamic interplay between the multidimensional facets of self and environment. The representations of self and object become more flexible and mobile, more easily projected or fused into external cues. The sign is a crystallization of an unconscious aspect of self, as if an image from the environment is "borrowed" to symbolize a hidden aspect of self that is to be catapulted to the level of consciousness. Insights are achieved by temporarily incorporating useful elements from the object world into selfobject systems, and thus applying them as fortuitous handles for stimulating intrapsychic change. The sign is a type of transitional object for transposing self structure, or a version of the "transformational object" (Bollas, 1986)—the signifier that promises a process of transformation to which the self regressively surrenders and fuses, in hopes of participating in a healing metamorphosis. As something the person sees, hears, feels, or does, the sign serves as a tangible, sensorimotor event, a "concretization of experience" (Atwood & Stolorow, 1984) that symbolically reveals and confirms an emerging configuration of self structure. For the American Indian, it was the appearance of the totem, the animal that represented one's essential nature. More powerful than simple introspection, the entrusting of oneself to a sign relies less on conscious efforts and runs deeper into the unconscious. For some people, the search for the sign is a search for the stabilizing center of the self:

I need to get in touch with some part of myself that used to be safe and secure . . . to delve into that part of me I hope I haven't lost forever. I have to take it back with me.

In psychoanalytic treatment, therapeutic gains occur as a result of the patient's need and motivation to relate to an object outside the self. The therapist fulfills this need, and with the patient, forms an intersubjective field of interlocking self structures that forms the basis for psychological growth. The presence of the empathic-introspective object stimulates the rich and powerfully therapeutic interplay within this transformational space. A fascinating aspect of the vision quest is its demonstration that the need to engage a transformational object, and the curative dynamic of the self/object field, also may be fulfilled between the self and the "physical" elements of the environment. This curative dynamic between self and object world is one of the key features of self-transformation in mysticism and Eastern religious systems.

Encountering a sign highlights a mode of experiencing the world that exemplifies the vision quest, a mode that taps Zen and Taoism. Our everyday style of consciousness grasps the environment as a collection of things to be used or manipulated, or as things that use or manipulate us. But during the vision quest, the self and world are not at odds with each other. The relationship feels communal, mutually rejuvenating and creating. Rather than being seen as a deadened or mechanical entity, the world is imbued with vibrant order and meaning. Some searchers sense that a higher realm or state of being is operating through the medium of the environment. The sign may be experienced as a direct manifestation of this higher influence. In his studies of primitive religions and rituals, Eliade (1959) described this as the experience of the "sacred," the realization of a higher, transcendent reality that penetrates this reality—a variation of B-cognition (Maslow, 1971), or sensing "the realm of the unseen" (James, 1902), or even a Buddhist awareness of the manifestation of the absolute within the relative, the no-self within the self. Though they are only distant inheritors of the ancient rituals studied by Eliade, the searchers during their quest sometimes feel this sacred quality of the environment and the forces that act through it. The sign may be considered a breakthrough of this higher realm, a concentration of sacred space into an *axis mundi,* an absolute point of support and meaning that puts an end to anxiety and disorientation. As Eliade stated, it can reveal a solution to one's existential problems, and, because it emanates from a transhuman world, it also can open one up to universal truths that transcend particulars. It gives one access to the world of spirit.

Individuation and Union

The vision quest facilitates individuation, the process of striving toward wholeness, completion, undividedness, of rediscovering one's uniqueness. This process is multilayered. The physical and psychological wanderings, punctuated by the manifestation of signs, enable unconscious components of the self to surface and begin integration into the personality structure. By physically returning to a locale from their childhood or by simply recalling their pasts (common occurrences in all the quests), the searchers also engaged in the process of "anamnesis" (Eliade, 1959), the act of returning, remembering, and reliving one's origins to fulfill the ontological need for restoring and recreating the self. They reflected on the relationship of their present life to their past and future, looking for causes and themes, ordering their life story into a "narrative" (Spence, 1982) that conveyed important truths about themselves and established a sense of self-continuity across time. The very act of reflecting on their past, present, and future served as a form of self-mirroring that strengthened their identity. For many searchers, the return to the past involved the need to recapture something that was lost (childhood innocence, according to the Indian tradition) and to idealize their child self-representations. Many participants remarked how the once-familiar place to which they felt drawn now no longer seemed the same, how the passage of time had altered it. They lamented and tried to reconcile themselves with the idea that industry and civilization contributed to the deforming of these treasured places, especially natural environments. By empathizing with the environment—and implicitly realizing the Taoist vision of the identity between self and world—these searchers used the quest as a vehicle for reconciling themselves with developmental losses and for destructuring toxic introjects and self-representations.

Being by oneself, away from home, observing people from a distance, tended to activate separation-individuation issues. It stirred in the participants feelings of loneliness and isolation, leading them to struggle with their needs and fears about relating intimately to others, to more fully realizing the importance of their object relations to their sense of self. They reenacted and grappled with conflicts from the practicing and rapprochement phases of development (Mahler, Pine, & Bergman, 1975). Memories of past separation achievements (traveling, moving away from home) were recalled with pride. Feelings of being unique and special, of having endured an exploration and trial of self-identity, were common, not unlike the Indian, who, after completing the vision quest, achieved a heightened self-esteem and sense of pride. One searcher, suddenly experiencing a boost of confidence about perambulating through the city streets, omnipotently stated that "I admire my courage to walk alone and be myself." Other searchers experienced considerable anxiety about being alone, as in one student's vivid reports of growing more and more distressed as she walked away from campus. The anxiety often was accompanied by worries about the unpredictability of life and the search for security. Of course, the developmental phase of young adulthood, in which these college students were located, naturally catalyzed their concerns about dependence, independence, and self-responsibility—in general, "growing up." In many cases the salient theme was the rapprochement conflict between the urge to separate and the fear of separating, the ambivalent balance of excitement and anxiety about individuation:

> I want to be everything. That's the problem. But when I step forward to achieve, my mind's doubt holds my foot back. This causes anxiety. I don't feel myself walking. I'll be on my way.

The fact that people can benefit from the vision quest with little or no assistance from an outsider, professional or otherwise, points to the existence of a natural, internal impetus toward separation and individuation—the kind of developmental force postulated in self-actualization theory and contemporary psychoanalytic paradigms such as object relations theory and self psychology. The curative dynamics of the sign could not exist if not for this inherent ability to enhance identity by immersing oneself into the world. The vision quest can tap these internal potentials.

Paradoxically, integrating and rejuvenating one's sense of self during the vision quest is attained by momentarily losing the self to a condition of unity that transcends it. The power of the quest lies in the experience of the interpenetration between self and no-self. The merging of self with environment that stimulates the surfacing of signs, as prescribed by the Indian tradition, may be considered a variation of the ubiquitous "search for oneness" that can yield therapeutic effects (Silverman, Lachmann, & Milich, 1982). It is similar to the quest for primary, total undifferentiatedness in psychoanalytic therapy, for the basic unity that provides the stillness at center from which arises the awareness of movement, perception, and identity, and the rhythm of differentiation and reassimilation (Little, 1986). In his analysis of ancient religions, Eliade (1959) described the sense of ontological rejuvenation and newness that ensues from this selfless state created through meditative rituals. According to Indian tradition, the sign will only appear and trigger this transformational process when the searcher lets things happen on their own accord, passes through a phase of self-abandonment in order to enter the overarching unity that renews identity—the same process of "letting go" described by Zen and other religious traditions.

Nearly all the searchers, at some point in their quests, felt drawn to natural settings, such as woods, lakes, and rivers, which represented an archetypal return to the origins of the self. Merging and losing oneself in these surroundings created feelings of oneness, peace, and contentment. Identity is refreshed and highlighted by its immersion into and emergence from states of basic unity. For the vision searchers, bodies of water, especially, conjured up associations of both the loss of self, and self-rejuvenation. Water—and the no-self it represented—was something to be feared, but it was also alluring. Although the searchers felt a strong attraction to gaze dreamily into lakes and streams, to feel their unifying and purifying powers, they also recalled people, sometimes friends and relatives, who had drowned. Nearly all the participants thought about the inevitable negation of self—death. Yet these reflections, consistent with a Heideggerian being-toward-death, provoked anxiety, as well as fueled the process of individuation. For those searchers who felt inspired by the juxtaposition of old, decaying houses and new homes being built around them, or by a few flowers blooming in an otherwise neglected and dead garden, the world provided a sign that revealed the Taoist vision of eternal change and the harmony and inseparability of all things arising and passing away:

> One particular house caught my eye. It was old, broken down, and virtually falling apart. Surrounding this house were more new and stable houses. Outside was a small garden with few flowers in bloom, yet some still seemed to survive. Like nature, life is revived, or faces death. Life is constantly changing around me, forcing me to change with it. Just as the house has become worn and old, and the flowers face the change of seasons, I too must enter into different stages in my life.

Vicissitudes of the Vision Quest

The vision quest can be a fascinating mixture of curative processes—psychodynamic, existential, spiritual. On various levels, the process of wandering in search of a sign—of settling down where there is no settling down—provides a transformational space to which the person surrenders, a space where the immersion into the ongoing experience of being revitalizes the self. Some aspects of the quest resemble meditative practice, others resemble psychotherapy. It is not easy to separate these processes into discrete categories. Although it may be true that meditation and psychotherapy are not identical in their effects, the vision quest project does suggest that any effective transformational process blends a variety of metamorphic functions. If the human psyche consists of multiple, overlapping dimensions, then the processes that transform the psyche must be a synergistic combination of forces.

Each vision quest is unique. Each unfolds as a story with a variety of plots and subplots as subtle, complex, and intertwining as the themes in the individual's life. The periods of doubt, hope, curiosity, frustration, boredom, impasse, and bravery embedded in the quest are but microcosms of the phases through which the person passes in the course of a lifetime. Whereas many of the searchers experienced moments of anxiety, depression, or other negative reactions, only a few felt they needed to talk to me in person about it; even then, brief counseling seemed sufficient to work through the experience. In fact, people who explored these negative reactions in their logs or in discussions with me seemed to benefit most from the project. Although it is possible that people with significant, underlying psychopathology might find the vision quest overly taxing, for most people their own intrapsychic safeguards seem sufficient for tempering the experience.

Evaluating the psychodynamic effects of the quest must take into consideration the fact that many of the participants were students in my psychotherapy course. The process and outcome were influenced by my providing guidelines for the project and offering feedback and interpretations of their experiences. Issues concerning the professor's implicit presence also may have affected the participants. Ideas about the professor may have stimulated and blended with unconscious transferential associations concerning parental figures and other significant object relations such as conflicts about pleasing, emulating, or challenging authority figures. Derivatives of such issues did appear in the logs. No transformational process, in the East or in the West, exists outside an interpersonal field. Either real or imagined, authority figures that heal, guide, or judge the person are inseparable from, and perhaps essential to, the process.

Some searchers benefit from the vision quest more than others. Similar to meditation and psychotherapy, the individual's character structure and the kinds of issues brought to the quest influence the process and outcome. Some students reached important decisions and insights; others simply felt the quest momentarily heightened self-awareness. Not everyone receives a sign or fully yields to the therapeutic potential of wandering, searching, and letting go. These individual differences can be explained in terms of the psychoanalytic concepts of defense and resistance; indeed, the searchers demonstrated wide differences in tactics that subverted the project (intellectualizing; dwelling exclusively on the past, present, or future; early termination; fleeing anxiety-arousing environments; pursuing activities that violated the spirit of the quest, such as reading). These individual differences in benefiting from the quest also may reflect differences in the ability to tap and reexperience an archetypal form of consciousness—differences that may be ascribed to the developmental level of the person's self structure and object relations, or to other factors that we don't yet understand. The strengths and weaknesses of the vision quest as a transformational practice (like those of psychotherapy and meditation) are determined by the personality dynamics and social-historical context of those people who devise, modify, and participate in the activity.

Practicing and benefiting from the vision quest do not require a belief in the realm of the transcendental; many searchers find the exercise worthwhile without sensing the presence of a transpersonal dimension. The personal experience of the unseen realm is but one of many potential links between the contemporary version of the vision quest and the ancient practice. Following the literal translation of religion, *religare*, "to bind back," the vision quest may offer the opportunity to enter the archetypal state of consciousness in which one subjectively experiences the rejoining of the self to the realm of the no-self that nourishes it.

Does the vision quest carry any long-term effects? For the first group of participants, a follow-up questionnaire administered four months after the project revealed varied results. When asked how often they thought about the experience, the replies ranged from "rarely" to "often." They reported that events during the day sometimes triggered memories of it, that they tended to think of it when they were alone, or in times of doubt, confusion, and conflict, as if the quest served as a reference point for self-cohesion and continuity. Everyone recalled the central theme or issue during his or her quest. Their most salient memories were of the emotions that had surfaced, the events (signs) that triggered them, and reaching a feeling of self-confirmation and acceptance. Only one person had undertaken additional vision quests on her own; however, several reported spending more time in self-reflection. They more often went for walks or drives; they felt more introspective about their dreams and daydreams. Whereas some students had told others about their quest, others considered it too personal to share.

There are significant individual differences in the long-term impact of a transformational experience, be it a meditative experience, psychotherapy, or a vision quest. The effects of any transformational process fade over time if it is not fortified and replenished by additional endeavors. Zen masters note that even the powerful effects of *satori* can dissolve into vague, stale memories if the experience is not cultivated by further meditative practice. The process is ongoing. If, indeed, there is an inherent impetus or drive toward psychological and spiritual development, there also exist inertia and resistance. The course of transformation moves along the path of the *yin* and *yang*.

Conclusion:
The Future of An Allusion

Arnold Toynbee once said that future historians will likely conclude that one of the most important events of the twentieth century was the introduction of Buddhism to the West. If this conclusion turns out to be true, what lies ahead for psychology and psychoanalysis as one sector of Western culture that rides the tide of this transition? What lies ahead for the Asian practices as they move westward? This book refers to a valuable transformation of both the psychoanalytic and Eastern disciplines as a possible outcome of the convergence between East and West. Indeed, it alludes to a *need* for such a transformation.

What will an Easternized psychoanalysis look like? Will clinicians be meditating as part of their professional development? Will patients be meditating as part of their treatment? Will therapists and theorists alike delve into the Buddhist sutras, Zen training methods, or the *I Ching* as religiously as they search Freud for guidance and inspiration? In some cases, yes—in fact, it is happening now. But in many cases, no.

The transformation, similar to many widespread cultural changes, will likely be gradual, subtle, perhaps almost imperceptible. But such changes are often powerful and enduring. Buddhist, Zen, and Taoist thought will seep silently into the mainstream of psychology and psychoanalysis without being specifically labeled as "Buddhism," "Zen," or "Taoism." The people who initially bridged the gap and continue to pioneer new, deeper paths of integration will know the Eastern terms and their original meanings, but others thereafter may not. It may not be necessary; it may even prove to be a good sign that they don't. When an idea or a system of ideas is truly assimilated, it becomes one's own; the old context may be superfluous baggage. The ideas themselves acquire fresh meaning in their new context. Words such as *spirituality, transcendental, enlightenment,* and *no-self*—which currently leave a bad taste in the mouths of many psychoanalytic people—may be translated into new words that signify similar, but somehow more psychoanalytically palatable, visions. Entire systems of Eastern ideas may be partially dismantled, reorganized, and assimilated into what become new systems, with some of the original ideas discarded, some retained, some transformed. A martial arts teacher said to his students, "Take what makes sense and develop from there." This is how Westerners will Westernize Eastern thought.

I once read a clinical case study of a patient suffering from AIDS. It was during the time when the medical community first began to realize that the disease could become an epidemic. The clinician described how the patient was at first overwhelmed by the horror that had seized his life. His body was disintegrating rapidly. He wanted an omnipotent figure who was unafraid of death to make sense of his nightmare. By the end of the first year of therapy, the clinician reported on the second page of the paper, they had succeeded in separating out the pathological aspects of his fear from the realistic aspects. With some relief from the anxiety about dying, he was then able to uncover his unconscious wishes and fears surrounding illness and death. He had wanted to be close to his mother, but was terrified of becoming dissolved in her psychosis. He could not detach from her for fear of losing her entirely. He had wished her dead to end his own suffering. Unfortunately, his wish came true. His subsequent guilt drove him to wish death upon himself as a means of punishment. He also longed to join her. Unfortunately, this wish, too, came true.

It was an interesting case study, but I was left feeling that something important was missing. What had happened during that first year of therapy? How does one separate out "pathological" from "realistic" fears about death? I wondered what a realistic fear of death was. What could have been a highly powerful theme in the paper— coming to grips with the ultimate existential anxiety, death anxiety— seemed to be only a brief prelude to the "real" analytic task of discovering ambivalence toward one's mother. Was that theme also a brief prelude in the treatment? Did the patient truly come to grips with his death anxiety, or did both he and the therapist escape it by delving into the more usual analytic work?

There is a tendency to cling to the familiar, especially when confronted by the unknown. Psychoanalysis may sometimes hold too tight to its theories while venturing into fundamental, unavoidable dimensions of human experience. People die: There is the possibility of no-self. And this possibility touches the psyche in ways other than those typically conceived by psychoanalytic theory. Here the Eastern disciplines can share their expertise. Their insights can help reveal other meanings concerning the negation of self, as well as the affirmation of self. They open a path to other possibilities that accompany the primary existential issues which psychoanalysis tends to overlook: the possibilities of relief from suffering through "spiritual" transformations. Because such ideas rest on questions that everyone, by simply being human, thinks about, consciously or unconsciously, partially or deeply, via his or her own unique experience, it is inevitable that they will seep into the mainstream of psychology and psychoanalysis. Such transformations are more basic and essential than high altered states or transcendental revelations. They entail the appreciation of the everyday mind and everyday life as it unfolds from its source background of endless variety and change. There is an appreciation of mystery and not-knowing, a sense of awe and respect, even passion, that only a few, rare clinicians and theorists discover as the inspiration for their work, while others retreat to the stale safety of familiar theories.

In exchange for their enrichment from the East, psychology and psychoanalysis offer an extensive knowledge of the human personality. The theories about development, interpersonal dynamics, psychopathology, and the therapeutic process are all sophisticated and highly valuable. As the Eastern disciplines slowly incorporate these Western theories, they will cultivate a deeper appreciation and understanding of the psychological aspects of the individual person who enters their traditions: that person's history, unconscious motives, interpersonal style, intrapsychic strengths and weaknesses. Eastern thought will refine its understanding of the object relations among teachers and students—a knowledge that can enhance the effectiveness of spiritual training methods. An improved comprehension of the psychological world of the individual person who seeks the process of realizing no-self will only enrich that process.

As the royal roads of psychoanalysis and the ancient ways of the East converge, the ultimate goal for each will be the same: To understand fully all dimensions of both the self and the no-self. On this path, the Eastern and Western disciplines will be complementary explorers of human nature and complementary healers of human suffering.

References

Aberbach, D. (1987). Grief and mysticism. *International Review of Psychoanalysis, 14,* 509–526.

Ahsen, A. (1987). Principles of unvivid experience: The girdle of Aphrodite. *Journal of Mental Imagery, 11,* 1–52.

Albers, P., & Parker, S. (1971). The Plains vision experience: A study of power and privilege. *Journal of Anthropological Research, 27,* 203–233.

Alexander, F. (1931). Buddhist training as an artificial catatonia. *Psychoanalytic Review, 18,* 129–145.

Allison, J. (1968). Adaptive regression and intense religious experiences. *Journal of Nervous and Mental Disease, 145,* 452–463.

Atwood, G. E., & Stolorow, R. D. (1984). *Structures of subjectivity: Explorations in psychoanalytic phenomenology.* Hillsdale, NJ: Analytic Press.

Bach, S. (1984). Perspectives on self and object. *Psychoanalytic Review, 7,* 145–168.

Balint, M. (1968). *The basic fault.* London: Tavistock.

Becker, C. B. (1989). Philosophical perspectives on the martial arts in America. In R. F. Nelson (Ed.), *The Overlook martial arts reader: An anthology of historical and philosophical writings* (pp. 97–110). Woodstock, NY: Overlook.

Becker, E. (1960). Psychotherapeutic observations on the Zen discipline. *Psychologia: An International Journal of Psychology in the Orient, 3,* 100–112.

Beebe, B., & Lachmann, F. M. (1988). Mother-infant mutual influence and precursors of psychic structure. In A. Goldberg (Ed.), *Frontiers in self psychology: Progress in self psychology* (vol. 3). Hillsdale, NJ: Analytic Press.

Benedict, R. F. (1922). The visions in the Plains culture. *American Anthropologist, 24,* 1–23.

Berger, D. M. (1987). *Clinical empathy.* Northvale, NJ: Aronson.

Bion, W. R. (1963). *Elements of psycho-analysis.* New York: Aronson, 1983.

————. (1970). *Attention and interpretation.* New York: Aronson.

Blanck, G., & Blanck, R. (1974). *Ego psychology: Theory and practice.* New York: Columbia University Press.

Bollas, C. (1986). The transformational object. In G. Kohon (Ed.), *The British School of psychoanalysis: The independent tradition* (pp. 83–100). New Haven: Yale University Press.

Bonanno, G. A. (1990). Repression, accessibility, and the translation of private experience. *Psychoanalytic Psychology, 7,* 453–474.

Breuer, J., & Freud, S. (1895). Studies on hysteria. *Standard Edition, 2.*

Brown, D. (1986). The stages of meditation in cross-cultural perspective. In K. Wilber, J. Engler, & D. Brown, *Transformations of consciousness* (pp. 219–285). Boston: Shambhala.

Brown, D., & Engler, J. (1986). The stages of mindfulness meditation: A validation study. In Wilber, Engler, & Brown, *Transformations of consciousness* (pp. 161–217). Boston: Shambhala.

Brown, N. O. (1970). *Life against death.* Middletown, CT: Wesleyan University Press.

Brown, V. (1974). *Voices of earth and sky: The vision life of the Native American Indian and their cultural heroes.* Harrisburg, PA: Stackpole Books.

Bruner, J. B. (1959). The art of ambiguity: A conversation with Zen master Hisamatsu. *Psychologia: An International Journal of Psychology in the Orient, 2,* 101–105.

———. (1964). The course of cognitive growth. *American Psychologist, 19,* 1–15.

Buckley, P. (1981). Mystical experiences and schizophrenia. *Schizophrenia Bulletin, 7,* 516–521.

Bugelski, B. R. (1970). Words and images and things. *American Psychologist, 25,* 1002–1012.

Butler, K. (1990). Encountering the shadow in Buddhist America. *Common Boundary, 8,* 14–22.

Campbell, J. (1972). *The hero with a thousand faces.* Princeton, NJ: Princeton University Press (Bollingen Series XVII).

———. (1976). *Primitive mythology: The masks of God.* New York: Penguin.

Castaneda, C. (1972). *A separate reality.* New York: Pocket Books.

Curtis, H. C. (1986). Clinical consequences of the theory of self psychology. In A. Goldberg (Ed.), *Progress in self psychology* (vol. 2). New York: Guilford.

Deikman, A. J. (1963). Experimental meditation. *Journal of Nervous and Mental Disease, 136,* 329–343.

————. (1966a). Implications of experimentally induced meditation. *Journal of Nervous and Mental Disease, 142,* 101–116.

————. (1966b). Deautomatization and the mystic experience. *Psychiatry, 29,* 324–338.

————. (1982). *The observing self: Mysticism and psychotherapy.* Boston: Beacon Press.

Doi, L. T. (1962). Morita therapy and psychoanalysis. *Psychologia: An International Journal of Psychology in the Orient, 5,* 117–123.

Ehrenzweig, A. (1971). *The hidden order of art.* Berkeley: University of California Press.

Eigen, M. (1986). *The psychotic core.* Northvale, NJ: Jason Aronson.

Eissler, K. R. (1953). The effect of the structure of the ego on psychoanalytic technique. *Journal of the American Psychoanalytic Association, 1,* 104–143.

Eliade, M. (1959). *The sacred and the profane: The nature of religion.* New York: Harcourt, Brace, & World.

————. (1976). *Myths, Rites, Symbols.* New York: Harper Colophon Books.

Elkin, H. (1958). On the origin of the self. *Psychoanalytic Review, 45,* 57–76.

————. (1972). On selfhood and the development of ego structures in infancy. *Psychoanalytic Review, 59,* 389–416.

Engler, J. H. (1981). Vicissitudes of the self according to psychoanalysis and Buddhism: A spectrum model of object relations development. *Psychoanalysis and Contemporary Thought, 6,* 29–72.

————. (1986). Therapeutic aims in psychotherapy and meditation. In K. Wilber, J. Engler, & D. Brown, *Transformations of consciousness* (pp. 17–52). Boston: Shambhala.

Epstein, M. D. (1981). Psychiatric complications of meditation practice. *The Journal of Transpersonal Psychology, 13,* 137–147.

————. (1984). On the neglect of evenly suspended attention. *Journal of Transpersonal Psychology, 16,* 193–205.

————. (1986). Meditative transformations of narcissism. *Journal of Transpersonal Psychology, 18,* 143–157.

————. (1988a). The deconstruction of the self: Ego and "egolessness" in Buddhist insight meditation. *Journal of Transpersonal Psychology, 20,* 61–69.

————. (1988b). Attention in analysis. *Psychoanalysis and Contemporary Thought, 11,* 171–189.

————. (1989). Forms of emptiness: Psychodynamic, meditative, and clinical perspectives. *Journal of Transpersonal Psychology, 21,* 61–71.

————. (1990a). Beyond the oceanic feeling: Psychoanalytic study of Buddhist meditation. *International Review of Psychoanalysis, 17,* 159–166.

————. (1990b). Psychodynamics of meditation: Pitfalls on the spiritual path. *Journal of Transpersonal Psychology, 22,* 17–34.

Epstein, M. D., & Lieff, J. D. (1986). Psychiatric complications of meditation practice. In K. Wilber, J. Engler, & D. Brown, *Transformations of consciousness* (pp. 53–63). Boston: Shambhala.

Erikson, E. (1963). *Childhood and society* (2d. ed.). New York: W. W. Norton.

————. (1969). *Gandhi's truth.* New York: Norton.

Fairbairn, W. R. D. (1952). *An object relations theory of the personality.* New York: Basic.

Farber, L. (1966). *The ways of will.* New York: Basic Books.

Fauteux, K. (1987). Seeking enlightenment in the East: Self-fulfillment or regressive longing? *Journal of the American Academy of Psychoanalysis, 15,* 223–246.

Federn, P. (1926). Some variations in ego feeling. *International Journal of Psychoanalysis, 7,* 25–37.

————. (1952). *Ego psychology and the psychoses.* New York: Basic Books.

Fingarette, H. (1958). The ego and mystic selflessness. *Psychoanalytic Review, 45,* 5–40.

Finn, M. (1992). Transitional space and Tibetan Buddhism: The object relations of meditation. In M. Finn & J. D. Gartner (Eds.), *Object relations theory and religious experience.* New York: Praeger.

Finn, M., & Gartner, J. (Eds.). (1992). *Object relations theory and religious experience.* New York: Praeger.

Fowler, J. (1981). *The stages of faith.* New York: Harper & Row.

Frankl, V. E. (1963). *Man's search for meaning.* Boston: Beacon.

————. (1967). *Psychotherapy and existentialism.* New York: Washington Square Press.

Freud, A. (1936). *The writings of Anna Freud II: The ego and its mechanisms of defense* (rev. ed.). New York: International Universities Press, 1966.

————. (1963). The concept of developmental lines. *The psychoanalytic study of the child, 8,* 245–265.

Freud, S. (1895). Project for a scientific psychology. *Standard Edition, 1,* 283–397.

———. (1900). The interpretation of dreams. *Standard Edition, 4 & 5.*

———. (1912). Recommendations to physicians practicing psycho-analysis. *Standard Edition, 12,* 111–120.

———. (1923). The ego and the id. *Standard Edition, 19.*

———. (1927). The future of an illusion. *Standard Edition, 21.*

———. (1930). Civilization and its discontents. *Standard Edition, 21,* 55–145.

Fromm, E. (1959). Psychoanalysis and Zen Buddhism. *Psychologia: An International Journal of Psycholology in the Orient, 2,* 79–99.

———. (1965). *Escape from freedom.* New York: Avon.

Fromm, E., Suzuki, D. T., & DeMartino, R. (1960). *Zen Buddhism and psychoanalysis.* New York: Harper and Row.

Fuller, J. R. (1988). Martial arts and psychological health. *British Journal of Medical Psychology, 61,* 317–328.

Funakoshi, G. (1981). *Karate-do: My way of life.* New York: Kodansha International.

Gedo, J., & Goldberg, A. (1973). *Models of the mind.* Chicago: University of Chicago Press.

Gill, M. M., & Brenman, M. (1959). *Hypnosis and related states: Psychoanalytic studies in regression.* New York: International Universities Press.

Gleser, J., & Brown, P. (1988). Judo principles and practices: Applications to conflict-solving strategies in psychotherapy. *American Journal of Psychotherapy, 42,* 437–447.

Goldberg, A. (1986). Preface. In A. Goldberg (Ed.), *Progress in self psychology* (vol. 2, pp. vii–x). New York: Guilford Press.

Greenberg, J. R., & Mitchell, S. A. (1983). *Object relations in psychoanalytic theory.* Cambridge: Harvard University Press.

Greenson, R. (1967). *The technique and practice of psychoanalysis.* New York: International Universities Press.

Grof, S. (1975). *Realms of the human unconscious.* New York: Viking.

Grotstein, J. S. (1980). A proposed revision of the psychoanalytic concept of primitive mental states. Part I. *Contemporary Psychoanalysis, 16,* 479–546.

———. (1981). *Splitting and projective identification.* New York: Jason Aronson.

————. (1982). Newer perspectives in object relations theory. *Contemporary Psychoanalysis, 18*, 43–91.

————. (1990a). Nothingness, meaninglessness, chaos, and the "black hole": I. The importance of nothingness, meaninglessness, and chaos in psychoanalysis. *Contemporary Psychoanalysis, 26*, 257–290.

————. (1990b). Nothingness, meaninglessness, chaos, and the "black hole": II. The black hole. *Contemporary Psychoanalysis, 26*, 377–407.

Guntrip, H. (1969). *Schizoid phenomena, object relations and the self.* New York: International Universities Press.

Haimes, N. (1972). Zen Buddhism and psychoanalysis: A bibliographic essay. *Psychologia: An International Journal of Psychology in the Orient, 15*, 22–30.

Haley, J. (1963). *Strategies of psychotherapy.* New York: Grune and Stratton.

Hartmann, H. (1939a). *Essays on ego psychology.* New York: International Universities Press, 1964.

————. (1939b). *Ego psychology and the problem of adaptation.* New York: International Universities Press, 1958.

Hendlin, S. (1983). Pernicious oneness. *Journal of Humanistic Psychology, 23*, 61–81.

Herrigel, E. (1960). *The method of Zen.* New York: Vintage Books.

————. (1971). *Zen in the art of archery.* New York: Vintage Books.

Hofstadter, D. R. (1980). *Gödel, Escher, Bach: An eternal golden braid.* New York: Random.

Hofstadter, D. R., & Dennett, C. (1981). *The mind's I: Fantasies and reflections on self & soul.* New York: Bantam Books.

Holt, R. R. (1964). Imagery: The return of the ostracized. *American Psychologist, 19*, 254–264.

Horner, A. J. (1979). *Object relations and the developing ego in therapy.* New York: Jason Aronson.

Horney, K. (1945). *Our inner conflicts.* New York: Norton.

————. (1950). *Neurosis and human growth.* New York: Norton.

————. (1987). *Final lectures.* New York: Norton.

Horowitz, M. J. (1983). *Image formation and psychotherapy.* New York: Jason Aronson.

Horton, P. C. (1974). The mystical experience: substance of an illusion. *Journal of the American Psychoanalytic Association, 22*, 364–380.

Hyams, J. (1982). *Zen in the martial arts.* New York: Bantam.

Ikemoto, T. (1971). Zen enlightenment without a teacher: The case of Mrs. Courtois, an American. *Psychologia: An International Journal of Psychology in the Orient, 14,* 71–76.

Jacobson, E. (1964). *The self and object world.* New York: International Universities Press.

James, A., & Jones, R. (1982). The social world of karate-do. *Leisure Studies, 1,* 337–354.

James, W. (1902). *Varieties of religious experience.* New York: Longmans, Green.

Jichaku, P., Fujita, G. Y., & Shapiro, S. I. (1984). Double bind and the Zen koan. *Journal of Mind and Behavior, 5,* 211–221.

Jones, E. (1913). The God-complex. In *Essays in applied psycho-analysis,* vol. 2. (pp. 244–265). New York: International Universities Press, 1964.

———. (1923). The nature of auto-suggestion. In *Papers on psychoanalysis.* Boston: Beacon Press, 1948.

Jones, J. (1991). *Contemporary psychoanalysis and religion: Transference and transcendence.* New Haven: Yale University Press.

Jou, T. H. (1980). *The Tao of Tai Chi Chuan.* Rutland, VT: Charles Tuttle.

Jung, C. G. (1961). *Memories, dreams, reflections.* New York: Pantheon.

———. (1971). On synchronicity. In J. Campbell (Ed.), *The portable Jung* (pp. 505–518). New York: Viking Press. (originally published 1951)

Jung, C. G. & Hisamatsu, S. (1969). On the unconscious, the self, and therapy. *Psychologia: An International Journal of Psychology in the Orient, 12,* 25–32.

Jwing-Ming, Y. (1989). *The root of Chinese chi kung.* Jamaica Plain, MA: Yang's Martial Arts Association.

Kahn, M. (1974). *The privacy of the self.* New York: International Universities Press.

Kahn, M., Kroeber, T., & Kingsbury, S. (1974). The I Ching as a model for a personal growth group. *Journal of Humanistic Psychology, 14,* 39–51.

Kapleau, P. (1980a). *The three pillars of Zen: Teaching, practice and enlightenment.* New York: Anchor Books.

———. (1980b). *Zen: Dawn in the West.* New York: Anchor Books.

Kauz, H. (1977). *The martial spirit.* Woodstock, NY: Overlook Press.

Kelman, H. (1958). Communing and relating. Part I. Past and current perspectives. *American Journal of Psychoanalysis, 18,* 77–98.

———. (1959a). Eastern influences on psychoanalytic thinking. *Psychologia: An International Journal of Psychology in the Orient, 2,* 71–78.

———. (1959b). Psychotherapy in the Far East. In J. H. Masserman & J. L. Moreno (Eds.), *Progress in psychotherapy* (vol. 4). New York: Grune & Stratton.

Kernberg, O. (1975). *Borderline conditions and pathological narcissism.* New York: Jason Aronson.

Kerouac, J. (1955). *On the road.* New York: Signet.

Klein, B. (1984). *Movements of magic: The spirit of Tai Chi Chuan.* North Hollywood, CA: Newcastle.

Klein, G. (1976). *Psychoanalytic theory: An exploration of essentials.* New York: International Universities Press.

Kohut, H. (1966). Forms and transformations of narcissism. *Journal of the American Psychoanalytic Association, 14,* 243–272.

———. (1971). *The analysis of the self.* New York: International Universities Press.

———. (1977). *The restoration of the self.* New York: International Universities Press.

———. (1984). *How does analysis cure?* Chicago: University of Chicago Press.

Kondo, A. (1952). Intuition in Zen Buddhism. *American Journal of Psychoanalysis, 12,* 10–14.

Kopp, B. (1976). *If you meet Buddha on the road, kill him! The pilgrimage of psychotherapy patients.* Toronto: Bantam.

Kovel, J. (1990). Beyond the future of an illusion: Further reflections on Freud and religion. *Psychoanalytic Review, 77,* 69–88.

Kris, E. (1950). The significance of Freud's earliest discoveries. *International Journal of Psychoanalysis, 31,* 108–116.

———. (1952). *Psychoanalytic explorations in art.* New York: International Universities Press.

Krynicki, V. E. (1980). The double orientation of the ego in the practice of Zen. *American Journal of Psychoanalysis, 40,* 239–248.

Kubose, S. K., & Umemoto, T. (1980). Creativity and the Zen koan. *Psychologia: An International Journal of Psychology in the Orient, 23,* 1–9.

Kurtz, S. (1989). *The art of unknowing: Dimensions of openness in analytic therapy.* Northvale, NJ: Jason Aronson.

Least Heat Moon, W. (1982). *Blue highways: A journey into America.* New York: Random House.

Legge, J. (1964). *I Ching: Book of changes.* New Hyde Park, NY: University Books.

Leonard, G. (1989). Aikido and the mind of the West. In R. F. Nelson (Ed.), *The Overlook martial arts reader: An anthology of historical and philosophical writings* (pp. 173–182). Woodstock, NY: Overlook Press.

Levine, D. N. (1989). Liberal arts and martial arts. In R. F. Nelson (Ed.), *The Overlook martial arts reader: An anthology of historical and philosophical writings* (pp. 301–319). Woodstock, NY: Overlook Press.

Lewin, B. D. (1950). *The psychoanalysis of elation.* New York: Norton.

Lhallungpa, L. P. (1982). *The life of Milarepa.* Boulder, CO: Prajna Press.

Liang, Z., & Ji, L. (1989). *Mastering the art of war* (T. Cleary, Ed. & Trans.). Boston: Shambhala.

Lichtenberg, J. (1983). *Psychoanalysis and infant research.* Hillsdale, NJ: Analytic Press.

Lichtenstein, H. (1977). *The dilemma of human identity.* New York: Jason Aronson.

Lindner, R. (1954). *The fifty-minute hour.* New York: Delta.

Little, M. (1986). On basic unity (primary total undifferentiatedness). In G. Kohon (Ed.), *The British School of Psychoanalysis: The independent tradition* (pp. 136–153). New Haven: Yale University Press.

Loewald, H. W. (1960). On the therapeutic action of psychoanalysis. *International Journal of Psychoanalysis, 41,* 16–33.

———. (1976). Perspectives on memory in psychology vs. metapsychology: Psychological issues. *Monograph, 36* (9, No. 4). New York: International Universities Press.

Lovinger, R. (1984). *Working with religious issues in therapy.* New York: Jason Aronson.

Luk, C. (1960). *Ch'an and Zen teaching.* London: Rider.

Mackett, J. (1989). Chinese hypnosis. *British Journal of Experimental and Clinical Hypnosis, 6,* 129–130.

Mahler, M. S. (1968). *On human symbiosis and the vicissitudes of individuation.* New York: International Universities Press.

Mahler, M., Pine, F., & Bergman, A. (1975). *The psychological birth of the human infant.* New York: Basic Books.

Malcolm, J. (1980). *Psychoanalysis: The impossible profession.* New York: Random House.

Maslow, A. (1954). *Motivation and personality.* New York: Harper and Row.

———. (1971). *The farther reaches of human nature.* New York: Viking Press.

Matthiessen, P. (1978). *The snow leopard.* New York: Bantam.

———. (1987). *Nine-headed dragon river.* Boston: Shambhala.

Maupin, E. W. (1962). Zen Buddhism: A psychological review. *Journal of Consulting Psychology, 26,* 362–378.

———. (1965). Individual differences in response to a Zen meditation practice. *Journal of Consulting Psychology, 29,* 139–145.

May, R. (1969). *Love and will.* New York: W. W. Norton.

McDargh, J. (1983). *Psychoanalytic object relations theory and the study of religion: On faith and the image of God.* Lanham, MD: University Press of America.

McDougall, J. (1989). *Theaters of the body: A psychoanalytic approach to psychosomatic illness.* New York: Norton.

McWilliams, N. (1984). The psychology of the altruist. *Psychoanalytic Psychology, 1,* 193–214.

———. (1991). Mothering and fathering processes in the psychoanalytic art. *Psychoanalytic Review, 78,* 525–546.

Meares, R. (1988). On boundary formation. In A. Goldberg (Ed.), *Frontiers in self psychology: Progress in self psychology* (vol. 3). Hillsdale, NJ: Analytic Press.

Meissner, W. W. (1978). Psychoanalytic aspects of religious experience. *Annual of Psychoanalysis, 6,* 103–141.

———. (1984). *Psychoanalysis and religious experience.* New Haven: Yale University Press.

Menaker, E. (1982). *Otto Rank: A rediscovered legacy.* New York: Columbia University Press.

Messer, S. B., Sass, L. A., & Woolfolk, R. L. (Eds.). (1988). *Hermeneutics and psychological theory.* New Brunswick, NJ: Rutgers University Press.

Miller, A., Issacs, K., & Haggard, E. (1965). On the nature of the observing function of the ego. *British Journal of Medical Psychology, 38,* 161–169.

Milner, M. (1957). *On not being able to paint.* New York: International Universities Press.

Morsbach, H. (1973). Aspects of nonverbal communication in Japan. *Journal of Nervous and Mental Disease, 157,* 262–277.

Mountain, M. (1983). *The Zen environment: The impact of Zen meditation.* New York: Bantam Books.

Musashi, M. (1982). *The book of five rings* (Trans. by Nihon Services Corporation: B. Brown, Y. Kashiwagi, W. Barrett, & E. Sasagawa). New York: Bantam.

Muzika, E. (1990). Evolution, emptiness, and the fantasy self. *Journal of Humanistic Psychology, 30,* 89–108.

Nardi, T. (1984). The tao of counseling. *International Journal of Eclectic Psychotherapy, 3,* 13–17.

Neihardt, J. G. (1972). *Black Elk speaks.* New York: Simon & Schuster. (originally published 1959)

Nicol, C. W. (1982). *Moving Zen.* New York: Quill.

Nietzsche, F. (1954). Thus spoke Zarathustra. In W. Kauffman, Ed., *The portable nietzsche.* New York: Viking Press. (originally published 1892)

Nitobe, I. (1975). *Bushido, the warrior's code.* Tokyo: Ohara.

Nosanchuk, T. A. (1981). The way of the warrior: The effects of martial arts training on aggressiveness. *Human Relations, 34,* 435–444.

Nosanchuk, T. A., & MacNeil, C. (1989). Examination of the effects of traditional and modern martial arts training on aggressiveness. *Aggressive Behavior, 15,* 153–159.

Nyanamoli, B. (Trans.) (1976). *Visuddhimagga: The path of purification by Buddhaghosha.* 2 vols. Boulder, CO: Shambhala.

Oremland, J. D. (1985). Kohut's reformulations of defense and resistance as applied in therapeutic psychoanalysis. In A. Goldberg (Ed.), *Progress in self psychology* (vol. 1). New York: Guilford Press.

Osmer, H. (1981). Paradoxical treatments: A unified concept. *Psychotherapy: Theory, Research, Practice, 18,* 320–324.

Parsons, M. (1984). Psychoanalysis as vocation and martial art. *International Review of Psychoanalysis, 11,* 453–462.

Perls, F. S. (1976). *Gestalt therapy verbatim.* New York: Bantam.

Pine, F. (1988). The four psychologies of psychoanalysis and their place in clinical work. *Journal of the American Psychoanalytic Association, 36,* 571–596.

Podvoll, E. M. (1979). Psychosis and the mystic path. *Psychoanalytic Review, 66,* 571–590.

Randall, R. L. (1984). The legacy of Kohut for religion and psychology. *Journal of Religion and Health, 23,* 106–114.

Randon, M. (1978). *The martial arts.* London: Octopus Books.

Rank, O. (1945). *Will therapy and truth and reality* (J. Taft, Trans.). New York: Alfred Knopf.

Rapaport, D., & Gill, M. M. (1959). The points of view and assumptions of metapsychology. *International Journal of Psychoanalysis, 40,* 153–161.

Reid, H., & Croucher, M. (1983). *The fighting arts.* New York: Simon & Schuster.

Reik, T. (1948). *Listening with the third ear.* New York: Farrar, Straus.

Rizzuto, A. M. (1979). *The birth of the living God.* Chicago: University of Chicago Press.

Rogers, C. (1961). *On becoming a person.* Boston: Houghton Mifflin.

———. (1963). The actualizing tendency in relationship to "motives" and to consciousness. In M. R. Jones (Ed.), *Nebraska symposium on motivation.* Lincoln: University of Nebraska Press.

Roland, A. (1988). *In search of self in India and Japan: Toward a cross-cultural psychology.* Princeton: Princeton University Press.

Ross, N. (1975). Affect as cognition: With observations on the meaning of mystical states. *International Review of Psychoanalysis, 2,* 79–93.

Rothpearl, A. (1980). Personality traits in martial artists: A descriptive approach. *Perceptual and Motor Skills, 50,* 395–401.

Rubin, J. B. (1985). Meditation and psychoanalytic listening. *The Psychoanalytic Review, 72,* 599–613.

———. (1992a). *Pathways to transformation: An integrative study of psychoanalysis and Buddhism.* (in preparation)

———. (1992b). Psychoanalytic treatment with a Buddhist meditator. In M. Finn and J. Gartner (Eds.), *Object relations theory and religion.* New York: Praeger.

Rubin, J. B., & Suler, J. R. (1992). *Self psychology and religion.* (in preparation)

Rutstein, J. (1985). *Psychoanalysis and the unity experience: Regression or progression?* Dissertation for the Graduate School of Applied and Professional Psychology, Rutgers University.

Sanders, J. (Ed.). (1990). Why spiritual groups go awry. *Common Boundary, 8,* 24–29.

Sandler, J., & Rosenblatt, B. (1962). The concept of the representational world. *Psychoanalytic study of the child, 17,* 128–145.

Sato, K. (1957). Psychotherapeutic implications of Zen. *Psychologia: An International Journal of Psychology in the Orient, 1,* 213–218.

————. (1968). Zen from a personological viewpoint. *Psychologia: An International Journal of Psychology in the Orient, 11,* 3–24.

Schafer, R. (1958). Regression in service of the ego: The relevance of a psychoanalytic concept for personality assessment. In G. Lindzey (Ed.), *Assessment of human motives* (pp. 119–148). New York: Rinehart.

————. (1968). *Aspects of internalization.* New York: International Universities Press.

Schroeder, T. (1922). Prenatal psychisms and mystical pantheism. *International Journal of Psychoanalysis, 3,* 445–466.

Searles, H. F. (1965). *Collected papers on schizophrenia and related topics.* New York: International Universities Press.

Sekida, K. (1975). *Zen training: Methods and philosophy.* New York: Weatherhill.

Seltzer, L. F. (1986). *Paradoxical strategies in psychotherapy: A comprehensive overview and guidebook.* New York: Wiley.

Shafi, M. (1973). Silence in service of the ego: Psychoanalytic study of meditation. *International Journal of Psychoanalysis, 54,* 431–443.

Silverberg, F. R. (1988). Therapeutic resonance. *Journal of Contemplative Psychotherapy, 5,* 25–42.

————. (in press). Working with resistance. *Journal of Contemplative Psychotherapy.*

Silverman, L. H. (1987). Imagery as an aid in working through unconscious conflicts: A preliminary report. *Psychoanalytic Psychology, 4,* 45–64.

Silverman, L. H., Lachmann, F. M., & Milich, R. H. (1982). *The search for oneness.* New York: International Universities Press.

Singer, K. (1989). The samurai: Legend and reality. In R. F. Nelson (Ed.), *The Overlook martial arts reader: An anthology of historical and philosophical writings* (pp. 16–29). Woodstock, NY: Overlook Press.

Sloane, J. A. (1986). The empathic vantage point in supervision. In A. Goldberg (Ed.), *Progress in self psychology* (vol. 2). New York: Guilford Press.

Smith, H. (1965). *The religions of man.* New York: Harper and Row.

Speeth, K. R. (1982). On psychotherapeutic attention. *Journal of Transpersonal Psychology, 14,* 141–160.

Spence, D. P. (1982). *Narrative truth and historical truth: Meaning and interpretation in psychoanalysis.* New York: Norton.

Sterba, R. (1934). The fate of the ego in analytic therapy. *International Journal of Psychoanalysis, 15,* 117–126.

———. (1940). Aggression in the rescue fantasy. *Psychoanalytic Quarterly, 9,* 505–508.

Stern, D. N. (1985). *The interpersonal world of the infant: A view from psychoanalysis and developmental psychology.* New York: Basic Books.

Stolorow, R. D., Brandchaft, B., & Atwood, G. E. (1987). *Psychoanalytic treatment: An intersubjective approach.* Hillsdale, NJ: Analytic Press.

Stolorow, R. D., & Lachmann, F. M. (1980). *Psychoanalysis of developmental arrests.* Madison, CT.: International Universities Press.

Stunkard, A. (1951). Interpersonal aspects of an oriental religion. *Psychiatry, 14,* 419–431.

Suler, J. R. (1980). Primary process thinking and creativity. *Psychological Bulletin, 88,* 144–165.

———. (1989a). Mental imagery in psychoanalytic treatment. *Psychoanalytic Psychology, 6,* 343–366.

———. (1989b). Paradox in psychological transformations: The Zen koan and psychotherapy. *Psychologia: An International Journal of Psychology in the Orient, 32,* 221–229.

———. (1990a). Wandering in search of a sign: A contemporary version of the vision quest. *Journal of Humanistic Psychology, 30,* 73–88.

———. (1990b). Images of the self in Zen meditation. *Journal of Mental Imagery, 14,* 197–204.

———. (1991). The Tai Chi images: A model of psychotherapeutic change. *Psychologia: An International Journal of Psychology in the Orient, 34,* 18–27.

———. (in press-a). Mental imagery in the organization and transformation of the self. *Psychoanalytic Review.*

———. (in press-b). Zen Buddhism and psychoanalysis. *Psychoanalytic Review.*

Suler, J. R., & Genovese, D. N. (1988). Psychodynamics of the vision quest. *Voices: The Art and Science of Psychotherapy, 24,* 83–90.

Sullivan, H. S. (1964). *The fusion of psychiatry and social science.* New York: Norton.

Sun Tzu (1971). *The art of war* (S. Griffith, Trans.). London: Oxford University Press.

———. (1983). *The art of war* (J. Clavell, Ed.). New York: Dell.

Suzuki, D. T. (1949). *Introduction to Zen Buddhism.* London: Rider.

———. (1956). *Zen Buddhism* (W. Barrett, Ed.). New York: Doubleday.

———. (1960). Lectures on Zen Buddhism. In E. Fromm, D. T. Suzuki, & R. DeMartino, *Zen Buddhism and psychoanalysis.* New York: Harper & Row.

Suzuki, S. (1970). *Zen mind, beginner's mind.* New York: Weatherhill.

Tart, C. T. (1987). Aikido and the concept of ki. *Psychological Perspectives, 18,* 332–348.

Tohei, K. (1966). *Aikido in daily life.* Tokyo: Rikugei.

Trungpa, C. (1988). *Shambhala: The sacred path of the warrior.* Boston: Shambhala.

Van de Wetering, J. (1978). *A glimpse of nothingness: Experiences in an American Zen community.* New York: Pocket Books.

Van Dusen, W. (1957). Zen Buddhism and Western psychotherapy. *Psychologia: An International Journal of Psychology in the Orient, 1,* 229–230.

———. (1958). Wu wei, no-mind and the fertile void in psychotherapy. *Psychologia: An International Journal of Psychology in the Orient, 1,* 253–256.

Vonnegut, K. (1975). *Breakfast of Champions.* New York: Dell.

Wachtel, P. L. (1977). *Psychoanalysis and behavior therapy.* New York: Basic.

Watts, A. (1957). *The way of Zen.* New York: Vintage Books.

———. (1958). *The spirit of Zen.* New York: Grove Press.

———. (1975a). *Psychotherapy East and West.* New York: Vintage Books. (originally published 1961)

———. (1975b). *Tao: The watercourse way.* New York: Pantheon.

Weber, M. (1947). *The theory of social and economic ogranization.* (A. M. Henderson & T. Parsons, Trans.). New York: Oxford University Press.

Weeks, G. R. (1985). *Promoting change through paradoxical therapy.* Homewood, IL: Dow Jones-Irwin.

Weis, P. (1960). The contribution of Geor Wilhelm Groddeck on Zen Buddhism and psychiatry. *Psychologia: An International Journal of Psychology in the Orient, 3*, 50–57.

Weiss, J., & Sampson, H. (1986). *The psychoanalytic process.* New York: Guilford.

Werman, D. S. (1986). On the nature of the oceanic experience. *Journal of the American Psychoanalytic Association, 34*, 123–139.

Wheelis, A. (1956). Will and psychoanalysis. *Journal of the American Psychoanalytic Association, 4*, 285–303.

White, R. (1959). Motivation reconsidered. *Psychological Review, 66*, 297–333.

Wilber, K. (1977). *The spectrum of consciousness.* Wheaton, IL: Quest.

———. (1980a). *The Atman project.* Wheaton, IL: Quest.

———. (1980b). The pre/trans fallacy. *ReVision, 3*, 51–73.

———. (1981). *Up from Eden.* New York: Doubleday.

———. (1986). The spectrum of development. In K. Wilber, J. Engler, & D. Brown, *Transformations of consciousness* (pp. 65–126). Boston: Shambhala.

Wilber, K., Engler, J., & Brown, D. P. (1986). *Transformations of consciousness.* Boston: Shambhala.

Wilhelm, R., & Baynes, C. F. (1967, Trans.). *I Ching: The book of changes.* Princeton, NJ: Princeton University Press (Bollingen Series XIX). (originally published 1950)

Wing, R. L. (1982). *The illustrated I Ching.* Garden City, NY: Doubleday.

Winnicott, D. W. (1953). Transitional objects and transitional phenomena. *International Journal of Psychoanalysis, 34*, 89–97.

———. (1958). *Collected papers—Through paediatrics to psychoanalysis.* New York: Basic Books.

———. (1967). The location of cultural experience. *International Journal of Psychoanalysis, 48*, 368–372.

———. (1969). The use of an object and relating through identifications. *International Journal of Psychoanalysis, 50*, 711–716.

———. (1971). *Playing and reality.* London: Tavistock.

———. (1974). *The maturational processes and the facilitating environment.* New York: International Universities Press. (originally published 1951)

Yalom, I. D. (1980). *Existential psychotherapy.* New York: Basic Books.

Author Index

Subject Index